Hare Krishna in America

# *Hare Krishna*

E. Burke Rochford, Jr.

Rutgers University Press, New Brunswick, New Jersey

*in America*

Second printing, 1991

*Library of Congress Cataloging in Publication Data*

Rochford, E. Burke, Jr., 1949–
  Hare Krishna in America.

  Bibliography: p. 305
  Includes index.
  1. International Society for Krishna Consciousness—
United States.   I. Title.
  BL1285.842.R63   1985      294.5'512      84–29819
  ISBN 0–8135–1113–5
  ISBN 0–8135–1114–3 (pbk.)

*To my Father and Mother with Love*

# Contents

# List of Tables and Figure

Tables

# Acknowledgments

This book is the result of the contributions of many individuals. Count-less people have freely given their time and energy to assist me in a number of indispensable ways throughout the eight years of research and writing required to complete this book on the Hare Krishna movement. Most important of these, of course, are the Hare Krishna people themselves.

This book would stand as no more than a dream without the coopera-tion of the many Hare Krishna devotees who took part in this research. Over the years, I have come to know as friends a number of devotees and former movement members and have spoken with dozens of others who freely told me about their life experiences, both prior to joining the movement and thereafter. In addition, over 200 of the movement's members took part in completing a questionnaire, which I distributed in 1980. As I sit here now, I only hope that I have not let down these many friends and acquaintances. Sociology is often considered and conducted as a cynical enterprise, and I fear that many who trusted me with their deepest thoughts and feelings will be disappointed and perhaps hurt. I am truly sorry for that. There are several devotees whom I would like to thank by name for their many contributions to my work, but I believe it best not to reveal their identities. Throughout the book, I have avoided using the true names of devotees to protect the individuals involved. Likewise, in respect for their privacy, I have substituted the names of some gurus and movement leaders with euphemisms, both in the text and in the extracts.

Several devotees thoughtfully read and provided a thorough critique of early drafts of the manuscript. Often they disagreed with portions of my analysis. While their criticisms were certainly taken into account in subsequent revisions, in the end there remain legitimate points of disagreement. Even so, my effort has profited enormously from these exchanges.

From the world of academia, many friends and colleagues have made contributions at various points along the way. First, I would like to thank the members of my dissertation committee at UCLA, Robert M. Emerson, Douglas Price-Williams, Ralph Turner, Melvin Seeman, and Thomas Weisner for their assistance, support, and trust. As for my mentor and friend, Robert M. Emerson, I lack the words to sufficiently express my gratitude for his many contributions to my training as a sociologist, and especially as a field worker. Bob encouraged me from the very beginning of this research, and when things became confusing, he was always there, pushing me to attend to specific aspects of the setting that I later realized were central to my analysis. Somehow he always "just knew" what the big issues were, even while I often remained blind to them. Ralph Turner and Melvin Seeman were always willing to listen patiently to any number of loose and sometimes incoherent ideas and partial analyses, many of which ultimately went nowhere. They also carefully reviewed early drafts of this monograph. Also from UCLA, I would like to thank Harold Garfinkel, Roderick Harrison, Melvin Pollner, and Linda Shaw for their continuing interest in my work and their willingness to struggle with me in trying to make sense of my data.

Thanks are also due to a number of other people who have read various parts of the manuscript and contributed their constructive criticisms of my emerging ideas. John Lofland carefully reviewed my dissertation and encouraged me to revise parts of the manuscript and to seek publication. Eileen Barker, David Bromley, Jeff Hadden, James Richardson, and David Snow each read all or major parts of the manuscript. David Snow, in particular, was influential in helping to shape my theoretical understanding of social movements. Diana Scully, David Franks, and Dan Johnson, from Virginia Commonwealth University, all provided assistance and support during what proved to be a personally trying and difficult year spent in Richmond, Virginia. Diana never let me give up on the idea of doing the book, and it was largely as a result of her direction that I was able to gain a contract to publish it.

I would also like to thank my colleagues in the Sociology Department of the University of Tulsa who tried to shelter me from many of the demands of university life so that I could complete this book. I know that they took on more than their fair share of the load, just so that I might have more time to write. I would especially like to thank Jean Blocker and Patricia Koski for their critical readings of various chapters of the book. In fact, under normal circumstances, they, along with Linda Shaw, would rightfully have co-authored the chapter on "Men, Women, and Membership." Each of them contributed significantly to my thinking about the issues discussed in this chapter. I also wish to thank the Society for the Study of Social Problems for permission to include my paper "Recruitment Strategies, Ideology, and Organization in the Hare Krishna Movement," *Social Problems*, 29 (1982): 399–410, which appears in a slightly different version in chapter six of this volume.

Sheri Jay, Kelly Peterson, Sheryl Purvis, and Leslie Swiggart provided valuable research assistance during the final phases of the project. Janice Brothers, Carol George, Cynthia Rea, and Maggie Scovil all typed various portions of the manuscript. Because of my tendency continually to make changes in the text, their efforts and patience often went far beyond the call of duty. I would also like to thank the University of Tulsa for providing the resources necessary to type the final draft of the manuscript.

Finally, and most importantly, I want to thank my family, who had to face many sacrifices so that I could complete the necessary research and write this book. My wife, Jean Burfoot, often was forced to place her own career on hold so that I could push ahead with my own writing. She contributed directly to the book in a variety of ways: most importantly, through her own theoretical insights, as well as by helping me to put together the case history of Devi that appears in chapter four. I am certain that I would not have persevered without her continuing support and assistance. Jean is my partner, friend, and colleague in every way and I am eternally grateful. My daughter, Holley, for whom I feel the greatest love in my life, helped me through the many times I felt like quitting. Her tendency to rise early also helped me in getting to work early every morning so that I could have a full day of writing. Last, but not least, I want to thank my parents, to whom this book is dedicated. Their love and continuing support I will cherish forever.

Hare Krishna in America

# 1
# *Introduction*

*F*ew social issues have been more controversial over the past decade than the growth and expansion of the new religions in America. Beginning in the mid-1960s, thousands of young people began to forsake their previous religious beliefs and cultural values to become adherents of new religious movements, such as the Unification Church (i.e., the Moonies), the Church of Scientology, the Children of God, and Hare Krishna. Yet the flowering of the new religions also spawned the growth of another movement whose sole purpose was to halt the cults' influence in America. From the view of the anticult movement and its members, the new religions posed a threat to society's values and to the many young people who were participating in the cults. Charges of brainwashing and the use of coercive and exploitative tactics were brought against the new religions. In rejecting these charges, the new religions openly questioned whether religious freedom and pluralism continue to be part of the American way of life.

This case study focuses on the growth and development of one of the new religions, the International Society for Krishna Consciousness (hereafter ISKCON), more popularly known as the Hare Krishna movement. The analysis centers on the young people who have joined the movement, on ISKCON's overall development and its career in the American context, and also on the larger society into which the Krishna movement has sought to expand its influence. In the broadest sense, my analysis centers on the range of processes that have influenced the efforts of the Hare Krishna movement to spread its message and to gain a following since its introduction in America in 1965. In this introductory chapter, I provide a brief overview of my analysis of ISKCON, I discuss in detail the research methods I used in this investigation, and I introduce the beliefs, lifestyle, and organization of the Krishna movement.

## Overview of the Analysis

This book is divided into three major sections. This and the next chapter are introductory. Chapter two details and analyzes my involvement with ISKCON over the course of a six-year period devoted to research. Chapters three through five address issues relating to membership and participation in ISKCON. This portion of the book analyzes processes of differential recruitment, or why some persons rather than others have joined the Krishna movement. The remainder of the book, chapters six through ten, focus on ISKCON's history as a social movement and organization in America. Here, I trace the history of ISKCON's development, identifying both those factors that have facilitated and those that have limited the movement's expansionary efforts and effected its overall viability as a movement and organization.

Chapter three (Searchers or Victims: Who Joins and Why) discusses various sociological explanations of why persons join movements such as Hare Krishna. The chapter begins by defining in demographic terms those who have swelled ISKCON's ranks. The discussion and analysis then turns to three other modes of explanation to account for recruitment to ISKCON: (1) macro-structural and social psychological analysis; (2) ISKCON members' own accounts of their reasons for joining; and (3) micro-structural and interactional approaches to the issue of recruitment to ISKCON. Instead of arguing for any one of these approaches, I view each as illuminating some aspect of the problem of differential recruitment as it relates to ISKCON's efforts to expand its membership.

Chapter four (Surrendering to Krishna: Devi's Story) presents the detailed life history of one woman who has become an ISKCON devotee. While this case study is analytically useful because it raises a number of issues relating to recruitment, commitment building, and the whole process of becoming a member, I believe it is of equal importance because it provides an insider's account of the whole experience of becoming an ISKCON devotee. Social science, in its efforts to be rigorous and systematic, sometimes forgets the personal human quality of the people it studies. Devi's story is meant to depict the personal and human dimensions of social movement participation.

Chapter five (Men, Women, and Membership) builds analytically on Devi's story by discussing the recruitment and membership process as it differently affects men and women who become ISKCON members. To date, there has been no research on the differences between the sexes with regard to recruitment in social movements. Students of social movements have assumed that the processes of movement recruitment and membership are much the same for men and women. My findings on recruitment into ISKCON, however, suggest that men and women make contact and are recruited into the movement through different influence structures, women through social ties and men through contacts made with ISKCON in public places. Because of these differences, I was led to analyze the roles of men and women in American culture with regard to their different degrees of participation in the private and public realms, respectively, of social life. In other words, I attempt to account for the differences in men's and women's recruitment into ISKCON by analyzing the role expectations that structure the different social worlds of men and women more generally.

Chapter six (The Growth of Hare Krishna in America) provides a point of transition. This chapter focuses on the range of factors which has influenced the recruitment strategies, ideology, and organizational development of ISKCON in America. I trace ISKCON's history in America with an eye toward how the ideological and structural development of ISKCON has influenced the recruitment strategies by which it has gained a following. Rather than conceptualizing movement structure, ideology, and recruitment strategies in global terms, I analyze each of these processes in terms of the local communities into which ISKCON has expanded. Because of ISKCON's goal of recruiting the masses to Krishna Consciousness, the movement has tailored its structure, ideology, and recruitment strategies to local conditions in an effort to maximize its appeal.

Chapter seven (Airports and Public Places) presents a natural history of ISKCON's use of public places as it has sought to garner resources—people and finances—critical to its survival and success. Few Americans have escaped the solicitation and proselytizing efforts of ISKCON members in public settings. In fact, these public place interactions between the devotees and members of the public constitute the only form of contact that most people have ever had with the Krishna movement. The movement's use of public places has been a major source of controversy, both within the larger society and within ISKCON. The controversy surrounding ISKCON's use of public places has had a major impact on ISKCON's development throughout the 1970s.

Chapter eight (Change and Adaptation) focuses on the adaptive patterns and strategies employed by ISKCON's leaders and members in the face of changes that have threatened the movement's survival. Because of the public setting strategies developed by ISKCON's leaders in the middle to late seventies, ISKCON faced a crisis of legitimacy by the end of the decade. Protest from inside and outside the movement grew, as the leaders' strategies came to be viewed by many as detracting from ISKCON's spiritual goal of spreading Krishna Consciousness. Here I use Bennett Berger's (1981) notion of "ideological work" to analyze how ISKCON's leaders and members dealt with the growing crisis of legitimacy within the movement. In light of ISKCON's history throughout the 1970s, I discuss critically existing theories and approaches to movement change and transformation.

Chapter nine (The End of Charisma) details the events which took place after the death of the movement's founding charismatic leader, Srila Prabhupada. As often occurs with the death of charisma, ISKCON faced a number of succession controversies following Prabhupada's death. ISKCON faced factionalism, defections, and schism, which brought the movement to the edge of crisis in 1980. Challenging groups, which were composed of former ISKCON members and of dissident devotees who remained within ISKCON, combined to mobilize support against ISKCON's new leaders. Further confounding the situation were two sources of authority who competed for power within the emergent reorganization structure. On the one hand, the gurus appointed by Srila Prabhupada sought power to dictate ISKCON's future, while, on the other hand, the movement's bureaucratically organized Governing Body Commission (GBC) challenged these leaders for power. Prabhupada's death left a power vacuum within ISKCON and power politics prevailed over a three year period before the succession crisis was finally resolved.

In the final chapter, (The Future of Hare Krishna) I bring ISKCON into the present and project this history into the future both in America and worldwide. I discuss and analyze several questions relating to ISKCON's future, including: Will the movement continue in its present form (as ISKCON) or will it fragment under the present gurus, as they splinter from ISKCON with their disciples and establish separate communities? Even if the movement does avoid fragmentation, will ISKCON alter its structure and ideology in an attempt to gain public acceptance and thereby move toward institutionalization as a religious denomination? To answer these questions, I explore four processes that will likely influence ISKCON's future course of development: (1) leadership; (2) recruitment and membership; (3) the relationship between financial resources and preaching; and (4) the impact of ISKCON's public definition on its ability to expand its influence in America. I conclude the chapter by contrasting ISKCON's expansion in America with the movement's pattern of development internationally.

## Research Methods

This investigation of the Hare Krishna movement in America has relied on a variety of methodologies of research. Since the fall of 1975, I have both observed and participated in Krishna communities throughout America. While the major part of this research was carried out in the Los Angeles ISKCON community (1975–1981), I have also visited and conducted research in nine other ISKCON communities throughout America. Because ISKCON's history has not yet reached the two-decade mark, I have had the good fortune of being able to observe the movement during the most significant portion of its North American history.

The major part of my research on ISKCON has involved participant observation. Over a six-year period, I observed and lived within the Los Angeles ISKCON community. During this period, I participated in the Krishna lifestyle and religious practices, and, over a four month period, I worked in the community's school as an assistant *gurukula* teacher. On several occasions I also lived for three- and four-day periods in the community's "*bhakta* program" for new recruits, and was thus able both to observe the recruitment process and be subject to it. From the very beginning of my involvement with ISKCON, my observations were recorded in detailed field notes, which over the years have grown to over 750 single-spaced typed pages. My field work has also involved interviews with dozens of current and former ISKCON devotees both in Los Angeles and in other ISKCON communities.

Participant observation was also carried out in an organization developed by a group of former ISKCON members in Los Angeles. In fact, I was a charter member of what came to be called the Kirtan Hall. This group was comprised almost exclusively of former ISKCON members who had left the movement in the late seventies, at least in part over policy differences with the leadership in Los Angeles. Under the leadership of four long-time devotees, the Kirtan Hall was developed as an alternative to ISKCON for the dozens of devotees who were defecting from the movement in Los Angeles. Most of these devotees remained at least somewhat committed to their Krishna beliefs, but felt that they could no longer live within the confines of ISKCON itself. A group of fifteen to twenty-five devotees and their families met two to three times a week in the house of the Kirtan Hall's founder. The meetings involved worship of Krishna, singing and dancing (*kirtans*), a class on Krishna theology, and the opportunity to meet with friends. I participated in this group throughout much of 1980 before the group finally disintegrated after its founder moved away from California.

My second source of data is derived from a non-random survey of six ISKCON communities in the United States. These data were collected in 1980 from a total of 214 adult devotees residing in ISKCON communities in Los Angeles, Denver, Chicago, Port Royal (a farm community in Pennsylvania), New York, and Boston. I had intended to survey two other ISKCON communities, but my request to distribute the questionnaire was denied, because it was held to be too controversial by the leadership. Even so, my sample of over two hundred devotee respondents represents approximately 10 percent of the total ISKCON population in the United States. Response rates to the questionnaires ranged from approximately 50 percent for the larger ISKCON communities (Los Angeles and New York) up to more than 90 percent for several of the smaller ISKCON communities.

The questionnaire focused on a number of issues, including how the devotees first made contact with ISKCON and/or Krishna Consciousness; the individual factors and circumstances that attracted the devotees to the movement and influenced their decisions to become ISKCON members; devotee involvements in other social movements prior to their joining Hare Krishna; and issues relating to the devotees' current commitments to ISKCON and Krishna Consciousness. The questionnaire also allowed me to gain systematic information regarding the devotees' previous lives with their families, including: the social class standings of their parents, their religious backgrounds and involvement, their educational achievements, and their employment histories.

The third research strategy I employed was systematic observation. I observed and counted specific behaviors of ISKCON members who were distributing religious texts at the Los Angeles International Airport. This observation involved recording whom the devotees approached on the basis of age, sex, and race, and what the specific style and outcome of each interaction was. I was interested in seeing whether the devotees were successful in establishing face-to-face interaction with the persons they contacted and whether those persons purchased a Krishna book from the ISKCON member. These observations allowed me to gain an understanding of ISKCON's changing use of public places and how these changes reflect ISKCON's overall development in America. Moreover, the data I collected allowed me to analyze male-female interactions in public settings and how the dynamics of these cross-sexed encounters have contributed to the processes of differential recruitment.

Beyond the specific methods used in this investigation of Hare Krishna, there are several other research issues that make this study noteworthy. As I suggested earlier, I have observed ISKCON's development in America over a prolonged period of time. This has allowed me to gain a first-hand historical understanding of the movement's career in America. Instead of cutting into the movement's history at one specific period and then trying to trace that history back in time in an effort to understand present circumstances, I had the opportunity to witness the actual process of much of ISKCON's development. This has allowed me to understand the factors that have together influenced ISKCON's efforts to grow and expand.

But this research has also taken place during a particularly critical juncture in ISKCON's history. When I began my research in the fall of 1975, ISKCON was reaching its peak in America. The numbers of its membership were high and the movement was economically prosperous. By the end of the decade, however, ISKCON faced decline. The movement's recruitment had dwindled, members had begun to defect, and many of ISKCON's communities faced serious economic problems. These developments led ISKCON leaders to develop a number of practices directed at bringing people and financial resources into the movement. In the short term, the leadership's strategies were largely successful, but, in the long run, they promoted considerable controversy and conflict both in and outside of the movement. Finally, in the fall of 1977, ISKCON's founding leader died, and the movement faced a series of succession crises that further threatened its existence in America and throughout the world.

Finally, because this research has involved varying degrees of participation in ISKCON, a number of issues are raised by this study regarding field work and field work roles. As I discuss at length in the next chapter, my involvement with ISKCON was often an emotional and personally trying experience. To gain access to the movement in 1975, I was required to participate in it as a nominal member in order to gain trust, and thereby access, to the devotees' social world. In the years that followed, my participation expanded. With continued involvement in ISKCON, the distinguishing line between researcher and researched became less clear, not only to ISKCON members, my family and friends, but also to myself. This in turn resulted in a variety of both positive and negative effects on the research. On the one hand, I was able to gain a close and detailed understanding of the movement and its devotees. For example, I learned what becoming a member was about practically and interactionally, by being subject to the recruitment process myself early on in the research. I was subject to many of the same processes that prospective members face upon first entering the movement. But while there were advantages to this participant role, there were a number of distinct disadvantages as well. Not only my family and friends, but also the university questioned my involvement and relationship with the Krishna movement. Was I after all a researcher-participant or a participant-researcher? Early on, I began to realize that these experiences were themselves worthy of analysis, and I began to attend to how my involvement with ISKCON influenced my relationships in and outside of the movement. In sum, I tried to maintain a reflexive stance toward the setting and my relationship to it in an effort to gain a deeper understanding of the Krishna movement, its membership, and the nature of field work as a research method.

## Hare Krishna's History, Religious Beliefs, and Organization

The presence of Hare Krishna in America comes from the inspiration of one man, A. C. Bhaktivedanta Swami Prabhupada.[1] Bhaktivedanta, or Srila Prabhupada, as he is fondly referred to by his followers, traveled to the United States from India in 1965, at the age of sixty-nine, to spread Krishna Consciousness to the western world. One year after his arrival, Srila Prabhupada founded the International Society for Krishna Consciousness (ISKCON) in New York City. Within a decade, Prabhupada and his disciples had established a worldwide movement with several thousand committed members and over seventy-five ISKCON communities and preaching centers around the globe. Before his death, in November 1977, Prabhupada had initiated nearly five thousand disciples into Krishna Consciousness. Today, ISKCON claims to have a membership of five thousand core members in America and ten thousand worldwide. The movement's membership also includes an additional congregation that numbers several million throughout the world.² ISKCON presently has two hundred centers and communities located on every continent, with over seventy in North America alone.

ISKCON's charismatic founder was born in 1896 with the name Abhay Charan De. Prabhupada grew up in a family that practiced a strict Krishna-conscious lifestyle. After graduating from the University of Calcutta with majors in English, philosophy, and economics, Prabhupada was employed as a manager in a chemical firm, where he worked until his retirement in 1954. In 1922, Prabhupada met his spiritual master, Bhaktisiddhanta, from whom he ultimately took initiation in 1933. Prabhupada thereby became a member of his spiritual master's organization, the *Gaudiya Matha*, which had over sixty temples in India, one in Berlin and another in London (Daner 1976). Prior to Bhaktisiddhanta's death in 1936, he instructed Prabhupada to carry the teachings of Krishna Consciousness to the West. In the years before his departure for America, Prabhupada raised a family and continued to help promote the teachings of Bhaktisiddhanta.

In 1944, Prabhupada started publishing the *Back to Godhead* magazine, which he would later use to promote his movement in America. At the age of fifty-nine, after his children were grown, Prabhupada took the order of *sannyasa* and retired from family life so that he could focus his remaining years entirely on spreading Krishna Consciousness. From this point forward, Prabhupada dedicated his life exclusively to Krishna and to his spiritual master. Prabhupada lived as a Hindu monk and worked daily translating and writing his commentaries on the ancient Vedic scriptures, such as the *Bhagavad Gita* and the *Srimad Bhagavatam*. Until his final days, Prabhupada continued to work on his translations and commentaries, which were published by ISKCON's press, the Bhaktivedanta Book Trust in Los Angeles. ISKCON claims to have distributed over one hundred million pieces of literature throughout the world containing Prabhupada's teachings of the Vedic scripture.

## *ISKCON's Roots in India and Religious Beliefs*

Prabhupada's Hindu beliefs derive from a tradition that originated in Bengal, India, in the sixteenth century. While aligned with orthodox Hinduism, the Krishna Consciousness preached by Srila Prabhupada traces its roots to the Krishna *bhakti* movement founded by Sri Caitanya Mahaprabhu. Caitanya revived the devotional form of Hinduism (*bhakti* yoga) emphasizing that love and devotional service to God (Krishna) were the means by which to gain spiritual realization. Instead of seeing him as one of several Gods, Caitanya and his followers made Krishna (Vishnu) the supreme manifestation of God. In another split from orthodox Hinduism, Caitanya preached that all people, regardless of their caste or station in life, could be self-realized through their activities performed in the service of Krishna. Caitanya's movement became popular among lower caste peoples in eastern India precisely because it did not tie salvation to one's position in the caste system. In this sense, Caitanya's *bhakti* movement was democratic, in that all people had an equal opportunity to reach spiritual salvation.

Caitanya also developed another practice that was unique to Hinduism, which has been the trademark of the Krishna movement in America. Growing out of his intense religious passion, Caitanya initiated *sankirtana*, a practice in which his followers ventured into the streets to dance and sing their praises of Lord Krishna. When Prabhupada began his movement in America, *sankirtana* (preaching, book distribution, and chanting in public) became the principal means of spreading Krishna Consciousness. Few people in America have not had the experience of seeing the devotees performing *sankirtana* in airports or in other public settings.

The Krishna movement's beliefs are derived from scripture contained in the Vedas, from which all Hindu beliefs stem. The central religious text of the Krishna movement is the *Bhagavad Gita*, because it is in this religious text that *bhakti* is first fully detailed (Judah 1974). The actual date of the *Bhagavad Gita* is somewhat open to question, but it appears to have been written somewhere between the fifth and second centuries B.C. (Daner 1976; Judah 1974).

Krishna Consciousness views the true spiritual self as an independent entity. Because of material contamination, however, the soul is forced to assume a continuous succession of material bodies. When the body dies, the soul transmigrates into another body, where the possibilities for spiritual advancement are greater (for instance, by being born into a religious family). If, however, an individual lives a life based on gratifying the senses, s/he may well be reborn into the body of a lesser animal as a consequence of forgetting his or her relationship with God. The human form is viewed within Krishna belief as the vehicle best suited for spiritual realization. To make spiritual advancement in Krishna Consciousness, an individual must avoid identifying with the body, since it ultimately is little more than a temporary covering for the soul. Only by denying the body certain earthly pleasures can the soul overcome the laws of karma and the cycle of birth, death, and rebirth and thereby become fully realized in Krishna Consciousness.

The *bhakti* yoga process, as practiced by Krishna devotees, involves a number of religious practices directed toward purifying the soul. Central to this process of self-realization is chanting the Hare Krishna mantra: Hare Krishna, Hare Krishna, Krishna Krishna, Hare Hare, Hare Rama, Hare Rama, Rama Rama, Hare Hare. In addition to chanting, there are a number of other religious practices and lifestyle restrictions that pertain to ISKCON members. The following statement of vows is based upon one posted in the *ashram* (living quarters) for new male recruits in the Los Angeles community:

1. He must chant sixteen rounds daily (on a string of *japa* or prayer beads).

2. He cannot eat meat, fish, eggs, or onions.

3. He cannot have any illicit sex. This means any sexual contact with women, except one's wife, and only for the propagation of God-conscious children.

4. He cannot take any intoxicants. This includes cigarettes and pipe smoking, alcohol, coffee, and tea.

5. He is not allowed to gamble.

6. He must rise early in the morning (four A.M.) daily, have a cold shower and offer a ceremony called *Mangala arati*. This ceremony entails offering the Supreme Lord some incense, a flower or leaf, and the recitation of specific Bengali mantras or prayers.

7. He must wear sacred neck beads, and have his head shaved, except for a small portion on top of the head (called a *shikha*). He must decorate his body twice daily in thirteen places with a mixture of clay and water called *tilaka*. While marking his body, he must recite Sanskrit prayers. He must wear religious robes.

8. He cannot take part in any activities connected with animal slaughter. This means the transportation of, handling of, preparation or serving of meat or animal food products.

## The Devotees' Lifestyle

The lifestyle of the Krishna devotees reflects the movement's religious beliefs. Priority is given to spiritual practices and activities in the devotees' daily rounds. Because of ISKCON's cultural and religious roots in Hinduism, the movement's communities reflect an ancient Indian tradition. The community centers around the temple where the devotees chant, worship, eat Krishna *prasadam* (spiritual vegetarian food), and meet together for childrens' plays and other cultural and community events.

The devotee men, whether married or single, dress in traditional robes called *dhotis*. The women wear *saris* which are long pieces of cloth gracefully worn around the body, including the head. Also,

ISKCON members wear beads around the neck to signify their status as devotees of Krishna. All devotees also have bead bags, worn around their necks, which contain *japa* beads on which to chant.

Because the movement attempts to regulate strictly contact between the sexes, single men and women (*brahmacaries* and *brahmacarinis*) live in separate *ashrams*. Marriages are arranged by community leaders. A devotee man or woman approaches the temple president and expresses a desire to marry, usually with a specific spouse in mind. The temple president then tries to bring about the match between them. Since marriage is predicated upon raising a Krishna-conscious child, the western notion of romantic love as a basis for marriage finds little relevance. Arranged marriages between ISKCON members usually occur only after a devotee has been in the movement for several years. Only after a devotee demonstrates an ability to live a strict Krishna-conscious lifestyle does he or she become eligible to take the sacred vows of marriage. While the percentage varies from community to community, it appears that somewhat less than half of the Krishna membership are married. Married couples and their young children live in separate living quarters, such as individual apartments, or they live with several other families in communal households.

Devotee children attend ISKCON schools either in the local Krishna community or at a nearby regional school. The schools are staffed by devotee teachers, at least some of whom have teaching credentials and/or college degrees. Krishna children are taught a variety of subjects, most of which any child would be exposed to in a public elementary school (reading, writing, arithmetic, geography) and they are taught the Sanskrit language and the Vedic scriptures as well. The movement is now planning for their childrens' secondary education, as a cohort of children aged thirteen and fourteen are now approaching high school age.

At the age of five, Krishna children leave the home of their parents to take up residence in an *ashram* comprised of other children of the same sex and approximate age. Usually childrens' ashrams include five or six boys or girls living in the household of one of their teachers. The teacher and his or her spouse oversee the children's day-today needs, instruct them in Krishna Consciousness, and see to it that each child attends all religious functions held in the temple. While there is no reliable source giving the number of children in the movement, it appears that the number must be a thousand or more. In 1980, the Los Angeles ISKCON community alone had one hundred and twenty-five school-aged children.

While the daily routine of the devotees varies to some degree because of the nature of each devotee's specific duties (i.e., job) within the community, the day is nevertheless structured similarly for all devotees because of the centrality of the movement's religious practices and beliefs. The daily schedule for new male recruits (*bhaktas*) to ISKCON's community in Los Angeles is indicated below.

3:00 A.M. Rise, Bathe, Dress

3:30 A.M. Go to temple, chant *japa* [Hare Krishna mantra]

4:30 A.M. *Mangala arati* [religious ceremony in temple]

4:55 A.M. *Tulasi* worship [religious ceremony in temple]

5:10 A.M. Finish chanting *japa*

7:05 A.M. Greeting of the Deities [religious ceremony]

7:15 A.M. *Guru Puja* [worship of the spiritual master]

7:30 A.M. *Srimad Bhagavatam* Class

8:30 A.M. Morning *prasadam* [breakfast]

9:00 A.M. Class in *ashram*

9:30 A.M. Prepare for duties [work in the community]

9:45 A.M. Duties

12:30 P.M. Lunch *prasadam*

1:15 P.M. *Bhagavad Gita* class

2:00 P.M. Prepare for *Hare Nam* [group chanting in public settings]

2:15 P.M. *Hare Nam*

5:00 P.M. Shower and read

6:00 P.M. Class in temple

6:30 P.M. Evening program [*arati* and class]

8:15 P.M. Krishna Book reading; hot milk *prasadam*

9:00 P.M. Rest

After waking early at 3 A.M., *bhaktas* join the other single men and women in the temple to begin chanting their rounds. By 3:30 each morning the temple is alive with the chanting of the devotees. Most married devotees rise somewhat later in the morning, arriving at the temple just prior to *Mangala arati*, the first religious ceremony of the day. *Mangala arati* begins at 4:30 A.M. and all members of the devotee community are required to attend. This ceremony is the first of six *arati* ceremonies performed each day. Devotees are required to attend only the early morning and evening *arati* ceremonies. During the *arati* ceremony, the devotees worship the deities, who are colorfully dressed and covered in flowers on the alter. While an unknowing outsider may see the devotees as worshipping idols, in fact, the deities are viewed by the devotees as incarnations of Krishna. Deity worship provides an opportunity for the entire devotee community to come together and collectively worship Krishna. Traditional Vedic music and dancing play a large part in the ceremony. One male devotee leads the others in singing various sanskrit verses to the beat of the music. Several devotees play *mrdanga* drums and *karatals* (small hand cymbals) while the other devotees dance in front of the deities. In the beginning, the collective chanting and singing of the sanskrit mantras is soft and deliberate, but, progressively, the pace increases until the devotees are enthusiastically jumping up and down with arms raised, loudly singing the verses. During the ceremony itself, one or more of the devotees positioned on the altar (the *pujaris*) offers a number of articles to the deities, including: incense, a camphor lamp, a *ghee* lamp, a small conch shell, a handkerchief, a flower, a fan made of peacock feathers, and a yak tail attached to a silver handle. For each offering, the *pujaris* stand in front of the deities with the object in hand and the arm raised moving in a circular motion. After offering the object to the deities, the *pujaris* then turn and offer it to the devotees. The *arati* ceremony lasts approximately twenty-five minutes. At the close of *arati*, the *pujaris* blow into large conch shells, signaling the end of the ceremony. The devotees then kneel, head to the floor of the temple, and recite a final prayer in honor of Krishna and the disciplic succession.

Immediately following *Mangala arati*, the devotees take part in a ceremony involving the worship of a sacred plant known as *Tulasi Devi*. *Tulasi* is worshipped because the spirit-soul of a pure devotee of Krishna is believed to reside in the body of the plant. By offering *Tulasi* worship, the devotees believe that their sinful thoughts and activities will be controlled. The devotees dance around *Tulasi* reciting sanskrit verses in her honor. Each devotee stops long enough to water *Tulasi* and to offer obeisances to her. As in other forms of worship in the temple, men and women are segregated. The *Tulasi* ceremony is in fact staged so that the women worship one *Tulasi* plant and the men another, in separate areas of the temple. During other forms of worship in the temple, men stand to the front nearest the alter while the women stand well behind them.

Following *Tulasi* worship, the temple once again becomes alive with the sounds of the devotees chanting the Hare Krishna mantra. Some devotees walk back and forth across the temple loudly chanting the mantra, while others sit before the alter softly chanting on their beads. For the average devotee, it takes an hour and half to two hours a day to complete chanting sixteen rounds on their string of 108 beads. While most finish chanting *japa* in the early morning hours, many can be seen chanting during idle periods that arise throughout the day.

Shortly after 7 A.M., the devotees again gather at the temple for the greeting of the deities. The devotees sing a number of sanskrit prayers, as the deities are revealed to the gathering of devotees one by one. Petals of flowers are offered to the deities by each of the devotees present. Immediately following the greeting of the deities, the devotees then perform the *Guru Puja* ceremony in honor of their spiritual master. The many disciples of Srila Prabhupada offer flower petals at the feet of their spiritual master, whose physical form has been skill-

fully reproduced in wax. Prabhupada's likeness (or, from the devotee's perspective, Prabhupada himself) sits in his chair (*vyasasana*) in
the temple. For the newer members, who have taken initiation from
one of the present ISKCON gurus following Prabhupada, a similar offering is made to a picture of their spiritual leader, which sits on
a smaller *vyasasana* next to Srila Prabhupada. Following *Guru Puja*,
the devotees remain in the temple for *Srimad Bhagavatam* class.
One male devotee leads the others in reciting the Sanskrit verses from
the scripture and then gives a lecture based upon Srila Prabhupada's commentaries.

After class the devotees eat their morning *prasadam* in the temple
and then begin their duties. Some devotees work within the community, while others go out in public distributing religious texts and other
Krishna-conscious literature. A few devotees who hold jobs outside
the community leave for their day's work. The schedule for the new
recruits varies from that of other members in that their day involves
several additional classes in the movement's theology as well as going
out in the afternoon to chant in public settings (*Hare Nam*). Upon returning from *Hare Nam* in the late afternoon, the new *bhaktas* and
*bhaktins* return to their *ashram* and prepare for the evening program in
the temple. After attending class in the temple, they join together with
the rest of the community for the evening *arati*, which is followed by
yet another class in the Vedic scriptures. After the evening program is
complete, most devotees have an hour or two to socialize with other
community members or to tend to their family obligations before retir-
ing for the night.

*ISKCON's Organization*

ISKCON is governed by the Governing Body Commission (GBC), con-
sisting of twenty-five senior devotees from around the world. This
governing body was established in 1970 by Srila Prabhupada to oversee the movement's day-to-day affairs and to set policy for ISKCON's
communities. Thirteen members of the GBC also serve as ISKCON
gurus, having been appointed to their positions following Prab-

hupada's death in 1977. ISKCON gurus initiate disciples into Krishna Consciousness, thereby maintaining the five thousand year old tradition of disciplic succession going back to Krishna Himself. Members of the GBC, whether initiating gurus or not, represent a specific area of the world where ISKCON has established communities. The GBC has full responsibility for setting policy for the movement and for directing the movement's future in America and internationally. GBC decisions are reached democratically, each member having a vote on issues brought before the commission. Each GBC member usually appoints one or more zone secretaries to be in charge of the various ISKCON communities in his zone. GBC members and their secretaries are responsible for informing the devotees in their zones of all GBC decisions.

Each of ISKCON's communities is incorporated separately as a nonprofit religious organization. Each community has its own board of directors and officers, including a temple president who deals with the day-to-day affairs of the community.

# 2
# Field Work and Membership

Since the 1960s, there has been an increasing interest by field researchers in the personal dimensions of field work (Emerson 1981, 1983). Attention has centered on how various personal characteristics and motives and feelings of the field worker influence his or her field relations and thereby the reliability of the data collected and the validity of the subsequent analyses. While the scholarly discussion has generally centered on the sources of distortion and bias that result from such influences (i.e., the problem of reactivity) more recently, some field workers have recast these personal and subjective experiences as sources of insight and understanding. Indeed, many of these field workers insist that access to members' worlds can only be gained by actively participating in the everyday lives of those under study (Bodemann 1978; Douglas 1976; Jules-Rosette 1975; Wolff 1964).

In this chapter, I describe the natural history of my field work and involvement with the Hare Krishna movement. This reflexive account of my field work with ISKCON speaks to the unique problems faced by field workers when they attempt to research highly charged ideological settings, such as are often found in social movements (see Thorne 1979). Because of strong pressures to participate in the activities of the group, it often becomes difficult to work out a role that is acceptable both to the researcher and to those under study. My discussion highlights the negotiated quality of field work roles and questions the principle prescriptions that are generally offered to define appropriate field relations, both those stressing role neutrality and those stressing active participation. In addition, I also discuss the personal consequences for the researcher of participation in a stigmatized group.

## From Observer to Participant: Early Field Relations with ISKCON

My initial research involvement with ISKCON began in the fall of 1975. At the time I was looking to become involved in a field research project as part of my graduate studies. Remembering two long-time friends who had become Krishna devotees several years earlier, I contacted them about the possibilities of conducting research on the Hare Krishna movement in Los Angeles. Without hesitation, they invited me to visit them at the nearby ISKCON community. My first entry into the community was thus informal, and although community authorities became aware of my presence and purposes, they never confronted me about my research. In large part, the reason for the lack of official interest in my research reflects the fact that during this early period I was seen by many, if not most, ISKCON members as a *potential convert* rather than as a researcher.

My efforts to conduct my research were very difficult and personally trying during the first year of my involvement with ISKCON. Instead of accepting my repeated assertions that I was a researcher, the devotees invariably refused to accept my explanation, seeing me instead as a "spirit-soul" who had been sent by Krishna. If I saw myself as being there to conduct research, that was my problem, and was of little or no concern to them. But being new to field work and somewhat frightened by the prospect of researching people who were attempting to convert me, I felt it to be imperative personally that I establish myself within the setting as a researcher:

> One of the most critical aspects of this research on the Hare Krishna devotees has been my inability to establish a 'researcher's role.' Since this was my first research experience, I did not have a clear conception of what a researcher's role actually was. Nevertheless, I had a vague idea of how people in my research setting were 'supposed' to respond to me. If I said that I was a researcher, I assumed that, after a period of getting to know the setting, I ultimately would be accepted in that role. The need to establish such a notion in the minds of those under study seemed particularly important. I thought the role of researcher might serve as a protective shield against forseen attempts at conversion on the part of movement members. I assumed that if the Hare Krishna devotees knew that my interest in the movement was purely for purposes of research, they would discontinue their initial attempts at conversion and accept me as a researcher (Rochford 1976).

I had hoped that my research role would become a "retreat" (Thorne 1979:87) allowing me to escape the risks involved in participating in the lives of the Krishna devotees. At this early point in my research, I wanted to maintain a role that was more like being a strict observer than a quasi-participant.

Early on in my research I was invited by the devotees to take a more active part in the life of the community, in particular, in the religious practices of Krishna Consciousness. For many weeks I steadfastly refused to participate in this way, however, fearing that such participation would only increase the strain and pressures I was feeling. Over and over the devotees asked if I was chanting the Hare Krishna mantra. While on some occasions I suggested that I was, to avoid a confrontation, I nevertheless refused to participate with the devotees as they chanted in the temple. Chanting was appropriate for someone who was becoming a devotee, not for a researcher:

> In the morning, when all the devotees were chanting their rounds in the temple, I refrained from doing so. It was very uncomfortable to be among all the devotees while they chanted. I observed for a while, but then realized that I was being observed more than I was observing. I could see that all the devotees were noticing that I wasn't chanting. I felt that I was being avoided (looked down upon) because of my refusal to take part in the chanting. I started wishing that I was somewhere else—anywhere. I had visions of the study coming apart at the seams. Several devotees stopped and suggested that I try chanting the mantras. I continued to refuse (Rochford 1976).

As the pressures continued to mount, on one such occasion, one of my main informants entered the temple. Within a few minutes he also noticed that I was not chanting. He walked over and asked if I had *japa* beads. Responding that I did not, he offered me an extra string of beads.

> At this point I felt I had better take the beads and try chanting. I succumbed to the pressure. I knew that by chanting, the devotees would be pleased and the pressures I was feeling would subside. Soon after I began chanting, things began to happen. First, a devotee came over to me and put a flower garland around my neck (flowers that had previously been on the altar and thus were very special to the devotees). He welcomed me to Krishna Consciousness. A few minutes later, another devotee stopped and showed me the correct way to hold the beads while chanting. Immediately after that still another devotee came over and asked if I wanted to water the spiritual plant *Tulasi Devi*. We went over to the plant and he showed me the proper way to 'offer' the water to *Tulasi* (Rochford 1976).

But while I had given in to the devotees' pressures, I nevertheless continued to interpret my actions in terms of my researcher's role. The following statement from my field notes, however, points to my growing sense of confusion:

> I should make the point that I was giving in to the pressures I felt, but not for the reasons the devotees imagined. I wasn't concerned with demonstrating my devotion to Krishna. No doubt many of the devotees observing my actions thought that I was beginning to 'surrender to Krishna.' Actually, I felt that I was surrendering more to the thought that if I didn't show my interest (as a potential convert) my relationship with the devotees would suffer, and my research would also. I sense that I am getting into a bind. I've got to think this out some (Rochford 1976).

After this initial period of frustration and anxiety about my role within the Los Angeles ISKCON community, I began more easily to accept the devotees' recognition of me as a potential recruit. After the chanting episode, I began to participate more freely in the ceremonial aspects of Krishna Consciousness, but again, the decision felt more like a research choice than like a personal decision reflecting my changing relationship to God (Krishna) or the movement. Rather than fighting the devotees' interpretation and treatment of me as a potential convert, I finally was able to see these as data allowing me access to the processes of recruitment and conversion to Krishna Consciousness. Indeed, because of the community's definition of me as a potential convert, I would have been hard pressed to have studied systematically any other aspect of the social life of the devotees. So, while recognition as a potential convert sustained my presence in the devotee community, it also cut me off from exploring other issues of sociological interest.

While being treated as a potential convert allowed me to gain an acceptable role within the setting, such a role has only a limited life for most persons who come into an ISKCON community. Because I was seen as a somewhat special recruit, I was allowed a longer period of time to convert. The devotee in charge of the *bhakta* program referred to me as one of his longer-term conversions. He spent considerable time explaining Krishna Consciousness to me because of my graduate status at the university. In short, he thought I was a "prize catch" (my words) and worth the extra effort. As he told me one day: "You're not like the young kids off the street who come to the community because they are in need of shelter. We expect them to convert quickly. We're willing to wait a while for you."

## From Participant to Member

After my initial year researching the movement, my relationship to ISKCON and Krishna Consciousness began to undergo a change. Once I had stopped actively researching the movement, I felt more at ease taking part in the religious practices of Krishna Consciousness. While it would be easy to say that I continued my involvement as a way of maintaining my research opportunities, I think it more accurate to say that I wanted to explore my spiritual self as I never had before. The research experience had not convinced me to join ISKCON, but it did awaken me as a spiritual being. For the next several years, I attended the evening *arati* ceremony in the temple once a week and continued to maintain my friendships with various devotees. It was during this time that ISKCON members began to see me as a "fringe" Krishna devotee (a person who appreciates Krishna Consciousness but who nevertheless refuses to make the commitment necessary to move into the community and become a disciple). Given the nature of this role within the community, I was not subject to the devotees' proselytizing efforts thereafter. Indeed, for the most part, I was left alone and allowed to come and go from the community without a great deal of interaction with the devotees.

Although my personal relationship with Krishna Consciousness changed during these initial years, changes also took place within the movement itself that facilitated my taking on a membership role. Prior to 1976 there had been little differentiation in the kinds of members in

ISKCON; one was either an insider (a devotee) or an outsider (a *karmie*). Persons residing in the Los Angeles ISKCON community were either on the path to becoming a disciple of Srila Prabhupada's, or they had already made the commitment to the spiritual master and were working toward their self-realization in Krishna Consciousness. Other kinds of members were not recognized. (This situation, of course, provided the source of the role strain I was feeling during the early period of my research.) The exclusivist structure of the movement made it nearly impossible for less committed persons to find an acceptable role within the community. But as the movement began to undergo structural and organizational changes, less committed persons were increasingly extended formal membership status within the devotee community, even if this status was not recognized as being in good standing. (These changes are discussed in chapters seven and eight.) Given the availability of such a role within the ISKCON community, I ultimately came to be defined as a fringe devotee.

By contrast, in less demanding and inclusivist movement organizations, such as the Nichiren Shoshu Buddhist movement, a researcher can more easily take on a role more closely aligned to being a core member. This consideration weighed heavily in Snow's decision to research Nichiren Shoshu rather than Hare Krishna:

> My involvement with Nichiren Shoshu had been participatory and much more consistent and intense than my involvement in Hare Krishna, which had been observational and occasional. [My] continued participation in Nichiren Shoshu wouldn't require me to drop out, shave my head, and assume an austere, communal lifestyle as would have continued participation in Hare Krishna. An additional and equally important consideration was my marriage, which made the latter course a highly untenable proposition . . . . Again, gaining membership in Nichiren Shoshu is not contingent on any such initial sacrifices. All that is required is that one pay a $5.00 shipping fee for the "Gohonzon," and be willing to risk, perhaps, a negative reaction by nonmovement significant others (1976: 10, 16).

## Membership as a Research Role: Recent Field Relations with ISKCON

Because of the changes in my membership status within the Los Angeles ISKCON community, my research experience became quite different during my later research activities (1979–1981). Instead of being seen as a potential convert to Krishna Consciousness, I was now seen as a person generally sympathetic to the beliefs of the movement, but even more importantly, I was defined by many of the devotees as a member of ISKCON. My work in the community school in particular, reaffirmed this latter understanding. Instead of taking part only in the religious practices of Krishna Consciousness, I was now seen as working for the benefit of the ISKCON community. Even so, my membership status within the community remained one of marginality because of my steadfast refusal to fully commit myself to the Krishna beliefs and way of life. I was of them, but clearly was never considered a committed devotee in the same way as community members were. My fringe status in the end resulted in an inability to fully mobilize the community in support of my research efforts. Or perhaps more accurately, I was only able to mobilize the Los Angeles ISKCON community within the limits imposed by my marginal membership role. The consequences of this marginal role for my research were perhaps best demonstrated when I distributed questionnaires in six ISKCON communities, including the one in Los Angeles, in 1980. Although I had expected trouble in gaining adequate response rates to the questionnaire in those ISKCON communities where I was *not* known, in the end, I received proportionally fewer completed questionnaires from Los Angeles than from any of the other ISKCON communities.[1] The reasons for this are two-fold.

First, because I was seen by the devotees in Los Angeles as a fringe devotee, I was unable to mobilize strong support for my research. Instead of being an asset, my marginal membership status became a liability for this part of the research. By contrast, just before I distributed my questionnaires in Los Angeles, another researcher visited the community to interview members about their involvements in Krishna

Consciousness. At the time I was struck, and actually felt hurt, by the degree of cooperation that he was given in his investigation. While he was able to mobilize the community in support of his research, I was not able to do the same, at least not to the same extent.

Second, although in Los Angeles I was accorded the status of a fringe devotee, in the other ISKCON communities that I visited I was seen as a researcher and/or as a devotee in good standing. My initial letter to each of the communities to be surveyed highlighted my continuing involvement with the movement. In addition, I sent each of these communities a letter from a well-known and respected devotee, who showed his support for my research and pointed out my general sympathies toward Krishna Consciousness and ISKCON. I quote from both of those letters:

I feel strongly that with your support, and that of the other devotees in your community, I will be able to write a book on ISKCON that is rich, detailed, and from the point of view of the devotees themselves. Given my sociological interests and my personal relationship with Krishna Consciousness, I feel uniquely qualified to carry out this work in an informed and serious fashion. I have been involved in the Los Angeles *New Dwarka* community for five years now, both in researching the movement and in uncovering my own spiritual consciousness. In addition, in recent months I have been working with the *gurukula* and over the past several years have taken part in the LA community's '*bhakta* program.' You can see that I am *not* the typical 'outside' researcher, but rather am a person with personal and practical interests in the future of ISKCON and its devotees.

Burke has been informally associated with the *New Dwarka* community for about five years, chants sporadically, attends temple functions, and performs service. He has also spent short periods of time in the *bhakta* program. Given this level of involvement, his approach to studying ISKCON goes a little deeper than that done by other 'outsiders.' His thesis could potentially be published and help to present ISKCON in a favorable light to the public. Kindly, therefore, cooperate with his efforts.

In sum, while I was taken seriously neither as a researcher nor as a member in good standing in Los Angeles, I was seen by most devotees in other ISKCON communities as a legitimate devotee-researcher. For example, consider the following exchange that occurred in Denver between myself and two devotees:

> A devotee and I were sitting outside the temple, talking about his involvement in ISKCON and various changes he had witnessed, when another devotee (Second Devotee) came along to turn in his questionnaire. He first inquired about a specific question on the questionnaire and then asked about my intentions:
> SECOND DEVOTEE: What are you going to do with all the results?
> EBR: Well first I'm going to be writing them up for my dissertation; then, hopefully, I will be writing a book on the movement. I want to write something that allows people to appreciate the devotees from their point of view.
> SECOND DEVOTEE: You should become a devotee.
> FIRST DEVOTEE: He *is* a devotee! (Denver 1980)

But my membership status in the movement created research problems in other ways. First, the number of topics of potential research both expanded and contracted as a consequence of my involvement. The devotees were more open and frank about their feelings and observations regarding ISKCON because of my involvement, but they also often omitted talking about certain basic subjects and issues regarding Krishna Consciousness because they saw me as both knowledgeable and committed. For example, when I began researching the movement in the later period for the dissertation, I was never subjected to the recruitment and conversion efforts of devotees, as I had been during my initial phases of research. I was no longer thought of as an inexperienced novice, who had to be taught the fundamentals of the philosophy or convinced of the righteousness of Krishna Consciousness. As a result, in the later period I had little or no access to the dynamics of the recruitment process as it took place interactionally within the community. What information I was able to gather on recruitment during the dissertation research was based largely on data derived from the questionnaire.

In trying to keep within my membership status, I was also very sensitive not to appear ignorant in the eyes of the devotees. I avoided asking certain questions about ISKCON and the Krishna lifestyle, because it was presumed that I had been properly socialized as an ISKCON member. Sometimes, I felt forced to guess at practices that would allow me to pass as a good member. Usually this involved faking competence to avoid revealing my overall marginality and apparent lack of seriousness toward Krishna Consciousness. One problem that often came up was my inability to sing the Sanskrit verses of various *kirtans*, which the devotees sang in the temple and elsewhere. As the following demonstrates, I occasionally got caught as an incompetent member:

On the way back from the beach with the *gurukula* kids, I got caught trying to act as a competent devotee. The situation involved singing various *kirtans* [Sanskrit songs] as we rode back to the temple. Some of the *kirtans* I knew fairly well and sang along with the kids without problems. There were a few, however, that I didn't know the words to, or at least I didn't know them all. As I often do, I faked it. I found a kid sitting in the front seat whose mouth I could see and I tried to sing along, following the words out of his mouth. After a few minutes of this, the young boy sitting on my lap turned to me and said: 'You're saying X [a particular phrase] and it's really Y.' Somewhat embarrassed, I leaned down and whispered in his ear: 'I'm just learning' (Los Angeles 1979).

On still other occasions, my membership was called into question precisely because I was acting more in a research capacity than in a membership capacity, again with embarrassing results:

This morning I attended class with the new *bhaktas* [I was taking part in the *bhakta* program for the new recruits at the time]. After reciting various Sanskrit verses, the teacher asked each of the *bhaktas* to recite a verse and give the proper translation. Each of the other *bhaktas* skillfully recited the verse and gave the translation. When my turn came I could neither recite the Sanskrit correctly nor give the translation. My embarrassment made me realize that I wasn't listening and taking seriously what was going on, as the others were. *Mainly I wasn't interested in learning Sanskrit.* That's not why I was there. I found myself searching for those moments when the conversation became 'worldly' and of relevance to being a new recruit. During the Sanskrit portion of the class, I thought about the other events and observations that I had made during the morning, which I didn't want to forget. I wrote a few brief notes while the others were attending to the class (Los Angeles 1980).

Even though my membership was called into question on numerous occasions during the course of my research, it would be incorrect to say that my presence in the community was best exemplified by these ongoing conflicts between member and research roles. On the contrary, my involvement was more often real, not simply acting in the best interests of the research. Like other ISKCON members, I had opinions about the movement's development and on occasion expressed them, *as a member*. In the following taped discussion between myself and a devotee in the Los Angeles ISKCON community, I used personal, inclusive pronouns in discussing ISKCON's book distribution tactics:

We have our primary mission, at least as this is given us by way of Srila Prabhupada: It is to distribute these books. If you're going to spread the word [about Krishna Consciousness], these books need to be distributed. And yet, as I understand it, some zones [portions of the movement] are making the decision not to distribute them, but to engage in picking [selling products] as their primary source of income, and, in a sense, these zones have stopped engaging in the most important practice set forth by the spiritual master, so that they can gain some political independence from the organization [ISKCON.] I really think that is sad. Prabhupada wasn't off [base] when he recognized the importance of distributing his books. There is no doubt about that. In other words, there are organizational things that are going on that are compromising the very thing that I think we want most. We want people to understand the ideal process of Krishna Consciousness, not some newspaper account. And if we are finding it difficult to do that job, then what in hell are we doing (Los Angeles 1979).

On other occasions, when I was working with the children in the *gurukula*, my genuine devotion again became apparent, in much the same way. On the way home from the beach the following discussion took place:

> DEVOTEE BOY: Did you ever see Prabhupada?
>
> EBR: Yes, the last time that he was in *New Dwarka* [the Los Angeles ISKCON community].
>
> SECOND BOY: I saw Prabhupada when I was a little baby. Prabhupada held me in his arms.
>
> THIRD BOY: Prabhupada held me in his arms too. Prabhupada said that I was going to be a great devotee.
>
> EBR: I hope all of us will become great devotees (Los Angeles 1980).

The difficulties of conducting research in a movement claiming a high commitment from its members, like Hare Krishna, are suggested by these descriptions of my field work experiences. While it was necessary to find an acceptable role within the Los Angeles community (not as a researcher, but as a participant) in order to develop the relationships necessary to conduct the research, these very relationships served to socialize me into ISKCON and Krishna Consciousness. From my earliest stance of avoiding participation at all costs, my position within the community developed into one in which I took on the status of a member. The task of adequately attending to both roles often produced difficulties for the research itself, and it also created personal dilemmas for me about what my involvement meant, both to me personally and to the persons who knew me apart from the movement.

## Personal Dilemmas Created by Membership in a Deviant Lifestyle

Researchers studying deviant lifestyles often come to be seen by their friends, acquaintances, and associates as having been somehow contaminated by their involvements with such denigrated populations. Investigators studying the lives of sexual deviants, such as the gay community, for example, often have their own sexuality called into question because of their research interest in these alternate lifestyles (Kirby and Corzine 1981). Researchers have sometimes chosen not to study such deviant groups precisely because of the resulting personal stigma, with the corresponding threat it poses to their professional lives. My involvement with Hare Krishna is perhaps different from other investigations of deviant lifestyles, because my membership role within that setting was consciously decided upon in the course of my research, instead of being imputed to me by others based on pure association.

   Membership in any deviant group is strongly dependent upon the relationships that an individual forms with other group members. However, while forming affective ties within the group is critical to the membership and conversion process (Lofland and Stark 1965; Snow and Phillips 1980) this process of assimilation is furthered, and reinforced, by the reactions of people outside the group or movement (Turner and Killian 1972; Snow 1976). As with other people who have chosen to become Krishna devotees, I was subjected to many of the suspicions that are often associated with taking part in a deviant lifestyle. Friends, family, acquaintances, and fellow students all questioned and evaluated the extent of my involvement with ISKCON. One long-time friend, whose brothers are former ISKCON members, told of his concern about my involvement with the movement and the means by which he calculated the degree to which I was being pulled into the Krishna lifestyle:

FRIEND: I saw the ways that you were becoming real defensive about the movement. The slightest criticisms, that before you just let pass by, now became a cause. You wouldn't allow me to criticize . . . I remember having a couple of conversations where I would jokingly criticize ISKCON, but I really meant it. I just wanted to see what your reactions would be so that I could judge the level of your involvement. I was gauging what your relationship was by how you would react. If you reacted very defensively, which you did, then I knew that you were real involved. But even more, I could see the ways that you were becoming more interested in the philosophy; you talked a lot more about it. Again that was a gauge that allowed me to see how involved you were. I could see the way that you were getting involved actually was skewing the way that you were interpreting what was going on. I just felt that it was increasingly difficult for you to be, not objective, but just critical. I mean ISKCON was certainly worth a little bit of criticism, but you wouldn't make it. You were trying to couch things in a way that wouldn't seem critical. So I just looked for markers because I could see that you were really becoming involved.

EBR: What were some of the other markers?

FRIEND: One was dress; you used to wear a lot of Krishna shirts. And your beads, are you still wearing your [Krishna] beads?

EBR: No.

FRIEND: Other things were that you were always saying 'Hare Bol' [a greeting used by the devotees] at the beginning and end of a conversation, just like the devotees. You said things like 'Ah Krishna,' or you would be singing various Krishna songs, things like that (Los Angeles 1981).

An exchange with my wife during the course of my field work points further to the ways in which I was becoming involved in the movement, and her fears about it. Late in the evening my wife (JB) and I sat down to a steak dinner. Two things came out of this.

EBR: I want to give up eating beef. I am just going to eat poultry and fish.

JB: Why?

EBR: Well, it's better for you if you eat less red meat. I have always heard it is bad for you, lots of cholesterol.

JB: [not satisfied pushes further] Is that the only reason?

EBR: [I stumble around in my mind looking for another reason, but then just say] I don't want to eat cows.

JB: That's what I thought!

JB: [After our talking a bit more, she finally says] Do what you like, but don't expect me to stop eating meat.

A few minutes later after a long silence,

JB: One thing I want to make clear.

EBR: What's that?

JB: None of our kids are ever going into the *gurukula*. I want you to understand how I feel about that.

EBR: I have no intention of ever putting a kid of mine in the *gurukula*.

JB: The way you are getting involved with these people, I don't know what you'll feel like in the future, so I just want you to know how I feel about this now (Los Angeles 1981).

Involvement in the movement created a variety of other personal problems. On numerous occasions during the course of my research, I was party to conversations about cults in general and Hare Krishna in particular. I often chose to avoid taking part in these conversations because to have done so would have brought my involvement with Hare Krishna into public light. My personal involvement made it difficult for me to take part in discussions about cults because of the burden of defense that I felt I would be forced to argue:

Towards the end of the seminar (group psychotherapy) a discussion emerged about cults. Members of the class began talking about the factors that led young people to take part in cults. The thrust of the discussion centered around the type of personality that would be attracted to the structured existence of cult life. There was considerable discussion as to whether the members of cults were brainwashed, or whether they had been psychologically 'unstable' to begin with. Many members of the class seemed to think that cults like Hare Krishna, which was mentioned specifically, were entrapping young people who were 'suffering psychologically.' During the discussion, I remained silent, but uncomfortable, feeling that I should intervene and set straight some of the notions being discussed, which I felt were incorrect. I continued to hold back, however. Finally, the woman sitting next to me, who was an acquaintance of mine, turned and said 'I really would like to hear what Burke has to say on this issue, since he is studying Hare Krishna.' Having been exposed, I then went on to talk about the changes in the kinds of people who were entering movements like Hare Krishna, and how it would be incorrect to assume that all, or most, of these people were in any way pathological. Persons joining the cults did so for many reasons. At this point, one member of the class remarked 'So why didn't you say something earlier?' (Los Angeles 1979).

But perhaps the most dramatic and emotional event that took place during my research occurred when I faced the Human Subjects Committee at the university in order to gain clearance to distribute my questionnaire. Having been awarded a small grant, I was required to get a "human subjects clearance" prior to administering the questionnaire. After several unsatisfactory written communications about specific procedures to be employed in distributing and having the forms returned, I was asked to appear before the committee. Initially, they addressed specific questions regarding the questionnaire to me. However, the committee's questions quickly turned to the Krishnas themselves and to my involvement with them. They asked questions like: Weren't these people involved in subjecting their members to something akin to brainwashing? How did I ever get involved in this movement to begin with? What did I think of their activities at the airport? Finally, after several minutes of being questioned in this manner, the chair of the committee announced that he had a question to ask on behalf of one member of the committee who wished to remain anonymous. At first I objected, saying that he/she should deliver the question in person. The chair refused and proceeded to say: "One member of the committee feels that this research is not for the purposes that you have stated. Specifically, he or she feels that you are doing the research for the Krishna movement, rather than for academic reasons. Further, he or she believes that you are involved with the Krishnas and hence would like you to specifically address the question of your relationship with them." I did not immediately recognize that the committee's work did not have anything to do with the specifics of my relationship with the movement. I went ahead explaining my religious views and describing the ways they had been influenced by my association with Krishna Consciousness. I assured the committee that, while I had gained an appreciation of the philosophy and lifestyle of Krishna Consciousness, I did not consider myself either a devotee or a "front" for ISKCON.

Several days later, after I had again been asked to address myself to still further questions regarding the questionnaire, I met personally with the chair of the committee. I told him in no uncertain terms that I felt that *my* rights had been compromised by the committee's reaction to my research. He then told me that two members of the committee (who were not themselves researchers) were afraid that I was about to involve the university in a possible Jonestown situation.[2]

## Leaving the Field: Membership Reconsidered

Although my membership status within ISKCON posed a number of personal and research-related problems during the course of my investigation, these problems continued, and became more complex and emotional, after I left the field and began analyzing my data. For several months after leaving the field, I struggled to find a way to write about ISKCON. While many students beginning the data analysis and writing phase of their dissertation feel overwhelmed for a time, I felt an additional sense of depression, which grew from my long-standing relationship with ISKCON. Being a group member and doing sociology are very different enterprises, and I felt that in many ways I was betraying my relationship with the movement and its members by now turning the devotees into objects of analysis. Furthermore, sociology often promotes a cynical way of seeing and analyzing the world, and I wanted to be respectful of ISKCON. As I began analyzing my materials, the analysis that began to take shape seemed critical of the movement, too critical, I thought. To write about the movement's controversial public solicitation efforts, for example, seemed important for sociological purposes, but wasn't I betraying the devotees by pursuing such a line of analysis? For a number of months I struggled with the issues to be analyzed as well as the proper tone to use in the analysis.

After I began analyzing my data and writing the dissertation, I avoided attending functions at the temple and more or less dropped out of sight. While I lived only blocks away from the ISKCON community, I would not allow myself even to walk past the community for fear that I would come upon a devotee on the street. At first I was afraid that the devotees would ask about the dissertation, what topics I was writing about and so on. Because I increasingly came to see the dissertation taking a more critical line of analysis, I wanted to avoid going into any details. But after several months these feelings gave way to more intense concerns. I felt that the devotees would in all probability feel betrayed by me. After all, many of them had given me open access to their lives primarily because they had seen me as a member and had understood me to be sincere in my feelings toward ISKCON and Krishna Consciousness. Also, by now I was unsure and confused about exactly what my true feelings toward ISKCON and Krishna Consciousness were. If I was a member with any conviction at all, shouldn't I be attending *arati* and other functions at the temple? Had I been lying to myself all this time? Had I really been sincere about my interest in Krishna Consciousness, or had I simply tricked myself into believing that I was for the sake of the research?

During the year that I was writing my dissertation, I only visited the ISKCON community in Los Angeles twice. On each occasion I was very uncomfortable; I consciously avoided devotees whom I thought would be inquisitive about my work or whom I thought might be particularly hurt by my apparent lack of sincerity.

> My wife and I walked to the temple this afternoon. We wanted to show our new daughter to one of the Krishna women who was a long-time friend. As we came into the community, I spotted the headmaster of the *gurukula* and his son on the other side of the street. He waved and with a smile said 'Hare Krishna.' I replied the same but continued walking. The young boy then ran over and asked when I was going to come and visit the *gurukula*. I didn't know what to say, but then said: 'Well I will be moving soon, so I'm not sure if I will be able to.' With that I excused myself, saying I wanted to attend the *arati*. I walked away feeling very guilty, wishing I hadn't come at all. The headmaster and his son were friends and yet I couldn't be friendly. While my wife went looking for the Krishna woman, I went to the temple where I would be less conspicuous, since this was Sunday and there would be a large number of visitors present.

## Conclusion

Field work, unlike other research strategies employed by investigators of social life, generally involves some level of participation in the everyday life of the people being studied. While the degree of participation is often a matter of choice or preference for an individual field worker, there are some settings which require active participation as a condition of the ability to do research. My investigation of ISKCON highlights the negotiated quality of field work roles. Instead of being predetermined, my relations with ISKCON members evolved over time as I became more deeply involved in Krishna Consciousness and as changes took place within ISKCON itself that accommodated the participation of less-committed members. My relationship with ISKCON was further reinforced as I became subjected to the suspicions and judgments of persons outside the Krishna movement.

But my field research on the Hare Krishna movement raises an additional issue regarding field work and the need and efforts made to gain understanding of a new social world. In the past several years a number of field workers have advocated more active, fully participatory roles for conducting field research. Some more ethnomethodologically oriented field workers have even proposed becoming a member of the studied group as a strategy for gaining insight into the members' worlds (Mehan and Wood 1975; Jules-Rosette 1975).[3] In this model of field work, emphasis is placed on the investigator participating as the members participate. While field workers may or may not actually become formal members of the groups they study, they nevertheless need to participate and to experience the members' everyday lives by "immersion in the natural situation" (Douglas 1976). This approach to field research is thought to yield the subjectively meaningful world of members, rather than an objective analytic account of their world. While I believe active involvement does facilitate access to the members' world, there are nevertheless limitations to this kind of field work.

First, many, if not most, settings that field workers study are characterized by local politics. To take on a membership role necessarily involves making choices about what sort of member the researcher wants to be. Field workers who embrace membership as a research strategy are forced to decide from what position they will gain an understanding of the events in a particular setting. For example, towards the end of my field work with ISKCON, I became a charter member of an organization that was composed of ex-ISKCON members who were challenging ISKCON policies under the new leadership. To become involved in this group was to publicly acknowledge and show my feelings toward ISKCON and toward the policies of the leadership. While I sought to hide my involvement in this splinter group from ISKCON members, some of the devotees did become aware of my membership in this counterorganization. As a result, my relations with some ISKCON members became strained. In the end, this became one factor that pressured me to leave the field when I did.

Second, while field workers may seek to become members in good faith, it seems unlikely that they can ever become more than marginal members. The interests and concerns of field workers ultimately are not the same as those of the people who are committed to the group. As Bittner (1973:121) states, the field worker "is the only person in the setting who is solely and specifically interested in what things are for 'them'." While I learned the religious practices of Krishna Consciousness and took part in the life of the ISKCON community, I nevertheless lacked the commitment that characterized other persons in the setting. Ultimately, I had come to study their world, even though I had become a member of it as a means to better understand it.

# 3
# Searchers or Victims: Who Joins and Why

**W**hy people act together collectively has long been a subject of debate among sociologists and other social scientists interested in social behavior. Yet not until the 1960s, when specific new collective movements became prominent in the United States, did sociologists begin to take special interest in differential recruitment—why some people rather than others join new and existing social movements. While studies in the 1960s tended to focus on the rise of political activism and dissent in America (Feuer 1969; Flacks 1967; Freeman 1979; Keniston 1967, 1971; Wood 1974) the focus of investigation tended to shift in the early 1970s to the growth and expansion of the new religious movements (Bromley and Shupe 1979: Downton 1979: Judah 1974; Lofland 1966; Snow 1976; Wallis 1977).

In this chapter I discuss and critically analyze sociological approaches to the issue of differential recruitment. Using quantitative and qualitative data, I describe and analyze how and why some young people in America have chosen to devote their lives to ISKCON and Krishna Consciousness. Critics of the new religions have argued that cult indoctrination, resulting in brainwashing, has allowed the cults to expand in America (Clark 1979; Conway and Siegelman 1978; Enroth 1977; Singer 1979). While my discussion of the processes of recruitment into ISKCON is meant to be objective and scholarly rather than emotional and one-sided, it nevertheless indirectly touches on issues relating to the brainwashing model of conversion. Those who have sided with the anticult movement and its ideology argue that the young people joining movements like ISKCON are ultimately passive, unknowing victims of the cults and their leaders. By contrast, the findings presented in this chapter on the young people who have become devotees of Krishna suggest that many were actively searching for an alternative lifestyle previous to their contact with ISKCON. Instead of being passive victims, ISKCON members were active creators of their own lives. The fundamental differences between the devotees and many other young people in America is that they have chosen to pursue a spiritual way of life, which stands outside the traditional institutions found in America.

My treatment of recruitment to ISKCON will involve discussing and analyzing four levels of explanation: (1) categorical-demographic analysis; (2) macro-structural and social psychological analysis; (3) members' accounts of their reasons for joining ISKCON; and (4) micro-structural or interactional approaches to differential recruitment. Instead of taking the normal stance of arguing for one approach at the expense of the others, I will view each instead as one part of the differential recruitment equation. From my perspective, any movement's growth is largely an outcome of a dialectical process, which is best depicted by some concepts and explanations central to each of the above approaches, operating together.

The starting point for traditional approaches to the questions of participation in social movements (categorical, social psychological, and macro-historical approaches) is that joiners differ from nonjoiners on the basis of some predispositional category. People who take up collective action are essentially different from those who do not on the basis of their subjective psychological states or their objective social positions and backgrounds. Each of these traditional approaches focuses specifically on demographic characteristics and/or predisposing cognitive states in trying to account for differential recruitment processes. Despite common assumptions involving the essential role of predisposing factors, each of these traditional approaches differs from the others in the central focus of its analysis: categorical-demographic analysis centers on identifying salient background factors and social categories (e.g., social class, age, religion) which are viewed as discriminating between joiners and non-joiners; macro-structural explanations seek to demonstrate how historical changes (e.g. economic deprivation, war, industrialization, urbanization) produce strains at the societal and individual level; and social psychological explanations of differential recruitment focus largely on participants' cognitive orientations and attitudes (e.g. alienation, relative deprivation, authoritarianism) and how they are linked to the goals and ideology of the movement.

Members' explanations for their decisions to join a group movement parallel the theorizing of these sociological approaches. Members' accounts also point to the connections between their pre-movement values and cognitive orientations and the ideology and lifestyle of the movement they joined.

The micro-structural or interactional approach takes a different view of the processes influencing movement recruitment. This approach sees movement participation as being strongly influenced by three factors: contacts with the movement, structural availability (i.e. a lack of alternative commitments and obligations that might limit an individual's ability to participate), and the alignment of recruits' cognitive orientations with the movement's ideology (Snow 1976; Snow *et al.* 1980; Snow and Rochford 1983). Instead of explaining movement participation largely in terms of one or more predisposing cognitive states or predetermined social categories, the micro-structural approach highlights the way group membership is ultimately an interactional accomplishment between a recruit and the adherents of a social movement. The motives for an individual's participation are viewed as largely emergent and (interactional) instead of the result of pre-existing factors that influence people's decisions to participate in a social movement.

## *Categorical-Demographic Analysis and Differential Recruitment*

Research on the activism of the 1960s focused in part on identifying the socio-economic strata, age distributions, and family backgrounds of political activists. Theories relating activism to permissive child-rearing practices among middle- and upper-class families (Adelson 1971; Flacks 1967; Keniston 1967, 1968) or as a response of the "conflict of generations" (Feuer 1969) emerged from analysis of categorical data on activists. Membership in the protest movement of the sixties was understood as resulting from developmental or lifecycle processes as well as from the family milieu in which the activists were raised.

Categorical analysis assumes that traditional demographic variables such as age, social class, religion, race, and family background are social categories that help to explain individual decisions to become movement members. While I will have more to say about the short-comings of this approach to differential recruitment later, for now, I want to use this demographic approach to describe who has joined the Hare Krishna movement. I will begin by discussing the ages of ISKCON members at the time they joined the movement and then consider a range of other characteristics that describes the devotees and the families in which they were raised.

*Age:* Perhaps more than any other single categorical variable, age best distinguishes those who have joined the Krishna movement in America. As the data reported in table 3.1 indicate, over half of the devotees joined ISKCON before their twenty-first birthday. Only one in five joined over the age of twenty-six. In this respect, the age composition of those joining the movement has changed little since its early days in San Francisco. Judah (1974) reports that 85 percent of the

Table 3.1.
Age Joining ISKCON

| Age in years | Percentage |
|---|---|
| 13–17 years | 9% (18) |
| 18–19 years | 15% (32) |
| 20–21 years | 27% (58) |
| 22–23 years | 15% (32) |
| 24–25 years | 14% (30) |
| 26 and over | 20% (43) |
| TOTAL | (100%)(213) |

devotees surveyed were twenty-five years or younger at the time of his survey.[1]

While those who have joined ISKCON in America have been predominantly young, many of the other social movements—religious, political, and otherwise—that emerged and expanded in the sixties and seventies also relied heavily on youth to help swell their ranks. Given the enormous number of post World War II baby boomers who came of age during this period, it is not surprising that they became the major constituents of numerous movements, pushing a variety of causes. (As I discuss later in this chapter, this is due largely to the structural availability of youth.)

*Ethnic Background:* Since ISKCON's earliest days, the movement has drawn its support almost exclusively from young Anglo-Americans (Judah 1974). As indicated in table 3.2, a large majority of ISKCON's adherents in America are white. Only 20 percent of the movement's ranks are nonwhites, and half of these are devotees who were originally from countries outside of the United States.

Although ISKCON's membership continues to remain overwhelmingly Anglo-Saxon in its ethnic composition, there have been changes

Table 3.2.
Race/Ethnic Background

| Race | Percentage |
|------|------------|
| White | 80% (165) |
| Black | 5% (10) |
| Hispanic | 6% (13) |
| Foreign born | 9% (19) |
| TOTAL | (100%)(207) |

since the mid-seventies in this composition. The movement's constituency is no longer limited to white youth. Increasing numbers of Hispanics (Mexican Americans and Puerto Ricans) and blacks have joined the movement's ranks. In fact, data from the devotee survey clearly underestimate the total number of ISKCON members from each of these groups. Observation of the ISKCON communities in New York and Los Angeles suggests that the number of Hispanic devotees is considerably larger than is reflected by the data in table 3.2. Many Spanish-speaking devotees were unable to complete the survey, and therefore the true proportion of Hispanics as opposed to blacks and whites is not reflected in the data reported. While the growth in the number of blacks in the movement appears not to have kept pace with the growth rate of Hispanics, again, the data do not accurately reflect the overall proportion of black devotees. In one ISKCON community in the midwest alone, the majority of the community's members were black in 1980. Unfortunately, the devotees from this community did not participate in the devotee survey, and therefore those twenty or more blacks were not part of the findings reported.

*Educational Background:* Given the youth of the devotees at the time they joined the movement, many had not completed college prior to their decisions to become ISKCON members. As reported in table 3.3, a majority had completed high school, but less than one-fourth

Table 3.3.
Educational Background

| Degree | Percentage |
| --- | --- |
| No high school degree | 13% (28) |
| High school graduate | 65% (137) |
| College graduate | 16% (34) |
| Graduate degree* | 6% (13) |
| TOTAL | (100%)(212) |

*Includes M.A., M.S., Ph.D. and professional degrees M.S.W., M.B.A.

had received a college degree or graduate degree. While most devotees had not completed college, most had attended for some period of time before dropping out. Sixty-one percent of the high school graduates in the movement had attended college for a one-year period or longer before dropping out. Over half of the devotees who had attended college had majored in the humanities and social sciences. Art, music, theater, English, and literature were the favored areas of study, with psychology leading the way in the social sciences.

One-fourth of the devotees (26 percent) were attending school at the time they decided to become ISKCON members; the majority were attending college. While some joined directly out of school, most became ISKCON devotees within one year of having dropped out, or of having graduated from high school or college. Half (49 percent) of the devotees surveyed had in fact joined ISKCON within the first year of leaving school. Some of these had decided to join the movement while they were still attending school, but they waited until they had completed their degrees before finally committing themselves to a Krishna-conscious lifestyle. But school also played another, more direct role in the recruitment process. A substantial number of ISKCON's members first contacted the movement at the educational institution they were attending. In part, this reflects the movement's conscious decision to target educational settings for missionary activities, but also the very nature of college life facilitates the diffusion of information about a range of subjects, including social movements.

*Family Background:* The Krishna devotees, like the adherents of many of the other new religions, come primarily from middle- and upper-middle-class families (Barker 1981; Downton 1979). As the findings shown in table 3.4 indicate, the fathers of ISKCON members tend to be employed in professional and administrative positions. One-third of the devotees' fathers are business and corporate executives or professionals (e.g., doctors, lawyers, accountants). An additional third are employed as business managers, as proprietors of medium-sized businesses, as administrators, or are small business owners. Of the mothers of the devotees who were employed, many worked as professionals, managers, and administrators. Somewhat less than half of the devotees' mothers chose not to work outside the family household.

The occupational standings of the devotees' parents are consistent with their levels of educational achievement. Nearly half of the devo-

Table 3.4.
Occupational Standing of Fathers and Mothers

| Occupation | Fathers | Mothers |
|---|---|---|
| Executive-professional | 32% (58) | 2% (4) |
| Managers-lesser professionals | 14% (25) | 18% (35) |
| Administrators-owners of small businesses | 20% (37) | 17% (33) |
| Clerical-sales | 10% (18) | 13% (26) |
| Skilled manual | 20% (36) | 2% (3) |
| Semi-skilled and unskilled workers | 5% (10) | 5% (10) |
| Housewives | — | 44% (88) |
| TOTAL | (101%)(184) | (101%)(199) |

tees' fathers had at least a college degree: a quarter of them had received an undergraduate education, and somewhat fewer (22 percent) had professional or graduate degrees. A third of the devotees' mothers had graduated from college with undergraduate or graduate degrees, but the majority had achieved only a high school education.

Not unexpectedly, given the occupational standings and education of the devotees' parents, most earned a good yearly income (see table 3.5). Over half of the devotees' parents had yearly incomes in excess of $20,000. Over a third of the respondents indicated that their parents' combined income was $30,000 or more. Clearly the devotees came from financially stable and relatively prosperous families. They did not come from economically deprived families, which might in some fashion have contributed to their desire to become involved in a communal movement that offered a secure way of life. In fact, just the opposite is true. They chose a lifestyle of renunciation, coming from family backgrounds of material and economic security.

*Religious Background:* A major question that arises in relation to the background of ISKCON members has to do with their previous involvements in religion. On the one hand, one might hypothesize that those pursuing the path to Krishna Consciousness are long-time reli-

Table 3.5.
Parents' Yearly Income

| Income | Percentage |
| --- | --- |
| Less than $10,000 | 13% (17) |
| $10,000–$15,000 | 15% (19) |
| $15,000–$20,000 | 13% (17) |
| $20,000–$30,000 | 20% (26) |
| Over $30,000 | 38% (49) |
| TOTAL | (99%)(128) |

NOTE: Sixty-six of the devotee respondents did not know their parents' yearly income.

gious seekers who have simply taken on a new faith by which they hope to gain spiritual salvation. On the other hand, investigators of the conversions of the young to the new religions have often implicitly assumed that the young people joining these groups were coming from a nonreligious worldview (see, for example, Judah 1974; Lofland and Stark 1965; Richardson and Stewart 1978; Snow and Phillips 1980). By definition, the phenomena of religious conversion involves an experience by which an individual's informing point of view is transformed from a nonreligious worldview (e.g., a secular or materialist one) to a perspective that sees the work of God and/or the spiritual world constantly operating in the world of everyday experience. Conversion involves a fundamental shift in one's sense of grounding (Heirich 1977) or what Kuhn (1970) refers to as a "gestalt switch." In the discussion that follows, I consider each of these possibilities as it relates to membership, and conversion to ISKCON and Krishna Consciousness. Were the youth joining ISKCON already converts to some religious worldview, or did ISKCON provide the context within which religious conversion took place?

*Religious Affiliation and Involvement During Childhood:* With few exceptions, ISKCON devotees were members of one of the established churches or synagogues during their childhood. Only a small minority grew up in households where religion had little or no importance, or where no specific religion was practiced. As indicated in table 3.6, most of the devotees grew up in Protestant or Catholic families. A substantial number also came from Jewish families. Since the time of ISKCON's early years in America, it appears that the number of Catholics joining the movement has increased. Judah's (1974) investigations in San Francisco found that less than 20 percent of the devotees surveyed were from Catholic backgrounds.

The fact that the devotees were affiliated with some religious faith ultimately says little about their degree of religious involvement or the overall centrality of a religious worldview during their early years. More than half of the devotees in fact reported that their parents stressed religious beliefs and practices throughout their childhood years. By comparison, only 17 percent felt that they had grown up in a family

Table 3.6.
Religious Affiliation During Childhood

| Religion | Percentage |
|---|---|
| Protestant | 35% (75) |
| Catholic | 33% (70) |
| Jewish | 15% (32) |
| Unspecified Christian | 6% (12) |
| Hindu | 5% (10) |
| None | 7% (14) |
| TOTAL | (101%)(213) |

where political involvement was stressed. With regard to religious training, three-fourths (77 percent) of the devotees had received formal education in the faith in which they were raised. For most devotees, this meant attending Sunday school, though many attended religious-affiliated educational institutions as well. One-fourth attended religious elementary schools, while 15 percent went to parochial high schools. A small number (5 percent) had attended religious-affiliated colleges prior to entering ISKCON.

Approximately half of the devotees attended religious services on a regular basis during their childhood (see table 3.7). Most of these attended services on a weekly basis, if not more frequently. About a third, however, rarely or never attended religious services, or their attendance was largely confined to major religious holidays such as Christmas and Easter.

Although the devotees generally came from families in which religion played a central role in their upbringing, few were practicing their family's faith at the time they contacted ISKCON. Only 12 percent had remained active in the faith they had grown up in when they were introduced to Krishna Consciousness. Over a quarter of the devotees were, however, practicing some other religious faith. All in all, 40 percent of

Table 3.7.
Frequency of Church Attendance During Childhood

| Frequency of attendance | Percentage |
|---|---|
| Rarely or never | 26% (54) |
| Less than once a month | 9% (19) |
| On average 1–2 times a month | 10% (22) |
| Weekly | 37% (79) |
| More than once a week | 10% (22) |
| Regularly as a child but rarely thereafter | 8% (16) |
| TOTAL | (100%)(212) |

ISKCON's members were practicing some religion when they joined the Krishna movement.

Taken together, these findings suggest that most of ISKCON's members came from family backgrounds in which religion played a relatively important role in their upbringing. Most had attended religious services regularly and had received formal training in their family's faith. While only a small number were practicing the faith of their family when they joined ISKCON, somewhat less than half were actively involved in some religious group or a religious organization of some kind. The pattern of religious involvement we have identified suggests two distinct types of recruits to ISKCON.

The first type of recruit is made up of those who are either largely unchurched or of people who had essentially rejected religion prior to contacting ISKCON. For these recruits, membership in ISKCON may involve a conversion to a religious worldview, though membership in the movement by no means guarantees that such a conversion experience will occur. As Bromley and Shupe (1979) have suggested in the case of the Moonies, some recruits never come to accept and internalize the movement's theology. Membership in the communal group and the social supports it provides for some members becomes an end in itself. For many recruits a conversion to a religious worldview may never be forth-coming. All too often, researchers have treated membership in a religious organization as *prima facie* evidence that such a conversion is underway, if not yet completed (see Judah 1974; Lofland and Stark 1965; Snow and Phillips 1980; Richardson and Stewart 1978). Consider, for example, the words of Stillson Judah regarding the Krishna devotees he studied in San Francisco, in regards to the question of how long it took them to convert after making contact with ISKCON:

> After their initial contact, almost 24 percent decided to surrender to Swami Bhaktivedanta immediately or during the following first week. Eight percent joined within a month of the first contact; 61 percent were devotees by the end of six months. Eleven percent waited up to a year before joining. *Thus most were converted within six months of the initial contact* [emphasis added] (1974:163).

For two decades researchers have tested and made refinements in the Lofland and Stark model without critically questioning whether it is, in fact, a conversion model at all. Despite its widespread acceptance, the model ultimately explains little about how persons come to experience a transformation in their state of consciousness. The conceptual strength of the Lofland and Stark model lies in its explanation of the processes involved in people becoming members of a religious group or movement. Yet conversion is not the same thing as membership, and, in fact, often stands in a problematic relation to it.

The second type of recruit is one who appears to be committed to a religious worldview prior to becoming an ISKCON member. By considering the notion of conversion careers or trajectories, it becomes clear that membership and conversion are different and distinct processes (Richardson 1980). Many of ISKCON's members were actively involved in some religion before they decided to become Krishna devotees. Many were raised in families that stressed religion. Others, having renounced the faith of their families, had nevertheless been involved in one or more religious groups or movements prior to their contact with

Krishna Consciousness. To argue that joining ISKCON for these people necessarily involves a religious conversion conceptually confuses the relationship between conversion and membership. While the content of their religious beliefs have certainly undergone a change as part of becoming a Krishna devotee, their informing spiritual view of the world may have remained largely unchanged. They continue to see God's work in the world, even though they now may refer to that God as Krishna. For recruits already committed to a religious state of consciousness, joining ISKCON involves a process of altering their established beliefs, understanding and practices of religion rather than conversion. Travisano distinguishes between the processes of alternation and conversion in the following way:

> Alternations are transitions to identities which are prescribed or at least permitted within the person's established universe of discourse. Conversions are transitions to identities which are proscribed within the person's established universe of discourse, and which exist in universes of discourse which negate these formally established ones (1970:601).

While it is perhaps impossible to clearly distinguish those recruits to ISKCON who are in the midst of alternation from those undergoing conversion, it nevertheless seems clear that either process may occur in relation to the religious background and experience a devotee brings with him or her into the movement.

In conclusion, theorists who attempt to explain differential recruitment by way of categorical-demographic schemes of explanation ultimately must assume that the objective categories that they use to describe members relate directly to these members' subjective experiences and actions and behaviors. In other words, they assume that peoples' experiences and actions are correlated with the characteristics that describe them as a social group. Yet the vast majority of the white middle-class youth of America with family backgrounds much the same as those of the devotees, have failed to join ISKCON, or even to have expressed any interest in doing so.

By assuming that objective categories determine indirectly subjective experience and behavior, categorical-demographic analysis leaves the real basis for participation in such movements largely unexplored. Speaking metaphorically, categorical analysis describes the features of a movement's landscape, without ever addressing itself to the ground upon which it sits. To assume that categories of actors largely share similar motivations for movement participation only glosses over the contents of members' subjectivity, and thereby overlooks the question of why and how people choose one course of action to the exclusion of others equally available.

## Macro-structural and Social Psychological Approaches to Differential Recruitment

Macro-structural approaches to the study of the growth and expansion of social movements generally combine the notions of "structural conduciveness" and "structural strain" to account for the forces underlying the mobilization and recruitment process (Smelser 1962; Gurr 1970). This approach to the issue of differential recruitment focuses attention on the fact that social movements do not emerge in a social vacuum but rather have their roots in problematical social conditions, which exist within society at specific points in history. While this approach to social movements tends to focus its analysis largely at the macro level, it nevertheless also incorporates a social psychological dimension in its attempt to explain why people ultimately take up collective action. Only when structural strains, such as "ambiguities, deprivations, conflicts, and discrepancies" (Smelser 1962:16), become internalized by individual actors do they serve as an impetus for decisions to become involved in a specific social movement seeking change.

Before turning to a discussion of the interrelationship between macro-structural and social psychological factors as these have influenced the growth and expansion of ISKCON in America, I first want to suggest how social discontent arising from changes in the larger social milieu ultimately is transformed into individual motivation, which then becomes the basis for movement participation.

*Social Discontent and a Sense of Injustice*

The study of collective behavior and social movements over the past several decades has largely been approached from within a macro-structural and social psychological framework. Movement participation has been explained in terms of fertile psychological and social predispositions such as frustration, alienation, relative deprivation and the like. These dispositions are seen as growing out of changes within the society, which ultimately promote strain at the level of the individual. As these sources of strain and their resulting discontent build up among a growing number of people within society, the potential for collective action increases. The actual emergence of a social movement, or the fact of many individuals deciding to join a pre-existing movement, however, requires that the source of discontent be generally recognized, so that those affected can band together in a common effort to promote or perhaps resist social change.

In emphasizing the importance of social discontent as a basis for collective action, some scholars working from within this approach (Turner and Killian 1972) have been pointing out a fundamental distinction between the concepts of misfortune and injustice. Individuals who interpret their feelings of discontent (i.e., alienation and deprivation) merely as a sign of misfortune have little or no motivation to take part in collective action. People who feel they have suffered from simple misfortune do not normally organize collectively in their own behalf. For example, short people face discrimination, yet they do not ordinarily constitute themselves as a group seeking fair treatment. There is no social movement championing the rights of short people because such physical characteristics are viewed both by the public and by those so afflicted as largely a matter of misfortune rather than injustice. As Charles Bedow, a spokesperson for Little People of America commented in a 1984 interview, his organization views short stature as "an inconvenience" rather than a disability. As a result, his organization exists largely as a social club for little people rather than a group pushing for the rights of its membership (*Los Angeles Times* 1984).

On the other hand, blacks, women, and other such social groups within society who face unfair treatment have constituted themselves into groups and have mobilized to protect their rights and overall group interests. For these latter groups, unfair treatment and discrimination constitute practices that are morally wrong and unjust. It is just such a sense of injustice that becomes crucial to individual and group decisions to take up collective action.

As Turner and Killian (1972:259) argue, "a movement is inconceivable apart from a vital sense that some established practice or mode of thought is wrong and ought to be replaced." Social discontent brought on by changes taking place within the social milieu is not sufficient in itself to spur people to collective action. It is only when individual misfortune becomes recognized as a collective misfortune that personal feelings of alienation and frustration begin to be seen and acted on out of a sense of injustice (Turner and Killian 1972).[2] Wood's study of student activism in Berkeley during the 1960s, for example, concluded that neither objective nor subjective forms of alienation were sufficient in themselves to account for those who were likely to become recruits to activism. While alienation perhaps provided an impulse towards action, there is no necessary causal relationship determining that this cognitive state will eventuate in a decision to take part in collective action.

But while a vital sense of injustice is crucial to movement participation, this still leaves unresolved the question of why persons join one type of movement to the exclusion of others that are equally available. In seeking to account for this part of the differential recruitment equation, the traditional approaches look to the linkages between individual cognitive states, which are seen as motivating action, and the ideology and objectives of the particular social movement chosen. For example, if individuals who are alienated from society view the source of their alienation as coming from structural inequalities embedded within American society, political action and organization would appear to be the logical choice for them to change such structures. Whether the individual chooses to become part of a reform movement or a more radical political movement depends largely on the kinds of changes that are viewed as necessary. A woman who feels a sense of injustice about the plight of women in modern society may choose to join a reformist movement or an organization that seeks to improve the economic standing of women (e.g., The National Organization for Women). Alternatively, should she see the unequal treatment of women as resulting from the capitalist economic system, she may make a decision to join forces with a socialist-feminist group. From this point of view, all forms of discrimination may be seen as deriving from the economic exploitation of workers—both male and female.

## The Counterculture and the Growth of Hare Krishna

From a macro-structural perspective, the sixties and early seventies in America were a period especially ripe for the emergence of collective movements seeking change. The war in Vietnam, and the peace movement that grew in opposition to it, sparked the growth of numerous movements—political, religious, humanitarian, and psychological. This was a period during which the youth of America were questioning the authority of the government to lead, as well as the entire established institutional system of American society. American values and ways of life faced critical questioning by many young people, who began exploring and experimenting with a range of alternative value systems and lifestyles. This social climate produced a general movement, composed primarily of youth who were seeking new values and hopes for the future, which ran counter to the values of the dominant society. Blumer describes the essential qualities of this general movement:

> People have come to form new conceptions of themselves which do not conform to the actual positions which they occupy in their life. They acquire new dispositions and interests and, accordingly, become sensitized in new directions; and conversely, they come to experience dissatisfaction where before they had none. These new images of themselves which people begin to develop in response to cultural drifts [gradual changes in the values of people], are vague

and indefinite; and correspondingly, the behavior in response to such images is uncertain and without definite aim (1951:200).

The counterculture, because it served to heighten people's awareness and their feelings of discontent without promoting any one ideology or organizational form, provided a constituency that helped feed the growth and expansion of numerous social movements during the sixties and early seventies. In a sense, the members of the counterculture were ripe for the recruitment efforts of specific social movements precisely because they were what Victor Turner calls "threshold people":

> The attributes of liminality or of liminal personae [threshold people] are necessarily ambiguous, since this condition and these persons elude or slip through the network of classifications that normally locate states and positions in cultural space. Liminal entities are neither here nor there; they are betwixt and between the positions assigned and arrayed by law, custom, convention, and ceremony (1977:95).

Members of the counterculture represent what Klapp (1969, 1972) terms "meaning seekers." The counterculture reflected a collective search for identity for its many youthful members. While a portion of the counterculture's members never actually became involved in any specific social movement as part of their quest for meaning, many did. Of course, many people participated in the peace demonstrations and various political groups and movements seeking an end to the war and a general restructuring of America's political and social institutions. Some members of the counterculture, initially seeking political solutions, ultimately turned their attention to religious and spiritual movements in their search for a lifestyle more congruent with their values.

Early studies of the Krishna movement in America stressed the role of the counterculture in the growth and expansion of the movement (Daner 1976; Johnson 1976; Judah 1974). The Krishna devotees were portrayed by these investigators as searching for greater meaning than was offered by the dominant institutions of American society. As

Daner observed in the early seventies, some youthful members of the counterculture saw Krishna Consciousness as an ideology and lifestyle that could potentially transform their own consciousness as well as the environment in which they lived:

> Young people appear preoccupied with personal consciousness and experimentation; the dropped-out, self-absorbed individual sunk in a narcotic stupor or lost in ecstatic contemplation is a common enough sight. It is to this task of remodeling themselves that the devotees of ISKCON dedicate themselves, attempting to strike through ideology to the level of consciousness in order to transform the deepest sense of self, relationships with others and even their environment (1976:14).

Judah's early account of the movement's growth and expansion in San Francisco also emphasized that primarily alienated and searching youth came to Krishna Consciousness from the counterculture:

> Hare Krishna devotees, whether remaining for a time in employed positions, going to school, or giving full time to being hippies, typically first became part of the counterculture principally because they were looking for meaning they could not find in the world of the establishment. They were, therefore, willing to experiment with an alternative style of life, which they hoped would liberate them from feelings of alienation that stemmed from conflict and rejection of the established culture (1974:110).

While these early studies of ISKCON suggest a direct link between the counterculture and the growth of the Krishna movement in America, I want to re-explore this relationship. A decade has passed since the publication of these initial studies of the movement. Many of the young people who joined ISKCON in the late seventies and early eighties have had little or no contact with the counterculture. The America of the 1980s reflects a much different culture from that of the activism that characterized the era of the counterculture. Because of this difference, the question arises as to whether present ISKCON members have their roots in the counterculture, and whether earlier images of the devotees as spiritual seekers continues to apply today.

*Meaning-seeking and Recruitment to ISKCON*

If ISKCÓN did provide a solution for the quest for meaning on the part of its members, we might logically expect that the devotees' pre-movement circumstances would have involved an active search for new values and lifestyles that might have held the hope of resolving their feelings of alienation from the larger society. One indication of how ISKCON helped resolve members feelings of alienation is suggested by the personal reports of ISKCON members. Consider the following remarks of four ISKCON devotees:

> I didn't know much about the philosophy, but I was suffering greatly, and when I met the devotees the second time I knew that I would join them. I distinctly heard from within: 'This is your opportunity to become happy and useful and perfect your life, to have all your questions answered . . . .' That voice was Krishna (Questionnaire 1980).

> Curiosity was one reason that I was attracted to ISKCON, but a big reason was the distress I was feeling. I was fed up with the material world and material life (Questionnaire 1980).

> My contact with the devotees came at a time when I was really searching. I knew the material way of life was without purpose, and everything I heard [from the devotees] seemed to fit perfectly into my own ideas. Krishna Consciousness gave a sense of purpose to life that was otherwise meaningless and ultimately leading nowhere (Questionnaire 1980).

> As a woman, the protection, security, and safety offered to me was appreciated. Also, I was tired of so many drugs and that sort of

lifestyle [sex, drugs, illegal activities, etc.] and found it difficult to live in the midst of such influences. I was just really materially exhausted. There was nothing worthwhile around, either in the wealthy suburban life of my family, the upper middle class hippie lifestyle offered in California, the sentimental fervor of so many religions, the eternal dreams of astrology, the mystic potencies of yoga, which came so easily. Everywhere the philosophies were incomplete, nothing was full and perfect and unlimitedly interesting like Krishna Consciousness (Questionnaire 1980).

In addition to such anecdotal accounts, we have more systematic evidence of the devotees' meaning-seeking behavior. Eighty-seven percent of the devotees surveyed said that they were "seeking spiritual knowledge prior to joining ISKCON." Only a handful felt that they had become spiritual seekers only after they had been exposed to Krishna Consciousness. More conclusive than these after-the-fact accounts, however, are the devotees' actual involvements in other social movements, religious organizations, and a variety of self-help groups prior to becoming ISKCON members. The findings reported in table 3.8 suggest the range of social movements and groups in which the devotees participated. Forty percent of ISKCON's members had participated in the counterculture of the 1960s. As might be expected, most who had participated in the counter-culture had also joined the Krishna movement during its early years in America. While nearly two-thirds of the devotees who had joined ISKCON between 1967–1971 had previously participated in the counterculture, only one-fourth of the devotees who had joined ISKCON after 1977 had taken part in the counterculture. A similar trend is apparent for members' participation in the peace movement. Over half of the early converts to Krishna had taken part in the antiwar movement, while only a small percentage of ISKCON members who joined after 1977 were so involved. These later recruits to ISKCON did, however, participate slightly more often in psychologically oriented groups as well as in religious movements, churches, and/or spiritual groups than did their more senior Godbrothers and Godsisters.

Table 3.8.
Involvements in Other Social Movements, Religious Organizations, and Self-Help Groups by Year of Joining
ISKCON

| Type of movement or group | ISKCON members joining 1967–71 | ISKCON members joining 1972–76 | ISKCON members joining 1977–80 | Mean % |
|---|---|---|---|---|
| Political movements[a] | 27% | 19% | 10% | 17%(37) |
| Anti-war (peace) movement | 54% | 23% | 15% | 26%(56) |
| Counterculture | 63% | 41% | 26% | 40%(85) |
| Self-awareness or psychologically oriented groups[b] | 37% | 35% | 41% | 37%(80) |
| Religious movements, churches, and/or spiritual groups[c] | 22% | 20% | 23% | 22%(46) |
| Therapy or counseling | 17% | 17% | 12% | 15%(32) |

[a]Types of political movements include: various radical groups (e.g., Students for a Democratic Society, Anti-war Groups, The Socialist Workers Party), traditional political groups and parties and an assortment of others including The Nixon Eviction Committee, Movement for a Democratic Military, and "No Nukes."

[b]Types of self-awareness and psychological groups include: Encounter groups, "T" groups, Erhard Seminar Training (EST), Esalan Institute, and a variety of less well-known self-help groups, such as the Berkeley Holistic Health Center and Morehouse.

[c]Types of religious movements, churches, and spiritual groups include: Traditional faiths (e.g., Catholic Church, Jewish, Methodist), Fundamentalist Christian Churches (e.g., Pentacostal Church), various forms of yoga (e.g., Hatha yoga and Kundalini yoga), other new religions (e.g., Self-Realization Fellowship, Divine Light Mission, Sri Chimoy, Satya Sai Baba, Scientology, and Transcendental Meditation), and a variety of other religious groups and faiths such as Sufism, Quakerism, and Buddhism.

The devotees who joined ISKCON during its early years in America (1967–1971) were involved as participants in more social movements and/or traditional religious and political groups than more recent recruits to the Krishna movement have been. If participation is defined strictly as active membership in a specific movement organization, our findings show that nearly two-thirds (63 percent) of ISKCON's early members were involved in one or more movements seeking social, spiritual, or internal personal change prior to becoming devotees.[3] The devotees who joined ISKCON during the middle years of its history in America (1972–1976) had participated less frequently in movements and groups seeking change. Only 40 percent of these devotees had been members of one or more groups or movements prior to joining Hare Krishna. Half of the devotees who joined ISKCON since 1977 have been participants in groups or movements seeking change.

While the devotees' previous involvements in groups and movements seeking change provide one measure of their search for meaning, another involves their use of and experimentation with mind-altering drugs. The use of drugs within the counterculture was commonplace and was part of the search for alternative forms of consciousness. The use of drugs can also be understood as an attempt by individuals to stand outside of society and its normative expectations. The early studies of the Krishna devotees stressed the fact that drugs played a central role in the devotees' lifestyles prior to their joining ISKCON. Judah's survey of the San Francisco temple in the early 1970s found, for example, that 91 percent of the devotees had smoked marijuana, three-fourths of whom admitted to using it regularly. Eighty-five percent of the devotees had at least experimented with LSD, and again, many were frequent users. One devotee who had joined the movement in 1970 reported that during the early days of the movement many devotees had felt that some previous experience with LSD was actually a prerequisite for understanding Krishna Consciousness.

The data reported in table 3.9 suggest that the use of drugs continues to characterize most of the young people joining ISKCON. Only a small minority of the devotees have never used drugs. The vast major-

Table 3.9.
Prior Use of Drugs and Other Intoxicants by ISKCON Members

| Type of Drug | Percentage |
| --- | --- |
| No drug use | 13% (27) |
| Alcohol only | 5% (10) |
| Marijuana only | 11% (24) |
| Hallucinogens (i.e., LSD, peyote) | 1% (2) |
| Alcohol and marijuana | 8% (18) |
| Marijuana and hallucinogens | 14% (30) |
| All types of drugs and intoxicants (i.e., alcohol, marijuana, and hallucinogens) | 47% (101) |
| TOTAL | (99%)(212) |

ity have at least experimented with some forms of drugs (i.e., alcohol, marijuana, hallucinogens) prior to becoming devotees. Eighty-one percent had used marijuana and nearly two-thirds (62 percent) had taken LSD at some point prior to joining the movement.

While most ISKCON members had used drugs of one kind or another prior to joining ISKCON, these findings must be interpreted with caution. Some observers might be tempted to argue that ISKCON has largely attracted drug users seeking just one more high through their involvement with Krishna Consciousness.[4] During ISKCON's early years in San Francisco (1967–1969) this kind of appeal was in fact used to attract young hippies to the movement: "Stay high all the time, discover eternal bliss" (Johnson 1970). While ISKCON was successful in attracting some of these youth, most never became involved with the movement even for a brief time. While drug use perhaps does suggest some degree of alienation from the dominant culture and shows a general willingness to experiment with altered forms of consciousness, it does not by any means provide an explanation for why people have taken up a Krishna-conscious lifestyle, particularly since the devotees' way of life strictly forbids drug use.

The data on ISKCON's members suggest that many, if not most, were seeking new meanings and alternative lifestyles prior to their decisions to join ISKCON. While this search for meaning best characterizes ISKCON's earliest members, the search for alternative lifestyles and values is not limited to this group alone. While the social climate of the sixties in America clearly facilitated the emergence and early growth of the movement, ISKCON continued to attract new members after this era in American history had passed. While the sources of discontent were perhaps different for the movement's early members from those that motivated the members who came later, each group, nevertheless, saw ISKCON and Krishna Consciousness as a viable alternative to the materialistic values and goals that characterize contemporary American society.

To conclude, macro-structural and social psychological approaches to differential recruitment highlight the dual roles of both larger social conditions and members' subjective motivations to explain movement participation. While predisposing cognitive states may be necessary in some way for participation in a social movement, this perspective overlooks the interactional processes by which recruitment actually takes place. Prospective recruits may be susceptible to a movement's message on cognitive levels, but they still must come into contact with a movement whose ideology and goals accord with their own views. Many people in society are predisposed to join some social movement or other, yet most do not in fact so participate.

## How Members Account For Becoming ISKCON Devotees

The accounts ISKCON members give for having joined the movement tend to emphasize the linkage between their pre-movement cognitive orientations and the movement's ideology and way of life. As indicated in table 3.10, most devotees accounted for their decision to join ISKCON in terms of the movement's philosophy. Well over one-third ranked the Krishna belief system as the major reason for their decision to join ISKCON. An additional third, while acknowledging that other factors had more of an influence, nevertheless ranked the movement's philosophy as one of the most significant factors contributing to their decision to join. Consider the following remarks offered by four ISKCON members for their decisions to join the movement:

I saw logically and scientifically that this philosophy explains the how and why of everything I saw in this world. I also saw that as in other religious philosphies that I approached there was no need for 'blind faith,' everything was provable logically and to a certain extent 'scientifically' (Questionnaire 1980).

It was actually only the [Krishna] books themselves that hooked me. I was actually hooked as soon as I saw them. Within two weeks after reading Prabhupada's books I moved into the temple. I took years to come to the movement after contact with the devotees, but no time at all after contact with Prabhupada's words. I have moved in and out [of the movement] at times, but never because of any disrespect for the philosophy. My absorption with the philosophy has remained constant in or out of the temple (Questionnaire 1980).

I read every philosophy I could get my hands on but none of them offered a practical solution to social and personal problems. I immediately saw how this philosophy actually filled in the missing link, the center; there were no loopholes; all my questions were satisfied (Questionnaire 1980).

I sincerely wanted to serve God—know who I was, what my purpose was in life in relation to God. The Church was no longer able to answer my questions. I believed in one supreme Lord and was wanting that strict spiritual life which the movement offered. I

Table 3.10.
Members' Reasons for Joining ISKCON

| Reasons for joining | % Ranked as first reason for joining | % Ranked second to fourth reason | % Ranked fifth or less as a reason for joining | Total |
|---|---|---|---|---|
| Philosophy of the movement | 39%(82) | 36%(77) | 25%(52) | (100%)(211) |
| Warmth and friendliness of the devotees | 16%(33) | 46%(98) | 38%(80) | (100%)(211) |
| Attraction to Srila Prabhupada | 12%(26) | 34%(71) | 54%(114) | (100%)(211) |
| Fact that my life was going nowhere and I wanted to explore another lifestyle | 8%(17) | 29%(61) | 63%(133) | (100%)(211) |
| Participating in the kirtans with the other devotees | 2%(5) | 27%(56) | 71%(150) | (100%)(211) |
| Movement offered a more secure way of life | 1%(3) | 15%(32) | 83%(176) | (99%)(211) |
| Attraction to my guru (not Srila Prabhupada) | 2%(4) | 7%(14) | 91%(193) | (100%)(211) |
| Deity worship | 1%(3) | 7%(14) | 92%(194) | (100%)(211) |
| Other* | 7%(14) | 12%(25) | 82%(172) | (101%)(211) |

*Many of the devotees who cited other reasons for joining reported that their decisions to join were largely based upon progressive realizations they experienced by practicing the Krishna-conscious lifestyle (i.e., chanting and adhering to the regulative principles). The fact that I did not include this as one of the choices on my questionnaire, I now consider a gross oversight. I suspect that many devotees would have chosen this as a basis for their membership, had it been included; at least, a number of devotees have said as much. A second reason mentioned in the "Other" category was the attraction of a number of devotees to *prasadam* (spiritual food). Several devotees mentioned this as the major reason why they joined ISKCON.

could perceive that what I was looking for was in ISKCON from hearing about the Krishna-conscious philosophy! Certainly not what I was seeing externally. I didn't know what the deities were. Why did the people [devotees] dress like that etc. (Questionnaire 1980).

The second reason members gave most often for the decision to join the movement involved social ties with ISKCON members. While not the single most significant reason for joining, nearly half of the devotee respondents indicated that the "warmth and friendliness of the devotees" contributed to their decision to join ISKCON. As two devotees explained:

ISKCON offered a lifestyle exactly the way I was looking to live. The devotees were the nicest people I had ever met (Questionnaire 1980).

I was attracted to the movement for many reasons (the philosophy etc.), but what was most important to me was the devotees themselves. I could see that they were sincere people, concerned about me and about each other. In a world so often uninterested in the plight of others, I felt a great sense of warmth which was very appealing (Los Angeles 1979).

The third factor influencing the decision to join the movement for a significant portion of ISKCON's membership—in particular, the early recruits to the movement—involved an attraction to the charisma of Srila Prabhupada. In the earliest days of ISKCON, the devotees were able to develop an intimate relationship with their spiritual master. As one devotee, who joined ISKCON in 1968, explained:

Srila Prabhupada was obviously speaking out of love for God and although I had no concept that God was a person, still I wanted to hear from Prabhupada because he was: (1) speaking authoritatively (quoting Sanskrit from the *Bhagavad Gita*); (2) inconceivably humble (Prabhupada wasn't trying to cheat me or to take my money;

he was only trying to serve Krishna); (3) obviously very self-controlled himself (Questionnaire 1980).

As ISKCON expanded throughout America and the world during the seventies it became more difficult for movement members to have a personal relationship with Srila Prabhupada. Many devotees did, of course, develop an indirect relationship with him through their worship of Prabhupada and by means of the occasional opportunity to see and perhaps speak with him prior to his death in 1977.

Another factor which entered into the decision to join the movement for a portion of ISKCON's membership related to the congruence between certain aspects of the Krishna lifestyle and the ways of life they were already accustomed to. For example, nearly a third (31 percent) of the devotees reported that they were long-time vegetarians prior to joining ISKCON. Another 17 percent had given up eating meat immediately prior to becoming an ISKCON devotee. Yet another third of the devotees had at least experimented with vegetarianism or had limited their consumption of meat at some point in their lives. All in all, 82 percent of the devotees either were vegetarians or had at least attempted to regulate their consumption of meat before joining ISKCON. While many devotees were attracted to the movement's strict vegetarianism, others also found the movement's stance against drugs and other intoxicants appealing. As one woman who joined the movement in Washington, D.C., explained:

My specific reason for joining was that I was attracted to the lifestyle of the devotees—particularly that they were vegetarian, did not take intoxicants, were thoughtful people, dedicated and renounced. I was a vegetarian and had rejected intoxication, and was searching for meaning to my life. There were very few people that I knew at the time who had similar beliefs. When I went to the temple and discovered a whole community of people living in this way, I became very attracted to them and found it impossible to continue attending art school (a very degraded place) in a city where there was no temple. So I left school and moved to the temple (Questionnaire 1980).

The contents of the devotees' accounts of their reasons for joining ISKCON stress in general the natural and logical nature of their decisions. Their participation was based consciously upon an attraction to the values and beliefs of Krishna Consciousness. In this sense, members' accounts of their reasons for joining the movement parallel the traditional accounts offered by sociologists to explain differential recruitment processes. A common feature of both kinds of explanation is the assumption that the members' pre-movement cognitive orientations must be somehow aligned with the movement's ideology and way of life if an individual is to become a movement member.

Without denying the existence of such linkages, for at least some recruits, I now want to suggest that such a view overlooks the way in which reasons for joining a movement are often no more than "motive talk" (Blum and McHugh 1971; Scott and Lyman 1968; Snow and Phillips 1980) and should not be taken as hard data, which reflect members' actual motives, predispositions, attractions, and feelings prior to joining. To accept uncritically members' accounts of the factors influencing their recruitments and conversions neglects the ways in which peoples' autobiographical stories are constantly being revised, redefined, and reconstructed to accord with their present experiences. Accepting such explanations at face value overlooks the way in which reasons and motives inevitably and necessarily reflect present circumstances.[5] Movements, by their very nature, provide their members with ideologically based explanations of why any person should join their ranks. To become a member of a movement means, in large part, learning the movement's rhetoric, its vocabulary of explanations and motivations about why and how the larger society stifles important aspects of existence, and relatedly, how the movement provides a necessary and meaningful alternative to that society. In this way, a movement's ideology serves as an interpretive screen used by members to reconstruct their own life stories to bring them into line with the movement's theories and to find a trajectory for their own lives which leads clearly to their present positions. Beckford's analysis of the Jehovah's Witnesses in England points out how this group's ideology served as a resource influencing the content of members' accounts of their conversions:

Jehovah's Witnesses' conversion accounts should be treated as skillful accomplishments of actors who have at their disposal the official version of their movement's rationale. The Witnesses are able to draw on this rationale and thereby make practical decisions about what to include and what to omit. The result is an intentionally persuasive, but implicit, statement about allegedly commonsensical feasibility of becoming a Jehovah's Witness. That is, Witnesses explain by implicit reference to the movement's rationale that it makes sense to have experienced certain things in the way that they claim to have done (1978:260).

## Micro-Structural Approaches to Differential Recruitment

Recent work by interactionists studying the processes of movement recruitment have been openly critical of the traditional approaches to this issue. Lofland (1977), Snow and Phillips (1980), and Snow *et al.* (1980) for example, argue that many persons in society experience alienation, deprivation, and tension, and yet few ever join a social movement.[6] Irrespective of people's cognitive states, they will not become movement participants unless contact is made with a movement representative offering some alternative ideological framework and/or way of life. As Snow *et al.* argue:

However reasonable the underlying assumption that some persons are more susceptible than others to movement participation, that view deflects attention from the fact that recruitment cannot occur without prior contact with a movement agent. The potential participant has to be informed about and introduced into a particular movement (1980:789).

In this interactionally focused approach to differential recruitment, analytic attention centers on the processes influencing how people make contact with a movement's participants. Such an approach recasts differential recruitment in interactional and relational terms rather than cognitive and social psychological ones. From this perspective, interaction and the micro- and macro-structural processes that shape insider-outsider encounters become the key to understanding the dynamics of differential recruitment.[7]

The traditional approaches to social movements implicitly assume that people with specific social psychological predispositions seek out social movements that promise to promote changes in their lives in line with their cognitive orientations. While it is certainly the case that some people do indeed seek out movements in this way, this view glosses over the range of interactional avenues available for making such contacts. In addition, by focusing too exclusively on the choices of individuals with regard to movement participation, this view overlooks the ways in which movements develop strategies to help assure that they have contact with potential recruits.

*Movement Contact and Interaction*

While contact with a social movement can occur in a variety of ways and locations, most such contacts are of four general types: (1) self-initiated contacts, in which an individual seeks out a movement and/or its representatives; (2) chance contacts made with movement members in public places; (3) contacts made through social network ties with friends, acquaintances, and family members who belong to the movement; and (4) nonmember network ties in which movement sympathizers influence people in their general sphere of social relations to join the movement. Sympathizers are those "who believe in or agree with the goals of a movement or movement organization, but who do not devote any personal resources to it" (Snow *et al.* 1980:789).

While contact with social movements can occur by means of any of the above paths, recent research has suggested that social networks are the path by which many, if not most, recruits come to join a movement organization. Snow *et al.* (1980) examined a variety of data sources relative to recruitment to a range of social movements and found that the vast majority of over 1700 participants in thirty-three different movements were recruited through social networks. Stark and Bainbridge (1980), Lofland (1966), and Beckford (1975) have also demonstrated the importance of network ties for recruitment to three religious groups—the Unification Church, the Mormons and the Jehovah's Witnesses.

The importance of social ties in the recruitment process is not limited to movement contacts. A variety of studies of the new religions has shown that the decision of a recruit to remain a member of the group often hinges on his or her becoming socially integrated into the community of believers (Lofland and Stark 1965; Snow and Phillips 1980). Snow and Phillips' (1980) reassessment of the Lofland and Stark conversion model, using data on recruits to the Nichiren Shoshu Buddhist movement in America (NSA), found that "cult affective bonds and intensive interaction are essential for conversion to NSA" (1980:444). Social ties, therefore, appear to be important not only for the diffusion of information leading to contact with the movement, but are also crucial to the initial phases of joining and becoming integrated into a movement both socially and ideologically. I will discuss the role of social ties in the processes of recruitment into ISKCON in detail in chapters five and six. For now, I only want to introduce the interactionist model as it pertains to recruitment.

The interactionist approach to differential recruitment does not limit its analysis to the contact process and to group interaction as the basis for movement participation. Not only do at least some of a movement's participants come into contact with the movement through channels other than social networks, but the presence of network linkages and of interactions with group members by no means assures someone's participation. Some recruits to a movement decide not to participate, despite social ties to group members. This raises the question of what other factors are the determinants of differential recruitment? One answer is that the joiners differ from non-joiners primarily in terms of the degree of their structural availability (Snow *et al.* 1980; Snow *et al.* 1983; Snow and Rochford 1983).

*Structural Availability and Recruitment to ISKCON*

The concept of structural availability suggests that decisions to pursue a particular course of action are strongly influenced by an individual's role obligations and relationships. The ability to pursue a particular line of action depends in large part upon the constraints put on an individual by other roles and social relationships. If people are entangled in many roles and social relationships, they naturally find it more difficult to expand their range of obligations and responsibilities into new realms. On the other hand, if a person is relatively free of role obligations and social ties, the time and effort needed to explore and consider a range of alternative courses of action become more available. These individuals possess both unscheduled or discretionary time and relatively few countervailing ties that would act to constrain their participation in the movement. It is to these qualities of structural availability and their influence on recruitment into Hare Krishna that I now turn.

The findings on ISKCON members' pre-movement life circumstances (table 3.11) suggest the overall importance of their structural availability to the recruitment process. As the evidence indicates, the vast majority of those joining ISKCON did so during a period in their lives when they were single, young, and were either attending school or were unemployed or only marginally employed in part-time and unskilled positions. Moreover, nearly half of the devotees reported that they possessed no occupational skills that would have allowed them to compete in the job market. An additional 35 percent had job skills that were limited to clerical and mechanical tasks. Taken together, over 80 percent of the devotees possessed either no occupational skills whatsoever or their abilities were limited to largely unskilled and semiskilled jobs.

If the employment history of the devotees is explored in further detail, this pattern of having little overall commitment to a career is apparent. Many of the devotees either had not worked at all prior to becoming ISKCON members, or their work histories were characterized by their having moved from position to position. About one in ten (12 percent) had never worked prior to their recruitment into the movement. Over one-third (39 percent) had been employed in five or more jobs before entering the movement. Of those who were employed immediately prior to joining ISKCON, two-thirds had worked in their job positions for a year or less. While this employment pattern is probably

Table 3.11.
Selected Socio-Demographic Characteristics of Hare Krishna Members
at the Time They Joined ISKCON

| Characteristic | Number | Percentage |
| --- | --- | --- |
| Age status | 213 | |
| Under 30 | 204 | 96% |
| Marital status | 211 | |
| Single | 164 | 78% |
| Employment status | 211 | |
| Not gainfully employed | 106 | 50% |
| Students only | 34 | 16% |
| Neither employed nor a student | 72 | 34% |
| Gainfully employed | 105 | 50% |
| Employed full-time | 65 | 31% |
| Employed part-time | 40 | 19% |
| Type of employment | | |
| Professional/business managers/ business proprietors/administration | 30 | 14% |
| Skilled manual/semi-skilled/ unskilled workers | 54 | 26% |
| Clerical/sales | 21 | 10% |

not too unlike that of other young people in America, the implication
of it is that youth are particularly good targets for the recruitment
efforts of social movements precisely because they are relatively un-
committed to ongoing careers and to other life situations that might act
to constrain their participation in a movement organization such
as ISKCON.

The above findings suggest that the Krishna devotees were not well
integrated into the mainstream of American life at the time they joined

ISKCON. Instead of having turned their back on society by taking part in the movement, it would appear that most were never really involved in or committed to the dominant institutions in the society in ways that might have constrained their participation. The devotees were not renouncing their commitments to the dominant society and its values so much as they were simply uninvolved in the system to begin with.

## Countervailing Ties and Movement Participation

While extensive social role obligations, such as those embodied in a career, provide one source that may limit the possibilities of a person participating in a movement like ISKCON, there are other countervailing forces that may also influence an individual's decision to join or not to join. Because those joining Hare Krishna are young, their parents, families, and friends may act as countervailing forces, limiting the prospect of their membership. These social ties outside the movement often become very important as recruits weigh the merits of joining and of continuing in their participation. As one woman explained, her continued involvement in ISKCON has often been difficult because of her ties to family and friends:

> I have had several spiritual crises since joining ISKCON because of problems arising from my past life with my parents and other family members. I felt attached to the area where I used to live and the people with whom I grew up. When I moved away from that area I found it difficult to adjust (Questionnaire 1980).

Another devotee, whose parents continue to be unfavorable toward the movement, reports how his parents reacted after first learning that their son had become a Krishna devotee:

> It was really a bolt out of the blue for my parents. When they heard they were shocked, surprised, but really didn't know what ISKCON was, just another 'cult' to them. They still don't really understand it (Questionnaire 1980).

Because of the often negative view of the movement held by members of the public, countervailing personal ties can serve as an influential deterrent to a recruit's decision to remain within ISKCON. Because of the potential for social control that is often exercised by a devotee's family and friends, we might expect that the recruits having the fewest extraneous social ties would have the best prospects for becoming Krishna devotees.

When we inquire about the social relationships of the devotees just prior to joining the movement, we see that many were more or less free of personal social ties that might have constrained their participation in the movement. As indicated in table 3.11, three-fourths of the devotees had never been married before joining the movement. Of those who had been married, a number of these had recently been divorced or separated from their spouses. In addition, some of the devotees had been separated from past network ties just prior to becoming Krishna devotees. For example, nearly one-third of the devotees reported spending time "on the road" or "on the street" within the year prior to joining ISKCON. Others indicated that they had had little or no contact with their parents during this period.

But even for those recruits who were in contact with their parents and friends prior to joining, sanctions against joining the movement were not always forthcoming from these sources. While only a minority of the devotees (17 percent) reported that their parents were "generally favorable" toward the movement when they joined, 35 percent stated that their parents had no particular feelings one way or the other toward their participation in ISKCON, or that their views had become more favorable within a short period:

My parents were unfavorable when I first called to tell them I had joined ISKCON, but they got used to it pretty quick (Questionnaire 1980).

My mother didn't exactly like it, but she knew it was genuine and therefore was generally favorable (Questionnaire 1980).

They [parents] were a little upset when I joined, but they were also respectful and I think overall generally favorable (Questionnaire 1980).

They were very thankful that I was no longer taking drugs and associating with hippies (Questionnaire 1980).

As the above remarks suggest, few extraneous social ties may well facilitate the recruitment process, but one cannot simply assume that the presence of such ties will inevitably constrain participation.

Although extraneous social ties can provoke problems for a movement's recruitment efforts, contacts with these outside sources of influence can be limited by the movement itself, as part of the recruitment process (Lofland and Stark 1965; Lofland 1966). For example, during the years when ISKCON was most closed in its dealings with the larger society (1972–1977), the leaders of some of the movement's communities attempted to limit contacts between neophyte devotees and their families and friends precisely because these ties were seen as threatening to the recruits' continued membership in the movement. Drawing on two examples from my early work on the movement in Los Angeles (Rochford 1976), it is apparent how the movement attempted to limit contacts between new male recruits, or *bhaktas,* and people whose perceived aim was to talk a devotee out of the movement[8]:

This afternoon while I was speaking with the devotee in charge of the *bhakta* program, two young women, approximately sixteen and eighteen, came looking for a devotee whom they claimed was their brother. Without any discussion, the devotee told them to sit down, that he wanted to show them a slide show on Krishna Consciousness and ISKCON.

The older girl protested, stating that she only wanted to see her brother.

GIRL: I came here to see John, can you please tell me where he is?

DEVOTEE: Only after the show. I will tell you then.

After the slide show (showing ISKCON communities in India and the New Vrindaban community in West Virginia) the devotee told them that their brother could be found in the temple. The *arati* would be starting soon and he would be there with the guests who had come for the Sunday feast. Within five minutes the women returned, stating that their brother was not in the temple.

DEVOTEE: Oh well, he is in the kitchen preparing *prasadam* for the feast. You can't see him now, but he will be at the feast. You can see him then.

The older of the women protested.

WOMAN: Where is John? Why can't we see him in the kitchen? We don't want to wait, we just want to see him.

Again the devotee insisted that they couldn't go into the kitchen, that they would have to wait and see him during the feast. They left visibly upset (Los Angeles 1975).

On this same occasion, another incident occurred along the same lines:

Half an hour or so after the young women had come looking for their brother, a devotee came in to speak with the head of the *bhakta* program.

DEVOTEE: There is a woman, she is pregnant, looking for *Bhakta* Thomas. She says *Bhakta* Thomas may be the father. What should we do? Some women have tried to convince her to leave, but she won't. She's waiting around to see *Bhakta* Thomas.

The two devotees then got into a discussion about what should be done. They decided to try to convince her to leave once more.

Within a few minutes, the devotee returned with the news.

DEVOTEE: She won't leave until after she speaks with *Bhakta* Thomas.

More discussion took place about what to do. One option mentioned was taking *Bhakta* Thomas to the beach right away so that he couldn't talk with the woman. But while this discussion was taking place, *Bhakta* Thomas apparently saw the woman and spoke to

her, because another devotee came in to report that the two of them
were talking out in front of the temple.

BHAKTA LEADER: Tell *Bhakta* Thomas I want to see him right
now.

*Bhakta* Thomas arrived a few minutes later.

BHAKTA LEADER: This woman has come to seduce you. She can
only interfere with your spiritual advancement.

*Bhakta* Thomas said several times that he wanted to speak with
the woman. The *bhakta* leader repeated that she had come to interfere with his spiritual progress. But *Bhakta* Thomas continued to
say that he wanted to speak with her (he never said exactly why).

Finally, the *bhakta* leader agreed, but said they may speak only
in the presence of other devotees.

BHAKTA LEADER: We are only thinking of your spiritual advancement. We are trying to help you get rid of this temptation.

Before anything could be arranged, however, a devotee woman
came in to announce that the woman had been persuaded to leave
by the devotee women (Los Angeles 1975).

As these incidents demonstrate, some ISKCON communities demanded
of their new members a sharp break with their previous life experiences and social relationships as a condition of membership. ISKCON's
restrictions in this regard were structured strategically in order
to offset countervailing personal ties that might have acted to constrain participation.

## The Alignment Process

While movement contacts and structural availability are crucial elements in movement recruitment from an interactionist perspective, it is
still necessary for members' cognitive orientations to become appro-
priately aligned with the goals and ideology of the movement, if membership is to be enduring rather than only temporary (Snow and
Rochford 1983). Forming social ties with group members is critical to

the initial stages of recruitment and remains important even thereafter, but recruits must ultimately come to accept the worldview of the group if they are to become deployable agents. The traditional approaches to social movements treat the alignment of prospective members' cognitive orientations with the group's ideology as a given. The recruit's very presence in the movement is taken as presuming a linkage between his or her beliefs and the movement's ideology. While some recruits to a social movement undoubtedly join with this kind of a cognitive alignment already in place, for others, the initial agreement to participate in the group may have little or nothing to do with the appeal of the movement's goals and values. Rather, the necessary alignment between the prospective member's cognitive orientations and the movement's ideology is born out of a process of interaction with other group members. In suggesting that members' motives for joining the group are largely emergent, interactionists are arguing that the alignment of member's cognitive orientations with the movement's goals and values is largely an outcome of their being socialized and integrated into that particular social movement.[9]

## Conclusion

My discussion and analysis of ISKCON's growth and expansion in America suggests the various contributions of many different historical, social, and psychological factors to the processes of differential recruitment. Clearly, no one mode of explanation in itself adequately addresses all the factors that have lead thousands of young people to become Krishna devotees. Rather, as Turner and Killian (1972) have long argued, social movements rely upon the contributions of many types of people acting in a variety of ways for a multitude of reasons. To favor one kind of explanation to the exclusion of all others is to impose an artificial structure of certainty on a reality that is complex and many-sided. In the next three chapters, I will draw on each of the four levels of analysis I have just discussed. My effort, however, will be to combine these approaches in order to present a more dynamic view of ISKCON's development in America. While the main approach used will be interactional, my analysis will incorporate both social psychological and macro-structural levels of analysis.

# 4
# Surrendering to Krishna: Devi's Story

*T*he description I have so far given of the devotees and of the circumstances leading up to their joining in Hare Krishna has been to this point largely static in character; it has not allowed for a detailed understanding of the processes leading people to become Krishna devotees. While the survey data presented in the last chapter provide useful descriptive statistics, which allow us to paint a broad and comprehensive picture of the devotees, such abstract findings inevitably gloss over the interactive processes that have influenced any particular individual's decision to join the movement. Yet recruitment and the processes involved in a person's becoming a member of a movement ultimately are outcomes of social interactions, rather than the result of some specific configuration of demographic and/or social psychological variables that might be interpreted as predisposing individuals toward collective action.

In this chapter, I take a very different approach, both methodologically and analytically, to the issue of recruitment into Hare Krishna. I will make use of a first person narrative to describe the experience of one devotee's surrender to Krishna. The life history method, because it is openly subjective in character and relies upon and respects a person's own story and analysis of his or her life, provides for a rich and detailed research strategy. The life history method may involve telling a person's life story in full, or it may involve telling simply a portion of that story, depending upon the theoretical interests and concerns of the investigator. While a life history is usually not viewed as conventional social science "data," which leads to the development of theoretical propositions, this method has the virtue of providing us with a wealth of richly detailed information about particular substantive topics from the perspective of the person under study. Becker thus explains the distinctive advantages of the life history, in particular its ability to gain a member's own perspective:

> This perspective differs from that of some other social scientists in assigning major importance to the interpretations people place on their experience as an explanation for behavior. To understand why someone behaves as he does, you must understand how it looked to him, what he thought he had to contend with, what alternatives he saw open to him; you can only understand the effects of opportunity structures, delinquent subcultures, social norms, and other commonly invoked explanations of behavior by seeing them *from the actor's point of view* [emphasis added] (1970:64).

This chapter tells the story of one woman who has chosen to dedicate her life to Krishna Consciousness. I have selected Devi's life history for a number of theoretical reasons. Like most ISKCON members, Devi was raised in a middle-class family where religion, particularly in her early childhood years, was an important part of her life. As she grew older, however, her involvements with the church lessened, as she became increasingly involved with the drug culture, men, and Eastern philosophy. In this sense, she comes from a quite typical background. In addition, Devi, like a number of other women recruits to ISKCON, first made contact with the movement through a social relationship, in her case as a result of her knowing a boyfriend who was himself interested in Krishna Consciousness. As it turned out, the two of them ultimately joined the movement together. Finally, Devi's career within ISKCON demonstrates the often problematical character of the recruitment and membership process: On two occasions Devi defected from ISKCON, largely as a result of outside ties that acted to compromise her full commitment to a Krishna-conscious lifestyle. In the end, however, her friendships within the movement, combined with her commitment to the Krishna beliefs, resulted in her rejoining the movement, in which she has now resided for some three years.[1]

## *Devi's Life History*

Devi was born in 1958 in Saulte Saint Marie, Ontario, Canada. At the time of her birth, her parents had only recently moved to Canada from Michigan, where they had met as students. Devi's mother wanted her new child to be born in Canada, where she had been born and raised before coming to the States. Her mother came from a large Canadian family of four brothers and a sister. After spending a year in Canada, Devi moved with her parents to Birmingham, Alabama, the homeplace of her father. Her father was well-educated and the only child of a well-to-do Southern family. His mother, according to Devi, was a typical Southern belle from South Carolina.

For the next six years, the family lived in Birmingham. Devi remembers herself as a spirited child during these early years. When she was aged four, Devi's brother was born. Soon after, her sister was born. In Birmingham, Devi completed her first years of school, completing the second grade before her family once again relocated. The family moved to Baltimore, Maryland, where her father took a government job.

In Baltimore, Devi attended the public schools, where she was a good student and very popular among her peers. She was an avid reader, her favorite books including the Nancy Drew stories and *Little*

*Women*, which Devi remembers reading "about a thousand times." A
Walt Disney fan, she watched all of the early Disney films on TV and
at the movies. Devi also loved music and dancing. She took ballet lessons beginning in the second grade.

Religion was always important to Devi and to her parents. She was
raised as a Protestant Anglican, attending church weekly with the family. Devi's father had been an altar boy in his youth, and although his
church involvement had waned since college, he resumed going to
church again after Devi's birth. Devi's mother, in her eyes, was always more religious than her father. She was humble and always active in the church where she sang in the church choir every week.
Devi remembers her early church involvement in the following terms:

> I always had a very big attachment at this time to Bible stories. I
> learned to read at a very young age. I was a very avid reader. . . .
> When I was between about seven and twelve, I wanted to be a
> prophet when I grew up. I always thought that I had somehow been
> born in the wrong time and place though: Why wasn't I born when
> Jesus was born? I really wanted to be a prophet. I always had a
> very deep feeling that that was what I was going to grow up and
> be—a prophet. I believed in Jesus. I believed in God. I believed
> everything the Bible had to say.

During her early years, Devi matured very quickly and in the sixth
grade she began to be aware of the development of her own sense
of identity.

> In the sixth grade is when my ego really began to take over. I really
> wanted to develop my own identity. You naturally wonder what
> other people are thinking about you and you want to develop
> your image.

As she entered her teenage years, Devi found herself being viewed
as both attractive and very popular by her classmates and friends. She

was significantly clever at her studies, so that she was an "A" and B" student despite little effort.

Then senior high school came and I got involved with boys and girls. Little clubs of various sorts and cliques, all that kind of thing. . . . This is when I really started to become a rascal. I started not wanting to attend my classes and not being serious about my studies.

But while her interest in school began to decline in her high school years, she remained committed to and involved in her church.

I still believed in God and I still went to church. I was an active member of the choir. I loved to sing and I so much enjoyed singing hymns in church every Sunday. Even during these years, it was no problem for me to go to church. I really liked it.

Even though she was active in the church, Devi looks back now on her involvement then as ultimately a shallow expression of her spirituality.

I can look back now and say it wasn't that deep a realization that I was experiencing at that time. Church was more like a social, extra-curricular activity. I enjoyed it, but it wasn't really fulfilling me spiritually.

Devi's first experience with drugs came at the age of twelve. On a visit to her father's parents in Florida, she was introduced to marijuana by some young people she met there. From this point forward, Devi became increasingly involved in the drug culture and the music and good times she associated with it. Her involvement in the drug scene ultimately took her still further away from school and from her parents. She desperately wanted to experience the excitement associated with this lifestyle, even if it created problems in other ways:

I was always a big music fan. I liked music a lot and played the radio every night and danced. I was smoking pot and going to parties. I would stay the night at a girlfriend's house, and Saturday nights we would go to the teen center and dance. Oh, how I loved to dance.

In the tenth grade, Devi became a cheerleader at her high school. She also became more and more involved in the drug scene, a situation which played havoc with her studies:

By this time I was very knowledgeable in the whole drug scene. I'd been going with a boy who was very rich and by now I had tried pot, cocaine, and some downers. I guess my first experience with LSD was in the ninth or tenth grade. I did [LSD ] a total of maybe five times in my life. I didn't like it. . . . It was in the tenth grade that I really started cutting classes regularly. What I would do was go to the park and get high with my friends. We were getting high on a lot of good dope, and that was where my life was at.

By this time Devi's parents had begun to suspect her involvement with drugs, and they suspected that it was linked with her recent performance at school. As Devi remembers:

I started seeing little pamphlets on the coffee table about marijuana and LSD. They must have been in touch with school groups—the PTA or something. They were trying to fight the problem, but they didn't really know what to do or how to effectively deal with it.

Devi's new lifestyle not only took her away from her studies and antagonized her parents, it also led her to become less and less interested in attending church and keeping up with her religious activities.

I wasn't reading the Bible anymore. I had finally stopped going to church by about the tenth grade. I still believed in God and at night I would pray to God, but I had lost my sense of direction spiritually. I wasn't thinking of being a prophet anymore, instead there was the pressure of the material world and I was definitely trying to take advantage of it. I was definitely in the fast lane, you might say.

At the age of sixteen, her boyfriend proposed marriage. His family was very successful; they owned a local jewelry store. Devi's parents approved of the marriage and at first she accepted his proposal. Within a few months, however, Devi decided that she was too young to be married and broke off the engagement. This was during the Christmas season of 1975. Soon after this relationship dissolved, Devi became involved in another that would prove important to her spiritual reawakening and ultimately to her coming to Krishna Consciousness.

After breaking off the engagement, Devi initially felt a need to avoid any involvement with men. She wanted to spend at least a few months by herself, unencumbered by the presence of a man in her life. As it happened, however, she visited an acquaintance whom she knew from buying drugs with her previous boyfriend. The dealer, Aaron, became a major influence on her life during the years that followed. He was five years older than the seventeen-year-old Devi, and as she describes it:

He was a very far-out person. To me he was a major force in my life. Aaron had a lot of experience about spiritual things, and he actually began my whole reinterest in spiritual life. He had been to India many times, because he was a dealer. He had been to Afghanistan and Nepal, bringing back all of these things like pictures and books and his whole house was like India. He had all these neat artifacts and he was into antiques. I couldn't help but be really impressed by that. So I fell in love with this person. I saw him every night. He really brought about a drastic change in my life.

Devi recalls the first evening she spent with Aaron and how she quickly became deeply influenced by him:

I went to his house one night and we were doing drugs. I remember being immediately captured by this person. He was attracted to me also, so we got involved. Within a few weeks time, I quit smoking cigarettes because he didn't like it. . . . Within two weeks after that I wanted to become a vegetarian like him. Aaron was such a neat person. He impressed me very deeply.

Aaron took a great interest in Devi and encouraged her to become a vegetarian. He taught her about health foods and how to cook various vegetarian dishes. Aaron was instrumental in teaching Devi about Eastern philosophy as well:

I had already been exposed to reincarnation. My father read many books by people who believed in witchcraft and ghosts. I believed in God. I believed in witchcraft. I believed in reincarnation. But this boy made it more understandable for me—reincarnation, karma, all these kinds of spiritual ideas which I knew so little about. He would talk to me for hours about these types of things. It was all so far out to me and I just was completely attached to him.

It was during these early days with Aaron that Devi first came upon Krishna Consciousness and Srila Prabhupada. Aaron had a number of books on Eastern philosophy, among them a copy of Prabhupada's translation of the *Bhagavad Gita*. Initially she took no special interest in the book and had no idea that there even was a movement in America that followed these teachings. Although she had been introduced to Krishna Consciousness, she had no knowledge of the Hare Krishna movement.

As Devi became more and more involved with Aaron, she became even less interested in school. In an effort to finish high school early—in the eleventh grade—she began attending a local college part-time. By this time she had fulfilled all her high school requirements and lacked only a few credits towards graduation. As she said: "At this point I just wanted to finish, get out of school and be done with it."

During Devi's final year in school, Aaron was arrested for dealing drugs. After receiving a light sentence involving probation, Aaron, Devi, and their friend Dwight decided to open a health food store in Ocean City, Maryland. When Devi explained to her parents their plan for starting a business and moving away, both parents were outspoken in their disagreement. They were already upset by Devi's involvement with drugs and by her decision to become a vegetarian, but now she wanted to move away with a man whom they disliked. When Devi broke the news to her father, he was furious:

> He didn't want me moving out. He didn't like this boy anyway and so I remember sitting around the kitchen table telling my father I'm going to Ocean City, and he was so upset. I wasn't even going to my high school graduation. I didn't care about my diploma; I disliked County High School. I mean there I was, their first child giving up everything and it just blew their minds . . . . The next week Aaron was at my parent's house and my father just said to him, 'If anything happens to her I swear to God, I'll kill you.'

Despite her parents' protest, Devi moved to Ocean City with Aaron and Dwight. With money from Dwight's savings and money contributed by Aaron's mother, they opened their health food store on the boardwalk. The three of them shared a large house in the woods and they enjoyed that first summer together.

Dwight was also interested in Eastern philosophy and both Devi and Aaron learned various yoga practices from him.

> Dwight was involved in a spiritual practice called *kriya* yoga. He practiced a kind of yoga called *agnihotra*. At sunrise and sunset, you recite mantras and meditate. There was also a pact you had to follow. You had to be a vegetarian, practice nonviolence, practice celibacy, and some other things I can't remember, but we were all doing these yoga exercises, basically deep breathing exercises and following the pact. It was an impersonal philosophy. The ideal goal was to merge into the absolute light situated between the eyes. I

mean I was really into it. I believed it. There was this little copper pot where you would burn wood and say a mantra and meditate. So we were all doing it.

While life in Ocean City involved practicing yoga, it involved a number of other things as well. Devi describes that first summer and her feelings about it:

We had our business going and we worked very hard. We were do-ing yoga and by this time I was a strict vegetarian. I didn't eat any meat, fish, or eggs. I didn't eat any cooked food at all. So we were practicing yoga every morning and night, smoking pot, doing co-caine now and then and laying on the beach. We were into jazz music and we would go to concerts all the time. I was young and free and it was really great.

During this time Devi also continued reading various Eastern spiri-tual texts. She had read the *Bhagavad Gita*, not realizing that Krishna was God. Even so, she was impressed by the continual search for truth that was embodied in the literature she read. She too was looking for truth, though she wasn't sure where to find it. While reading these texts brought her closer to spiritual matters, she also felt a sense of disappointment in them:

I felt very disappointed from my readings because I thought that here again I had been born too late. I was born at the wrong time and missed it. It was the same experience I felt from reading the Bible. After reading the *Bhagavad Gita*, I said to myself, 'Well there are no people that live like this, or if there are, they are all in India.'

One day Devi expressed her sense of disappointment to Aaron. She wanted to meet people like those in the *Bhagavad Gita*, but felt sure she would have to go to India. It was then that he told her about the Hare Krishna movement:

So he told me about the Hare Krishna people. He had seen them in India while he was there, but also in Baltimore. That's how he had gotten all the books about Krishna. He had gone to the temple there. I mean here he had already been there and he hadn't told me! So he told me about them, how they lived and everything and about their Sunday feasts. I just kept asking him why he hadn't ever told me before. He just said that it never occurred to him. The funny thing was that he had given me the Hare Krishna album George Harrison produced and I would play it all the time, even before we moved to Ocean City. I was playing it and singing Hare Krishna every morning when I got up. Even my mother was walking around the house chanting Hare Krishna. There I was chanting this Hare Krishna and I didn't even know there was a group of people with shaved heads and with women wearing saris that were called Hare Krishnas.

It wasn't until the following summer that Devi finally met the devotees firsthand. After spending the winter in Baltimore, they returned to Ocean City to start the business again. One day Aaron walked into the store and announced that the Krishna devotees were giving out magazines on the boardwalk.

I said 'Really. I've got to go and meet them.' I ran out and up to the boardwalk. There were all of these [Krishna] women and I ran up to them. I said: 'Hello who are you? I've read these books about you, I want to talk.' So this one mother started talking to me and they could all see that I was enthusiastic and very favorable toward Krishna Consciousness. I was ripe. So they were preaching to me. I was like the big attraction for them that day. I was a ripe person and all the mothers [Krishna women] were coming and talking to me. Now, as it turns out, I am very close with all these women. So they were offering the books, telling me to come to the temple. I was so excited. They came to the store and met Aaron. Everyone was so excited. They parked their van just outside the store and I stayed in the van talking with them all day. They gave me some *prasadam* [vegetarian food] and while it was only cashews and almonds with raisins I will never forget it. It was the best food that I had ever tasted in my entire life.

Devi's initial attraction to the movement was based largely upon her immediate feelings for the Krishna women.

These women had real understanding and foresight. I appreciated that immediately. They knew what they are doing in life and knew what the purpose of life was. They were not afraid of death; they weren't afraid of anything in the material world. Nothing could affect them, it seemed. I just felt like I wanted to be like that too.

Over the next two days Devi spent most of her time with the devotee women. Aaron was also enthusiastic toward them and they decided to invite the women to stay at their house. After calling the temple president to gain permission, the Krishna women stayed over the weekend and nearly every other one that summer. Both Devi and Aaron avoided smoking pot on the weekends when the devotee women stayed at their house. Under the devotees' influence, they began offering their food to Krishna before each meal. One weekend the devotee women returned from Baltimore with japa beads for each of them to chant on, and they took to chanting "Hare Krishna." The women also gave Devi a sari to wear, which she liked very much.

In the coming months, Devi and Aaron both became increasingly involved with the devotees and with the devotional practices of Krishna Consciousness. Not only would they get up early every morning to chant with the devotees, but they also walked on the beach every night, chanting the mantra on their beads. As Devi explains:

We knew by the end of the summer that we wanted to be devotees. As the summer went by, we were very much involved with the chanting. We were into it and realized it would only be a matter of time. We were ready.

But while Devi and Aaron were attracted to the devotees and Krishna Consciousness, Dwight was entirely disinterested. Devi felt hurt by Dwight's lack of interest, since she had always considered him a spiritual teacher in his own right. She wanted him to become in- volved in the movement with them. But he continued practicing *agnihotra* yoga. Before the summer was over, Dwight decided he wanted to get out of the business and finally he left Ocean City altogether.

In contrast to the previous two years, Devi and Aaron decided to stay in Ocean City for the winter. Devi had already made plans to attend a local college to study art and music. As it turned out, these plans were never realized. Devi's attraction to the movement grew throughout the summer and she became more and more convinced that she wanted to become a Krishna devotee. On a number of occasions over the course of the summer, Devi and Aaron visited the temple in Baltimore, when they would travel there to pick up supplies for the store. They usually stayed overnight at the temple and participated in the movement's religious practices and rituals. Devi describes her first experience of the temple that summer:

I walked into the temple and the moment that the incense entered my nostrils I was completely attracted. It smelled so good and so clean. The atmosphere was so mystical. The devotees were chanting and I was wearing my sari and Aaron was wearing his yoga pants and it was just wonderful. The whole morning was so wonderful.

Devi's involvement with the movement intensified later that summer when she visited ISKCON's New Vrindaban community, in West Virginia, to celebrate Krishna's birthday. She had decided to go because several of her women friends at the Baltimore temple were to receive initiation into Krishna Consciousness as disciples of Srila Prabhupada. Since Aaron was unable to attend, she traveled to New Vrindaban with the devotees from the Baltimore temple.

I went to see their initiation. It was going to be a really big thing
and I didn't want to miss it. I remember we had to sleep in a barn
and it was so different from anything I had been used to; it smelled
like a barn and there were children running all over the place. I remember thinking how could anyone get any sleep in this situation.
I was so excited, I couldn't sleep anyway. I couldn't eat any of the
food either because I had been eating nothing but raw food all summer. . . . That was the first time I ever chanted a full sixteen
rounds and it was very heavy for me. After finishing chanting I was
so high. I couldn't believe it. It wasn't like any drug high. It was
all such a new experience for me. When you chant Hare Krishna
you become purified. Your awareness is acutely intensified. Your
awareness of everything: your spiritual awareness, your physical
awareness, your awareness of everything around you. It was almost
more than my senses could take.

The remainder of Devi's stay at New Vrindaban was no less
memorable.

Here I was in the hills of West Virginia chanting Hare Krishna
dressed in a sari. I helped decorate the temple for the initiation and
it was so beautiful. I had never seen anything like this. The whole
thing was just heaven and I remember before the actual fire sacrifice [initiation ceremony] I danced [to the kirtan music] so much I
couldn't stop. I was eighteen and full of life. I danced so much that
I was feeling a spiritual high, a high that I had never experienced
before.

These religious experiences were much more profound than anything Devi had ever felt from practicing other forms of yoga.

When I practiced *agnihotra* yoga I would sit there and meditate, do
the breathing exercises, waiting for something to happen, but nothing really ever did.

In addition to her religious experiences, Devi also became very attracted to many of the devotees she met and talked with during her stay at New Vrindaban. They were helping her understand Krishna Consciousness and she felt a sense of belonging.

> It was all very attractive to me. The devotees were preaching to me and I was really understanding what they were saying. . . . I believed in them right away because I could see that they were truthful people and knew what they were talking about. It all made sense to me. Krishna Consciousness somehow just seemed like a natural, logical, spiritual progression for me. I had been reading all the books and I could understand that I wasn't my body, reincarnation, birth, death, chanting the Lord's name. I knew God was a person, he wasn't just a light (like in some other forms of yoga). I wanted a loving relationship with God, whoever he was. Ever since I was a little girl, I wanted to find God. Now here he was.

After the festivities at New Vrindaban, Devi returned to Ocean City to help Aaron close the business for the winter. She excitedly told Aaron about her experiences and it was then that they both decided to join ISKCON and become Krishna devotees.

> We had made a conscious decision to move into the temple. It was just the right thing to do and we both realized it. . . . I remember the first day of school. My girlfriend knocked on the door and said 'It's time to go' [to school] and I said, 'I'm not going; we're moving into the Hare Krishna temple.'

On September 7, 1977, Devi and Aaron moved into the ISKCON community in Baltimore. For Devi the decision to join was not a difficult one.

> Joining was a real natural sequence for me. It wasn't a situation where we sat down and were thinking should we do this or not.

What about our lives? What are we giving up? It wasn't like that. It was a real easy decision based on a natural progression that we both understood. We liked the devotees. We agreed with the philosophy. There was nothing we disagreed with in the whole philosophy—nothing. It made perfect sense to us. We were ripe. We were ready. We were on a path and the next attainable level spiritually was before us. So we just moved in. . . . I had no personal crisis. I had plenty to do, I had a lot going for me. I was no misfit. I was very much what a lot of people wanted to be at the time I joined.

Even though they had become ISKCON devotees, Devi and Aaron had decided not to tell their parents immediately of their decision. Only after several weeks did they finally break the news. Aaron's mother, although she was somewhat shocked at first, became more accepting when Aaron and Devi explained what the movement was about. Devi's parents, however, were another matter altogether. Devi called her mother and then went to visit her to break the news of their change in lifestyle. Devi explains what happened:

I went over to my parent's house with this [devotee] girl. I should have gone with Aaron I suppose. I really shouldn't have gone with this devotee girl. We went over in the afternoon, since I knew my father wouldn't be home on a Friday afternoon. I walked in wearing my sari and said 'Hi.' Mother hugged me then said, 'What do you have on?' I said, 'Mom, its a sari. I joined the Hare Krishna movement and it's really far out. Wait until you hear all about it.' And she just freaked out immediately. What it was, was actually a communication gap created by my garb. Just because of my dress, she couldn't relate to me anymore. She didn't know what to say. She just freaked out, went off the deep end. She acted like an insane person, no logic, no sanity at all. Her reaction was so extreme . . . like total anger . . . First she yelled at the [devotee] girl, 'What have you done to my daughter?' I tried to tell her that she hadn't done anything. But my mother was totally against us. It just blew her away. She ran next door and told the neighbors. I went after her and told her to come and talk with me. . . . That night I went back to the temple really shaken.

Upon returning to the temple, she sought out the temple president for his advice. He pursuaded Devi to call her parents. Devi thought that perhaps her father would be more understanding and reasonable.

He is very well read in everything. I knew already that he believed in reincarnation. I just thought, well my father will understand this. He'll be proud and I thought he would think it was neat.

As it turned out, her father's reaction was not unlike her mother's.

I said, 'Daddy. I guess Mom told you I joined the Hare Krishnas.' He said, 'Yes. She told me.' I couldn't tell from his voice where he was at, but the more we talked, the more apparent it was that he was really just mad. He, in the end, couldn't control himself he was so mad . . . He had traveled all over the world, in and out of airports, and he had seen a lot of Krishna devotees. He had been approached by them, so his image was really shaped by that. He said, 'So you think you're going to save the world by standing on the street corner and passing out magazines?' I actually didn't even know he knew that they did that. So he took it in a very bad way. He was very emotional. He said, 'You are causing us to get a divorce. How can you do this to us?' I kept trying to tell him that I had just chosen a new way of life. I asked him over and over, 'Aren't you interested? Why don't you want to know what this is about?' But neither one of them wanted to hear what it was about, and that just crushed my image of what parents were about. I mean why didn't they respect what I thought? . . . After awhile I was over it and it made no big difference to me. I would call and say, 'Well you know where I am. You know what I am doing. If you want to find out more about what I am doing, please come and see.' They never came. I gave them books, but they would just throw them away. So I just decided to let them be. I didn't want to have anymore contact, if they didn't want to be fair. I wasn't going to let their feelings hamper my spiritual development.

Even Aaron's mother called Devi's parents in an effort to help them understand their daughter's involvement with the movement. This attempt at persuasion didn't help, and Devi's parents remained firmly against Devi's decision to become an ISKCON devotee. In the months ahead, however, as it became more and more clear that Devi was going to stay in the movement, her parents began to be at least more tolerant toward her involvement in the movement.

They were not happy, but they finally decided they weren't going to change me. If that's what I was going to do, OK. They couldn't help but think how I had so much potential and capability to make a success in the material world. They just couldn't understand why I was willing to throw it all away.

While Devi's parents were upset and confused, so too were her brother and sister. Being the oldest, Devi was looked up to and admired by her siblings. She had always been an important role model to them. Her decision to join the movement, however, left them both in a state of confusion.

My brother thought I had deserted him. Here I had set the example of how to make a big material life. And then suddenly I just cut it all off. My sister was also upset. They both looked up to me, since I was the eldest. When I became a devotee, they didn't know what to make of it. They felt like, 'My sister has left material life to become a devotee. What does this mean? What do we think now? What do we do now?'

Despite the reactions of her family, Devi remained committed to her spiritual quest. She was convinced that Krishna Consciousness was a true spiritual path, which would lead her to spiritual realization. In the months ahead, she continued to work towards that goal even though she was only a neophyte devotee.

When Devi and Aaron joined the Baltimore temple, they moved into separate residences: she in the women's ashram and he in an ashram with other men. Because the movement's philosophy stressed a separation between men and women, Devi visited Aaron only infrequently. After being in the movement less than two months, it dawned on her one day that she had not seen Aaron over a period of several days. After making several inquiries, someone told Devi that Aaron had recently taken to going to his mother's house. Devi called Aaron at his mother's. She asked when he was coming back to the temple and why he had been leaving the community. Aaron explained that he was unhappy in the movement and that he was uncertain whether he was coming back to the temple at all. He was seriously considering leaving the movement altogether. In the weeks following that call, Aaron visited the temple now and then, but finally, just before Christmas of 1977, he quit the movement completely. Devi explained his reasons for leaving and her reaction to them this way:

I think he left because he felt I was Krishna's devotee. There was that restriction on our association. He didn't want us to be separated. Our relationship had really gone in different ways since joining the movement. Plus at that time in Baltimore it wasn't so easy for a man. There were a lot of women living at the temple at that time and there were very few men. The women were gone a lot on *sankirtana* . . . . Aaron was helping the temple treasurer, but it was plain to everyone that the temple president really liked me. I was the new girl who was doing really well in spiritual life. The devotees liked me and I was making a real good adjustment. I was getting a lot of attention and instruction in spiritual life, a lot more than Aaron was. That, coupled with the fact that he was getting a whole lot less of my attention, made it really difficult for him. He was really hurt by the situation. He was definitely hurt, so he left because of that. . . I was upset that he left, but I was so into what I was doing that it didn't really make that much difference to me. I was going on to do my service. I knew I wanted to be a devotee, whether he was there or not.

As Devi suggests, she was now committed to the extent that her relationship with Aaron had become secondary to pursuing Krishna Consciousness. She had readily adjusted to the devotee's lifestyle and was committed to her spiritual goals and to the possibility that they would be realized as a Krishna devotee:

> By this time I was already doing full-time *sankirtana* [literature distribution]. I was getting up for the morning [worship] program, chanting my rounds, eating breakfast, and then going out to distribute books . . . . That was my whole life. But I was developing spiritually very quickly. In the temple I had responsibilities for specific duties, so my [devotional] service was going well. I learned all of the [Sanskrit] songs really quickly. I had nice relationships with the other devotees and everything was going really well for me.

Devi worked hard in spiritual life, looking forward to the day when she would take initiation from Srila Prabhupada. She worshipped Prabhupada as the spiritual master every day and felt that she was already gaining a close relationship to him.

Even as Devi was entering the movement, Prabhupada's health was failing. Finally, after Devi had been in the movement for little more than two months, news came that Prabhupada had passed away in Vrndavana, India, on November 14, 1977. Like the other devotees, Devi was stunned and heartbroken. Devi recalls the day of Prabhupada's passing and her feelings:

> All the devotees knew that Prabhupada was sick. We'd been praying for him regularly. Special prayers were being sung and kirtans [singing and dancing] were always going on for Prabhupada's health. While we knew of his condition there was still talk that he was going to come to America one last time. I was thinking I'm going to get to see him; take initiation from Prabhupada. . . Then I

came home from *sankirtana* one day and there was this guy and he came running out saying 'Did you hear? Did you hear? Srila Prabhupada has left his body.' I had never experienced anything like this before at all. My heart just went to my stomach. It was such a weird thing. I was numb; I couldn't believe it. I didn't even know Prabhupada. I was so upset I was crying. It was a very traumatic experience because here I had joined his movement and Prabhupada was going to be my spiritual master. I had already cultivated a little attachment from worshipping him every day. So when it happened, I thought, 'Oh no, oh no.' I was crying and it was like being in a dream. I walked into the temple and I was watching. I was watching myself walk inside the temple and all the devotees were there. It was like there was a film in front of me and everything had a yellow cast. All the devotees were crying and everybody's eyes were red and everyone was taking the pictures off the walls. We stayed up all night dusting and cleaning the temple. We were all thinking, 'What is going to happen now? What are we going to do without Prabhupada?' It was just so heavy and everybody was crying.

Though she experienced tremendous grief and disappointment over Prabhupada's death, this event did not shatter Devi's growing commitment to Krishna Consciousness. Even though the months ahead were uncertain for the movement, she continued her devotional efforts, and she was now looking forward to the day when she would take initiation from one of the newly appointed gurus. Within months after Prabhupada's death, Devi had decided who would be her spiritual master. She describes her first encounters with the man who would later become her guru:

The devotees from Baltimore went to Washington, D.C. to see North East Guru. He gave us class and it was then that I came to see him as the true spiritual master. . . . In February [1978], or thereabouts, he came to the Baltimore temple and I asked him a question during class. He liked my question and I knew then in my mind that this person was going to be my spiritual master. I had a lot of faith in the movement. I believed in it and my faith was strong. I believed in the authorities when they said that the movement would go on. And North East Guru was going to be my spiritual master.

Devi continued to work hard, looking forward to the day when she would become North East Guru's disciple. But on Memorial Day of 1978, after she had been in the movement for nine months, Devi's spiritual advancement came to a sudden halt. On this day she had traveled to Ocean City with a number of other women from the temple to distribute literature on Krishna Consciousness:

> We went to Ocean City on *sankirtana*. It was summer and Aaron was there. He had gone back to do the business again. So the situation was kind of like a test for me. When we arrived we all went to see him, to get free juice and stuff. I sat down and talked with him.

After talking with Aaron, Devi found herself making plans to leave the movement, at least for a while. She felt overworked, but her decision to leave the movement was more spontaneous than planned. It was only at that moment, as she sat in Ocean City with Aaron, that the thought of leaving the movement occurred to her.

> It was really whimsical. I wasn't even meditating about leaving. I hadn't even thought about it until that weekend in Ocean City. It wasn't like I wanted to leave. I wasn't feeling dissatisfied with the movement or anything like that. I wasn't being mistreated, or feeling separation from Aaron, nothing like that. It was more like, here I am with all my old friends and I thought, 'Oh this is far out, I don't think I'm going back today.' So I asked Aaron if I could stay with him for a little while. He said, 'Sure you can stay at my house for a while.' But he asked, 'Are you sure this is what you want to do? You really want to leave?' I just talked myself into it, I guess.

It was really weird. I knew it was wrong, but when you get in *maya* [materially minded and contaminated] you just shut out your intelligence. I knew what was right and what was wrong. Just like a little child does something when his mother tells him not to. He knows not to do it, but he does it anyway. So I was like that . . . But I was at the same time scared to death. I knew that I was going out from the protection of Krishna. If I do this [discontinue practicing Krishna Consciousness] and a car hits me, and I die, I'm in trouble. Whereas if I'm in the movement and I go out and a car hits me and I die, I'm saved.

Devi went back to the devotees' van to pick up her belongings. She then went with Aaron to his apartment on the bay. Aaron was smoking marijuana again and Devi somewhat hesitantly decided to try some. She explains what happened:

It was so heavy it flipped me out. I was tripping from one puff. My body was so clean that I took just one hit and my body was flipping out. I was actually hallucinating . . . So I was sitting there looking out at the bay and I was praying to Krishna. I was saying, 'Krishna, Krishna just let me come down.' I was so scared—'just let me come down.' I was thinking the police were going to catch me and throw me in the crazy house. I was scared. I was so scared.

But being at Aaron's house meant more than just being around marijuana again. It also involved being around all the temptations of the outside world that she had left behind when she joined the movement. Here she was staying in an apartment with men for the first time in many months.

I had not had any association with men for nine months. I was living a completely celibate life and you actually become shy and chaste. Its like the process reverses itself. You actually develop these qualities after a while. So that night I wouldn't stay inside the

house. I didn't want to stay where men were staying. So I slept
outside on the porch. The whole time I was so scared to death, because I knew I wasn't under the protection of Krishna. I slept that
night with the *Bhagavad Gita* over my head. I was thinking, you
are contradicting yourself. You're living outside the movement,
thinking you can somehow maintain a devotee way of life. But you
can't have both. But I was thinking I could have it all I guess. Here
I was, I couldn't sleep and I had this *Bhagavad Gita* over my head
and I was feeling horrible.

The next morning her adjustment problems continued.

I didn't want to take a shower in the same bath where the men had
been taking theirs. I told Aaron, 'Men have been in this bathroom.
I don't want to use this bathroom because I have been living such a
pure existence.' Of course I later forced myself because I stayed at
the ocean for two weeks.

Even though she was staying with Aaron, it was clear to Devi that
their relationship had changed from the early days of their romantic
involvement.

Nothing happened between us while I stayed at the beach. We were
just friends. I didn't have any rights to this person anymore, because here I had been living a spiritual life and he had been living a
*karmie* life. We didn't have anything in common anymore.

Even though she was now out of the movement, Devi continued to
have ambivalent feelings about her decision to re-enter the outside
world. She constantly thought about her commitment to Krishna Consciousness, not least of all when her parents found out that she had left
the movement.

Then I called my mother to tell her that I was living outside the
temple. She was so happy, to the point that it made me so mad. I

finally just hung up on her. She was so happy that she started crying and I said, 'Mother if you don't stop crying right now I'm going to hang up the phone' because I knew in my heart that I was a devotee. . . . My sister later told me that my parents went out and got a bottle of champagne that night to celebrate. I couldn't believe that. I couldn't believe that they would be celebrating my leaving the spiritual life to come to a life of meat-eaters, intoxication, and illicit sex. They were celebrating these things; I couldn't believe that.

Despite Devi's feelings about her parents' reaction, she moved back to Baltimore and spent the next several months living with them.

I went back to my parents' house and I thought that I would get a job and work; just check out material life for a while. I was a young girl and I wasn't ready to make that lifelong commitment to Krishna Consciousness. . . . I knew that I was a devotee though. I knew that I was going back one day. I was going back and I always knew that. I just wanted to give the material life one more last good try.

During that first summer, Devi divided her time between her parent's house and Ocean City. Her parents supported her financially through the summer months until she finally started working in the fall in a shoe store. Even though she spent time with her parents, she couldn't help feeling distant from them emotionally.

I was mostly only there to sleep. I ate at health food stores or cooked my own food. I didn't eat dinner with them because I was still a strict vegetarian. . . . I cared about my mother and father and I was very kind to them, but I didn't have a deep attachment. . . . I didn't do any activities with my parents. I mean we had a pool in our back yard and I would go swimming and they would go swimming, but that would be about as far as it would go.

During the whole time of her stay with her parents, Devi constantly thought about returning to ISKCON. She often expressed this desire to her parents.

> They knew after a while that I might go back [to the movement]. I told them, 'Don't get attached to me being here, because I'm going to be moving back to the temple.' . . . I had my saris and I had my [Krishna] books on my bookshelf. I didn't hide them and they knew that one day I'd go back.

In the fall of 1978, however, Devi became involved in a relationship, which made it extremely difficult for her to decide between Krishna Consciousness and the lifestyle she had been living since she had left ISKCON. After Aaron had asked her to marry him—an offer she refused—he introduced her to a man with whom Devi would soon become deeply involved and who was to become a major influence in her life in the years to come.

> Aaron introduced me to this person and he was the one who really got me entangled into the material life. I fell completely in *maya* [entangled in material life] over this person. Ben was very successful, a very successful musician and very handsome.

In a short time, Devi and Ben fell in love. Even though Devi was firmly committed to her relationship with Ben, she continued to believe that some day she would return to the Krishna movement. Her hope at this point, however, was that Ben would join her in her spiritual life and that the two of them would become ISKCON devotees together. In the months to come, she tried over and over again to interest Ben in Krishna Consciousness.

> I wanted Ben to become a devotee. I wanted him to visit the temple and I told him all about Krishna Consciousness the very first time we met. . . . I took him to the temple and we would sometimes go

to the Sunday feast. He loved *prasadam* [spiritual vegetarian food-stuffs]. But he didn't want to shave his head and move into the temple. He was very attractive and very vain. He didn't want to shave his hair . . . that would be a final surrender and he wasn't ready for that.

Under Devi's influence, Ben did become a vegetarian, and the two of them also avoided marijuana and other intoxicants. As it turned out, however, this was as far as Ben was willing to go. Despite Devi's preaching, Ben refused to consider participating in ISKCON as a real possibility. He was far more interested in continuing his already successful musical career.

Meanwhile, Devi continued to maintain her friendships with the devotees at the Baltimore temple. She frequently visited the temple to talk with them and to take part in the Sunday feast and other religious activities. The new temple president, in particular, played an important role in Devi's life during this period.

Prabhu used to preach to me whenever I visited the temple. He is a very potent preacher. . . . So one day I went to the temple and he was preaching to me. I realized that everything he was saying to me was true and I couldn't turn him down. I couldn't defeat him philosophically. He just stood there and said finally, 'When are you going to move in?' And because I was a devotee in my heart, I couldn't fight him. I didn't know what to say.

At about this time, Ben was getting ready to leave for Los Angeles where he and his brother were going to produce their first record album. While they were gone, Devi decided to move back to the ISKCON community in Baltimore. This was in May of 1979, a year after Devi had left the movement in Ocean City. Devi was torn between her love for Ben and her belief in Krishna Consciousness. She had chosen once again to commit herself to a spiritual path, despite the grief she was feeling at the loss of Ben.

> I knew I couldn't go on in the material world any more. I was un-
> happy and I had insomnia. Every night I kept thinking, 'Oh
> Krishna, Krishna, what if I get hit by a car tomorrow and I'm not a
> devotee?' I was aware that death could come at any moment and
> even though I was enjoying the material life I still believed in
> Krishna. I still knew that North East Guru was my spiritual master.

While determined once again to become an ISKCON devotee, Devi's
commitment to the movement was no more than provisional this time
around, since Ben continued to be an emotional force in her life.

> Every single day the temple president would preach to me. I would
> cry because I was so attached to Ben. I just kept saying, 'I can't
> give up this attachment.' And he would preach and preach every
> single day to me. His preaching was the only thing that kept me
> there. . . . I knew he was telling the truth, but my heart and emo-
> tions were all tied up with Ben and our relationship.

As the days went by, Devi began to feel more at ease being back in
the devotee community and she was feeling less sorrow about Ben and
their failed relationship. After several weeks, she was back into her
spiritual routine again and was beginning to return to her old devotee
self. Then Ben returned from his trip to Los Angeles. His return
proved to be a major test of Devi's commitment to the movement.

> I told Prabhu, the temple president, that I wanted to visit my
> mother for Mother's Day. But really I wanted to go because I knew
> that Ben was coming home. The temple president knew me very
> well and told me that if I went I wouldn't come back. But I prom-
> ised, 'I'll come back.' And he said, 'If you don't come back I'll
> be upset.'

Devi describes what happened when she saw Ben:

It was very traumatic for both of us . . . We were both crying. I kept saying that we could live here [ISKCON community] and do so much in the movement. He could still have his music. But he said, 'No, I just can't do it.'

As it turned out, Devi did not return to the temple that night. She had decided to remain with Ben and give up her membership in ISKCON. Once again she felt the pain of being caught between two worlds. She was in love and was committed to her relationship with Ben, but even so, she wanted to maintain her ties to ISKCON and Krishna Consciousness.

So we went through the whole thing again, for another two years. And of course, I couldn't stay away from the devotees. Even as embarrassed as I was, I would go back to the temple for the Sunday feast and see the devotees.

At the same time, Devi lived with Ben and thought about the day when they would marry. She got a job and the two of them resumed their previous lifestyle together. Unlike the last time, however, Ben now refused to attend the Sunday feast with her at the temple. Although Ben continued to resist Krishna Consciousness, Devi continued to hope and to lay plans for the day when he too would join the movement as her husband.

I knew that if I married him and had his child, that he too would come to the movement. That was my whole goal. I'll have his child and he'll be attached. That's how he is, and he'll come if we only have a child. But he knew what I was thinking and he wouldn't marry me. He knew I wanted to move into the temple again. He knew that I was just waiting for Krishna to work with him.

For the next two years, Devi and Ben struggled to work out their relationship. Always the issue that divided them was Devi's desire to return to the movement. As Devi reflected:

> Krishna came in between us always. Always I knew that I was a
> devotee and he knew that I was a devotee too.

In January of 1980, Devi traveled with Ben to Las Vegas and Los
Angeles where he was performing. While in Los Angeles, she persuaded Ben to visit the ISKCON temple. The movement's recording stu-
dio was located in Los Angeles, and she thought his interest in ISKCON
might be aroused if he saw the possibilities for music making that
existed within the movement. She tried to explain to Ben that his
musical life could continue as a devotee. He could work for Krishna
through his musical abilities.

> But he wouldn't do it. He wouldn't join. He would say, 'I believe
> in the spiritual life and I believe that God should be the center of
> my life, but I don't want to give up everything.' . . . He was at-
> tracted to the idea that he was the source of his musical ability. I
> mean he was a musical genius. In the end, he had a stronger attach-
> ment to his music than he did to me.

Upon returning from Los Angeles with Ben, Devi again sought out
her friends at the Baltimore temple. Ben was going to leave for Japan
in the days ahead and, as before, she sought out the support of the
devotees. On one of these visits to the temple her long-time friend,
Radha, who had also joined ISKCON in 1977, gave her a tape recording
of a conversation that had taken place between Devi, several other
devotees, the temple president, and North East Guru. The conversation had taken place during her last abbreviated return to the movement some two years ago. The tape reminded her of North East
Guru's words that morning.

> He said, 'What's the matter? Why can't you give up these material
> attachments?' He was preaching to me about Krishna Conscious-
> ness. Later the tape was entitled, 'Yes to Krishna, No to Maya,'
> and the whole tape was about me!

Radha also gave Devi a picture that had been taken that morning as she walked alongside North East Guru. Devi took both the tape and picture that day when she left the temple.

During this period, Devi was working for Ben's brother, who had recently opened a hair shop. She was working at the shop cutting hair. She began taking the tape of her conversation with North East Guru to the shop every day and she would listen to it while she worked. With Ben in Japan, and with the words of North East Guru in her mind, she began to feel more and more pulled toward returning to the movement.

> I was ripe now. I was again really ripe. I started listening to the tape and I thought, wow, that's what he means, yea. I knew it was just a matter of time, so I decided to give myself a permanent. . . . I knew I was going back. I was finally going to graduate and leave all these things I was attracted to behind. I told myself then, 'You're going to start chanting and you're going to cooperate with Krishna Consciousness.'

Before Ben returned from Japan, Devi had already made up her mind to return to the movement. To her surprise, however, she then learned that the authorities at the Baltimore temple were in India and that when they returned to the States, they would be transferring to Philadelphia to help manage the ISKCON community there. At first she thought this would disrupt her planned return to the movement. However, the temple president, Prabhu, asked her to join them when they moved to Philadelphia. Devi was relieved for more than one reason.

> I needed to get away from Baltimore. I needed to get away from Ben. I felt like if I didn't get away, I'd never make it away from him and back to Krishna.

When Ben returned from his trip, Devi informed him of her decision to rejoin the movement. While the decision was certainly painful, they both had realized this had been coming for some time. Devi's commitment to Krishna had finally won out.

It was strange because, as I was preparing to go back, Ben and I tried not to get emotional about it. I said, 'O.K. here are a few things I need. Can you buy them for me?' He took me out and bought me a tape recorder, socks, tee-shirts, a sleeping bag, all the things I would need. I was real organized and thoughtful about what I needed. He helped me put my suitcase in the car. By then the situation was real heavy as I left.

While he was sad to see Devi go, Ben did not try to dissuade her from joining the movement again. He understood by this time that Devi was seriously committed to Krishna Consciousness, even if he wasn't. Nor did her parents react negatively toward her decision. By this time, all those people who were close to her had come to realize that Devi's faith in Krishna and her commitment to the movement were real and were the most important forces in her life.

With my parents, through all these years in and out, they had come to accept that they couldn't do anything to get me out of Krishna Consciousness. They understood that mentally I was going to be into Krishna Consciousness forever. So when I decided to move back in, they just said 'O.K. if that's what you want, we won't stand in your way.'

So on April 5, 1981, after two years away from the movement, Devi once again turned her back on the material world to resume her spiritual journey. With little difficulty, Devi resumed her life as a devotee. Within a month after her return, she had reestablished her bond with North East Guru and was once again looking forward to her initiation as his disciple.

I developed a really close and wonderful relationship with North East Guru and he wrote me letters. I wrote him letters about var-

ious things and I was asking him, 'How can you guide me back
to God?'

Even though she was back in the movement, Devi was not able simply
to put Ben out of her life altogether. She often called Ben in those first
days, encouraging him to visit her in Philadelphia. North East Guru,
however, advised Devi no longer to see Ben because he could only interfere with her spiritual advancement. Reluctantly, but determinedly,
she agreed no longer to see or to talk with Ben.

Not long after rejoining the movement in Philadelphia, Devi was
asked to return to the Baltimore temple to act as temple secretary. Although she avoided seeking out Ben, she felt sure that just being in
Baltimore again would mean that their paths would naturally cross, especially since Ben continued to visit and be friendly with her parents.

It was Krishna's arrangement that I move to Baltimore at that
point. I went to all the same places where Ben and I used to drive
around as part of my work. But I never saw him. I kept waiting for
the day I was going to run into him. But I guess it was Krishna's
plan that I never ran into Ben. It was a confrontation that in many
ways I dreaded.

Only weeks after moving to the Baltimore temple, Devi was made the
temple treasurer. While she lacked formal training in accounting, she
nevertheless learned quickly. Because of her treasury work, she became involved with a number of the leading devotees in the movement, including North East Guru, with whom she began to communi-
cate regularly regarding matters related to her work as well as her own
spiritual progress. Because of this growing relationship with her guru
and her growing dedication to the spiritual life, she became less and
less concerned about Ben.

Because I was serving the spiritual master through my service
[work] and because I was putting my whole heart and mind into
Krishna, my attachments outside the movement began to wane. I

was chanting sincerely and doing a lot of service. Plus I had the association of the devotees who were preaching to me all the time. My friend Radha and I were very very close and she was such a big help. She was my crutch for a while and I leaned on her as a friend.

Devi's growing skills as temple treasurer led to her being sent to the Washington D.C. temple to help establish a movement business. While she was there, however, the Baltimore temple received word that they were to be audited by the Internal Revenue Service. Devi quickly returned to Baltimore and took over the responsibility for handling the audit.

I had this whole audit thing on my shoulders and it was up to me. Everyone was looking to me, this woman, to make this audit come out right. Everything was very heavy, very tense, and I was definitely praying. But the audit went well.

Because of her success with the IRS audit, Devi was sent back to Philadelphia to serve as temple treasurer for the ISKCON community there. She became informally involved in learning business and corporate law in an effort to help the movement gain effective management strategies and overall financial planning for the future.

In February of 1982, Devi took her first initiation from North East Guru. She had finally made the step she had been seeking in spiritual life for nearly five years, ever since the day she had met the devotees on the boardwalk in Ocean City. Finally, after leaving ISKCON twice, she had become initiated into Krishna Consciousness as a disciple of North East Guru. In December of that year, Devi took her second initiation. She described her feelings about being initiated this way:

Taking initiation from a bonafide spiritual master is the perfection of spiritual life. By accepting instruction from a self-realized soul and serving him, all the imports and meanings of the Vedic scriptures are revealed. So this was a wonderful occasion to formally accept a spiritual master. 'You are my teacher and I'm your student. Please guide me on this path back to the spiritual world.' It is very rare to find a living example of one who has actually understood that serving God—Krishna—is the highest goal and has practically attained that steady platform of performing wonderful devotional service without any tinge of personal motivation.

Even though she was now a committed and valued member of the movement, Devi continued in her struggle to maintain a spiritually pure life. From time to time, she still thought of Ben, continuing to believe that the day would come when he would join her in the movement as a Krishna devotee:

Time has made a lot of difference, of course. I still wish that Ben had become a devotee and I still have hope that he will in the future. I have faith that he will become a devotee because he ate so much *prasadam* [spiritual food], worshiped the deities, sang the *kirtans*, and took to chanting. So in my mind there is no doubt, he is going to come to Krishna Consciousness one day. . . . I told Ben just before I left him, 'You must promise me that every time you see a devotee in an airport that you will give . . . [him or her] a dollar.' And he promised that he would, so he will continue to gain some advancement in Krishna Consciousness.

As she looks to the future, Devi sees her life as continuing in Krishna Consciousness. She plans to do whatever she can to help advance the movement's message. Her immediate plans include going back to school to become a Certified Public Accountant or perhaps a corporate lawyer. By becoming a professional, she not only hopes to provide the movement with needed skills, but she also plans to use this training as a way to preach Krishna Consciousness:

I think it is such an important step for the movement to begin preaching to the professional people in America. It is really needed by our movement, since these are the people who have the money and power in society. They are controlling the government and the laws. We need to reach these people and I hope that we can.

While it is not in her immediate plans, Devi also looks forward to the day when she will be married and raise a Krishna-conscious family.

I'm pretty sure that I'll get married. I'm still a young girl and my guru has told me that I will get married. I'm not real anxious right now. When you are married, it isn't so easy to do a lot of service. I'm doing a lot of service right now and I feel if I was married I wouldn't be able to do as much as I want. I really want to dedicate myself to my service for the movement, for North East Guru, right now.[2]

In terms of her spiritual future in Krishna Consciousness, Devi explains:

I want to learn to perfect the chanting of the Hare Krishna mantra. That's a main goal. I want to learn to chant Hare Krishna and actually become pure. I've been making spiritual advancement, so I want to make more progress. I want to actually realize that Krishna is God and that everyone won't be happy until they are situated back into the practice of serving God, serving Krishna.

# 5
# Men, Women, and Membership

The processes that result in persons joining social movements of various types have received enormous attention from scholars in recent years. Even though there have been numerous substantive studies and theoretical treatments of differential recruitment, all of these investigators have failed to address the question of what significance, if any, gender plays in the recruitment process. Empirical and analytic discussions of movement recruitment have implicitly assumed that gender is without explanatory significance: that men and women join social movements for much the same reasons and in much the same ways.

Even though research in various realms of social life has demonstrated the importance of gender differences for social behavior,[1] and even though our natural folk understandings of social life suggest that the worlds of men and women are at least somewhat differentiated, if not profoundly different, mainstream social science theory has implicitly assumed a society essentially undifferentiated on the basis of gender. As two sociologists explain:

Sociology often assumes a 'single society' with respect to men and women, in which generalizations can be made about all participants; yet men and women may actually inhabit different social worlds, and these must be taken into account (Millman and Kanter 1975:xiii).

Evoking a vision of the social world as it is portrayed by phenomenologists, Jessie Bernard suggests a more radical formulation of the differences between men's and women's experiences of social life and the implications of such differences:

The underlying premise is that most human beings live in single-sex worlds, women in a female world and men in a male world, and that the two are different from one another in a myriad of ways, both subjectively and objectively. R. D. Laing tells us that, 'Insofar as we experience the world differently, in a sense we live in different worlds.' A major theme here is not only that women and men do indeed experience the world differently but also that the world women experience is demonstrably different from the world men experience (1981:3).

In this chapter, I want to address the different processes involved in men and women coming to surrender to Krishna Consciousness and ISKCON. Instead of assuming that the factors involved are much the same for both sexes, and that gender differences are therefore without analytic significance, I will assume gender differences to be problematic and make them a focus of sociological inquiry. My findings on recruitment into ISKCON suggest that influences on recruitment are different for men and women, and that the whole experience of surrendering to Krishna and becoming an ISKCON member is in many ways unique for men and women. Because of these empirical differences, I then address the more general question of how the different social worlds experienced by the two sexes affect differential recruitment processes as they relate to participation in Krishna Consciousness.[2]

## Gender and Movement Contacts

The findings reported in table 5.1 suggest significant differences in the ways men and women have made contact with ISKCON and Krishna Consciousness. For the most part, men and women have been recruited into the movement through different influence structures: men are more often recruited into ISKCON after they have initiated contact with the Krishna devotees in public places, while women are more apt to be recruited through social network linkages with ISKCON members or movement sympathizers. As the data indicate, more than half of the male ISKCON members were recruited in public places, while conversely, nearly two-thirds of the women joining the movement did so as a result of ties with friends, family, or acquaintances who were either ISKCON devotees or movement sympathizers.

However, while the findings reported in table 5.1 point to distinctly different pathways and interactional processes by which men and

Table 5.1.
Gender by First Contact with ISKCON

| Gender | Devotee network[a] | Non-member network[b] | Public places | Other[c] | Total |
|---|---|---|---|---|---|
| Men | 15% | 19% | 51% | 15% | 101%(110) |
| Women | 32% | 28% | 33% | 8% | 101%(104) |
| Mean % | (23%) | (23%) | (42%) | (12%) | 100%(214) |

[a]Devotee networks are contacts leading to membership initiated through social ties with persons who are already ISKCON members.

[b]Nonmember networks are contacts initiated with movement sympathizers that lead to persons taking up membership with ISKCON.

[c]Contacts coded as "other" include being picked up hitchhiking by ISKCON members, visiting a Krishna community for a school project, and meeting the devotees at an Antinuke rally. Since only 6% of the devotee respondents indicated that they had initiated contact with the movement on their own (i.e., attended a Sunday Feast at a local temple or read ISKCON's literature) I have grouped them in the "other" category.

women are recruited into ISKCON, these data ultimately tell us little
about the particulars of the recruitment process as it operates differentially between the sexes. The question to be addressed in the
remainder of this chapter is: How do men and women take part
differently in the public and private spheres of social life, and how
might each sex's use and experience of these social forms influence its
possibilities for contacting social movements such as Hare Krishna?

## Gender, Social Networks, and Differential Recruitment

Despite a history of controversy over the relative involvements of men
and women in kin and friendship networks, recent studies suggest that
basic differences do exist between the sexes with regard to the quality
of their relational ties (Bernard 1981; Bell 1981; Horwitz 1977; Weiss
and Lowenthal 1975) if not with regard to the number of such ties
(Bell 1981; Booth 1972; Tiger 1970). Overall, it appears that women
are both more active in kin and friendship networks (Adams 1968;
Booth 1972) and that women's network ties tend to emphasize "per-
sonalism, self-disclosure, and supportiveness" to a greater degree than
men's network ties do (Wright 1982). As one recent investigator of
the respective worlds of men and women concludes:

> The evidence clearly indicates that the friendships of women are
> more frequent, more significant, and more interpersonally involved
> than those commonly found among men. The friendships of women
> are more often based on trust and involve more revealing of the self
> to the other. . . . Women more typically come from within them-
> selves in their friendships with other women, while men typically
> function outside themselves. The woman reveals her feelings, emo-
> tions, and insecurities. Often the man guards against letting out
> anything that reveals his feelings, especially if he sees them as
> threatening to his sense of masculinity (Bell 1981:60–61).

The differences between men's and women's participation in social networks to a large degree reflect fundamental differences in the everyday social worlds experienced by each. As Bell (1981) concludes, the social world of men—especially middle-class men—very often mitigates against self-disclosure and the forming of close ties with other men:

> For many middle-class American men, it is the competitive world of work that is both the cause and effect of many of their behavior patterns. In the competitive world the male typically believes he has to stay away from revealing much about himself . . . in general, the greater the competition, the less the affectional relationships (1981:84).

Having been socialized into a culture of competition, which stresses achievement and getting ahead, men tend to place little trust in friendships with other men—viewing them more in terms of their potential threat than as agents of support, understanding, and friendship or warmth. Conversely, women have more often been socialized into being "unselfish, altruistic, and self-sacrificing" (Sorokin 1950:21).[3] While different personality characteristics distributed between the sexes provides one logical explanation for women's greater participation in and reliance on social networks, I want to argue that these differences are largely structural, reflecting the general marginality of women in contemporary society.

As a number of investigators have suggested, women as a status group are largely marginal (Hacker 1951; Sapiro 1983). While women are part of the dominant culture, their relationship to it is ultimately paradoxical: they both live in a social world structured by the values and objectives embodied in patriarchy and capitalism (i.e., values associated with the structures and functions of a man's world) and, at the same time, they are strongly influenced by a separate cultural system with distinctive and different values and objectives, which are associated with their gender.[4] As Komarovsky explains, the marginality of women in contemporary society creates a situation in which:

The goals set out by each role [associated with the two cultural systems] are mutually exclusive, and the fundamental personality traits each evokes are at points diametrically opposed, so that what are assets in one become liabilities for the other, and the full realization of one role threatens defeat in the other (1946:184).

As a consequence of their marginality as a status group, women face a choice between two relatively unattractive alternatives. As Sapiro (1983) argues in a slightly different context (the political participation of women), women may join the public (masculine) realm only at the cost of being considered unfeminine. On the other hand, if they choose to confine their activities to the private feminine world of household and family, they lose both power and status.

In the past, one "solution" to the dilemma of marginality has been for women to define the traditionally female realm as necessarily carrying the appropriate status for them, recognizing that their status and power does not compare with those of men. In terms of that solution, their experience of social life by necessity has been characterized by those social and personal qualities associated with being feminine: altruism, interpersonal support, nurturing, and depth of feeling. Moreover, the loss of social power and prestige associated with these personality characteristics has been buffered by the recognition of, and the virtual glorification of, the importance of these feminine qualities for serving crucial societal needs (as in stabilizing the family).

Because of this traditional solution to women's marginality in social life, female social networks play a particularly critical role in their lives. Social networks provide the structures by means of which private roles within society are enacted (Bensman and Lilienfeld 1979). The basic structure of women's worlds rests on a myriad of network ties that link women to one another. The prominence of female social networks, therefore, should be understood as a result of the marginal status of women in modern society instead of as a simple or direct reflection of personality characteristics peculiar to women. Social support systems need not be inherently the cultural work of women, but they are the work of a status group within society that continues to be largely relegated to the private realm to the exclusion of full participation in the public realm. Investigators of social life have long noted that marginal and powerless groups within society tend to turn inward, finding support and comfort within their own community or culture (Becker *et al.* 1961; Best and Luckenbill 1982; Cohen 1955; Horowitz and Liebowitz 1968; Kanter 1972, 1977; Warren 1974). As Becker notes with regard to deviant groups:

> Many people have suggested that culture arises essentially in response to a problem faced in common by a group of people, insofar as they are able to interact and communicate with one another effectively. . . . Where people who engage in deviant activities have the opportunity to interact with one another, they are likely to develop a culture built around the problems arising out of the differences between their definitions of what they do and the definition held by other members of the society (1963:81).

The web of social relationships critical to the maintenance of any culture is ultimately held together by a bridgework of network ties that facilitates contact and interaction among members (Bensman and Lilienfeld 1979; Finc and Kleinman 1983). In the case of women in modern society, however, female networks serve not only as the social infrastructure for women's culture, but also serve as the social infrastructure for the dominant culture as well, because women, unlike deviant groups, remain largely committed to society's norms and values.

Recent reforms associated with the status of women in American society, which have grown out of the efforts of the Women's Movement, have brought traditional strategies for dealing with female marginality under fire. Increasingly, women have not supported adopting a traditional, private and feminine role in society to the exclusion of participating in the public realm. For women who have been unable or perhaps unwilling to enter the public sphere of social life, ongoing feminist attacks on their previously valued women's images have become problematic. Ironically, some of these traditionalist women have recently been pulled into the public realm in order to defend the private roles carried by women in society (for a discussion of this aspect of the ERA battle, see Burris 1983, and see Ehrenreich 1981 regarding the social characteristics of anti-ERA women). This whole conflict, in itself, points to the deep structural roots of women's marginality, rising from the split between the private and public worlds and its basis in gender. The resulting dilemma for women who choose to hold onto their traditional (private) roles in the face of ongoing changes that promise to further expand women's domain into the public realm (principally, the work place) has served to deepen the overall sense of marginality and isolation of these traditionalist women from the dominant culture. Their status in the society is no longer beyond reproach: they remain marginal, but now their selfaffirming ideology has been progressively threatened and stripped away. All other things being equal, these women appear to be particularly susceptible to social movements like ISKCON, which offer a message extolling the virtues of traditional, private and feminine roles.

Because of the overall importance of interactional social networks in the lives of women, it seems logical that these pathways would serve as the readiest conduits to participation in social movements. Women appear to be more likely to join social movements (particularly communally organized utopian societies) when significant others whom they know join, because a movement provides affective ties with other people, and/or because a movement provides a potential solution to the problem of marginality faced by women in contemporary society. It is to each of these possibilities and their respective roles in the recruitment of women to ISKCON that I now turn.

*Women's Ties to Family and Friends*
*as a Basis for Joining*

Although social networks have played a major role in facilitating women's contacts with ISKCON, they have also proved important to the recruitment process in other ways as well. Some of the women who have joined the movement did so primarily because of relationships with friends, family, or a spouse who had also decided to become an ISKCON member. In these cases, the social ties leading to the decision to join were not directly linked to movement members, but were linked to the decision of a significant other who wanted to become a Krishna devotee. Thirty-five percent of the women surveyed joined ISKCON with a significant other, as compared with less than 20 percent of the men. Moreover, nearly one-fourth of the women who joined, joined together with a spouse or boyfriend. While it was not always clear who was the party most responsible for the decision to join (if the decision was really not mutually decided upon) at least in some cases, a woman's decision to join was linked directly to her mate's desire to become an ISKCON member. Some women, in fact, were reluctant or even openly against the idea of joining the movement, but did so in the end only to maintain a relationship with their husband or boyfriend. As one woman who joined with her husband and two children explained:

It actually took me three months to decide to join, even though I had already moved into the [ISKCON] community. I actually moved in before I was ready to. My husband moved in and, if I didn't come, I was going to get left behind. So I was kind of stuck there prematurely. I didn't want to move in. I really didn't want to move in at that point. I had all kinds of arguments right from the beginning. We lived near the temple and I couldn't understand why we couldn't stay there; I mean we have two kids, why can't we just stay here [she says to her husband]. But in those days you were either in or you were out. To me at that time I still felt it was an unnecessary step. There was some taste for Krishna there, within me, but still I just didn't want to move in. But what was I to do really (Philadelphia 1983).

A man who joined ISKCON with his wife in 1971 suggested the way in which his decision to become a devotee resulted in his wife reluctantly joining the movement as well:

I actually became involved with the movement while I was experiencing serious marital problems. My wife had left, and I became
deeply involved in the movement. I was going to the temple, chanting, reading the books, the whole thing. So she came back and she
freaked out. I mean there was this whole new person. I literally
told her, I am going to join, if you want to tag along, that is up to
you. Within a few weeks, she started going to the temple. She was
also attracted. She really wanted to just taste it [Krishna Conscious-
ness] but did not want to become involved. That was her attitude.
. . . But she actually saw the way I was changing and finally just
said: 'Hey I want to get involved too.' So she finally got hooked
too (Los Angeles 1979).

## Recruitment and Affective Ties

Social relations play a role in the recruitment of women to ISKCON in a
more enduring way than by simply facilitating contacts and by influencing women's initial decisions to join. A dozen or more studies of
recruitment and conversion to religious groups and movements have
emphasized the crucial role played by affective group bonds (Downton
1979; Judah 1974; Lofland and Stark 1965; Lynch 1978; Richardson
and Stewart 1978; Snow and Phillips 1980). While group affective
bonds do without question strongly influence the decisions of both
men and women to remain within ISKCON, the beliefs of the movement
dictate that affective ties assuring membership are gender-based. Because the movement attempts strictly to limit sexual contacts between
men and women, ISKCON's communities are segregated along gender
lines. New recruits, therefore, are integrated into gender-based cultures, rather than into the movement as a whole.

   While group affective bonds are normally understood to be outcomes of the recruitment and conversion process (Lofland and Stark
1965; Snow and Phillips 1980), it is often the case that women recruits
to ISKCON make their initial commitments to the movement on the basis of an almost immediate attraction to the other Krishna women. The
fact that women are more often recruited through social network ties

than through any other means of recruitment suggests immediately the importance of affective ties as the basis for their initial decisions to become at least provisional members. As discussed in chapter three, the second most important factor to influence the devotees' initial decisions to join ISKCON (for both men and women) was their initial attraction to "the warmth and friendliness of the devotees." Moreover, one-fourth of the devotees surveyed—men and women equally—reported that during the period just prior to joining ISKCON they were "looking for new friends and social contacts." One devotee woman, who joined ISKCON within weeks of her initial contact with the movement, suggests the importance of affective ties to her decision to join:

When I first met the [Krishna] women I was so impressed. I really liked what I saw in them. . . . I knew immediately after spending time with them that I wanted to be a devotee woman. I was very impressed by their knowledge, but also their sincerity and warmth (Philadelphia 1982).

But while some female recruits form affective ties with the other devotee women almost immediately, for others the development of such social relationships is born out of an interactional process that is less certain and immediate. Most new recruits to the movement—men or women—remain as provisional members or perhaps verbal converts (Lofland and Stark 1965) for a prolonged period of time. For most of the women who join ISKCON, it takes time to form commitments and relationships with other women. In addition, the early days of participation in the movement normally involve problems adjusting to the devotee's lifestyle and gaining command of the movement's religious practices and routines. Furthermore, joining the movement involves losses as well as gains, and many women find it difficult to adjust to the loss of social relations they valued prior to joining the movement. In recognition of these losses and their possibly adverse effects on a new woman's commitment to the movement, the devotees begin immediately to build meaningful and intimate relationships with new recruits. As two devotee women explain:

FIRST DEVOTEE WOMAN: I think most women, as compared to men, think more about what they are going to give up. What will my parents think, what will my boyfriend think. So they tend to be more hesitant.

SECOND DEVOTEE WOMAN: They also tend to be more protective of their domain. Their possessions and so forth. I know I was.

FIRST DEVOTEE WOMAN: My experience with taking care of women who first join is that they are much more emotional than are men. You have to talk to them a lot and keep good communication going. You have to preach to them and keep doing it because they do forget. They get emotionally overwhelmed and sometimes they make their decision to join or to leave strictly on the basis of their feelings. You have to keep constantly reassuring them that that's not everything (Philadelphia 1983).

Another woman, who has been a devotee for eleven years and who has both witnessed and contributed to the recruitment of dozens of women during her tenure in the movement, likewise suggests how the decision to join for women often hinges on their becoming integrated into the women's community:

For a lot of women, they find it difficult initially to join our movement. There is a tremendous amount of restrictions on their interactions with men and they don't always like living with other women. Many, at least at first, are not attracted to joining the community. But after a woman has been a devotee for a while, then that sense of belonging and feeling good about being a part of a women's community comes; you actually start to value the relationships with the other women as your Godsisters. You feel that there is some spiritual relationship. You look forward to seeing them and being a part of them (Philadelphia 1983).

The presence of a woman's culture within ISKCON remains important to the women's commitment to the movement throughout their tenure with ISKCON. Commitment, after all, is never final, but instead is continually renegotiated over the course of an individual's history in a social movement. One woman, for example, who has considered defecting from ISKCON on several occasions, points to her relations with other devotee women as the major factor influencing her commitment to the movement in both positive and negative ways:

> I joined ISKCON because of the warmth and friendliness of the devotees, particularly the other women. Recently though, I have had personal problems relating to the other women, which sometimes makes me feel like I should leave [the movement]. But, in the end, I realized that I was too attached to some of them [other devotee women] and so I didn't want to leave (Denver 1980).

The presence and overall importance of the women's culture within the Krishna movement not only serves as a basis for its members commitments, but also serves as a mechanism allowing some women in contemporary society to work out the crisis of meaning resulting from their marginal status. ISKCON's lifestyle, however much it may have little or no appeal for many contemporary women, nevertheless provides a traditionalist solution to the marginality faced by women in modern industrial society.

## Krishna Consciousness and the Resolution of Women's Marginality

As the traditional solution to women's marginality has come under attack in recent years, there have been relatively few alternative options available for women who seek to solve the problems associated with their marginality. One course of action, which women with a feminist orientation are taking, is to push politically for structural changes that would put an end to sexism. For these women, the goal is for men and women to share equally in both the private and public realms of social life. While some women view political action as an appropriate strategy to help resolve women's marginality, for others the solution lies in living traditionalist lifestyles that are given legitimacy and purpose as a matter of ideology. It is precisely this possibility that serves as the source of attraction for many women joining the Krishna movement. ISKCON's traditionalist lifestyle, as reflected in its gender-based cultures, affords a unique opportunity for some women to solve the dilemma of marginality. It is just this solution that leads some women to commit themselves to ISKCON and Krishna Consciousness.[5] As an illustration of how ISKCON may serve as a solution to the problem of women's marginality, consider the words of one devotee woman who has been in the movement for approximately five years:

> It was a relief to join the movement really. There was a certain sense of liberation. For me it was just the feeling of being freed from anxiety. Just the anxiety that comes from living in the material world—from having to do so many things like work, as well as being expected to get married and have children. I think anyone who is a little thoughtful will feel this general anxiety of 'where is my life going?' So for me the movement was a perfect solution for my life and one I appreciate more and more (Philadelphia 1983).

As this woman suggests, the dilemma of trying to integrate both the private and public realms of social life into a unity is a major source of discontent for many women in society. For at least some women, the appeal of ISKCON's lifestyle lies precisely in its traditionalist way of life. The everyday lives of devotee women are more or less confined to the private sphere of social life, to the relative exclusion of public roles. While the division is not always exact because some devotee women (such as Devi) hold positions critical to the functioning of the movement's communities, women's overall role obligations are nevertheless largely confined to the household. After all, it is in this realm that the movement's theology provides women with the greatest status, legitimacy, and potential for spiritual realization in Krishna Consciousness. As one devotee woman explains in an ISKCON publication addressing the role of women in Krishna Consciousness:

> Devotees respect women as valuable members of society, not only for their own distinctive value as human beings, but also for their

contribution as wives and mothers. We don't consider those functions to be insignificant. The quality of human society will to a large degree reflect the quality of families people are raised in. Wifehood and motherhood are crucial social functions, so we don't feel there is anything demeaning about being a good wife or mother (Devi Dasi, 1982:12–13).

The Krishna movement is even more appealing to some young women because joining it involves rejecting the society's material values and goals and replacing them with values and a lifestyle more in keeping with the traditional female world.

## Men, Marginality, and Social Ties

My interest up to this point in the analysis has largely centered on the processes by means of which women take up membership in ISKCON. While the public realm clearly is more instrumental for men in making contact with the movement (to be discussed in the next section), the concept of marginality and the overall importance of social ties are, nevertheless, also important to men joining the Krishna movement. I want to discuss briefly each of these as it relates to men becoming ISKCON members.

As the findings reported in table 5.1 indicate, social ties have played less of a role in the case of men being recruited into ISKCON than they have for women. Although social ties seem to be relatively unimportant in the contact process, social ties, nevertheless, play a crucial role in the membership process for men. As previously discussed, forming group affective ties within sex-based cultures appears to be necessary to both sexes, if they are to become sufficiently committed to the movement to insure their continued participation. In this sense, becoming integrated into the male or female world found within the movement is essential to sustaining the membership of any neophyte member, irrespective of gender.

The importance of social networks for the membership process for men is also linked to social psychological processes reflecting the marginality felt by many men in modern society. Some men join ISKCON out of a desire to take part in a *Gemeinschaft* way of life. They seek a lifestyle more in keeping with the female world. For these men, the competitive and self-centered nature of the men's world found in the larger society promotes a sense of isolation, of marginality, and perhaps of alienation. The Krishna movement represents a break from the dominant (male) worldview prevailing in the outside society. ISKCON's appeal lies largely in the value it places upon the interpersonal intimacy and support to be found within the men's culture. In contrast to the plight of men in general, ISKCON provides a lifestyle for men that maintains a greater balance between the public and private realms of social life. Consider the comments of one male devotee of seven years who resides at one of ISKCON's farm communities:

> Before I joined, I was very much wanting to meet people who were very open and loving. I saw this immediately in the devotees I first met. I found it difficult to relate to people before I became a devotee. With women, sexual things always seemed to interfere. With men, it just never felt comfortable. I always felt like I had to be on guard. But the devotees weren't like that. They were warm and friendly and I appreciated that right off (Port Royal, Pennsylvania 1980).

As this man's words suggest, part of ISKCON's appeal for male recruits lies in the quality of the relationships they are able to establish within the movement. For men, the experience of becoming an ISKCON member entails being socialized into ways of behaving and feeling that are more or less consistent with the female world. Although the social world found within the movement has its appeals, shedding the values associated with being male in the larger society is not always easy. As one male ISKCON devotee explains:

> A lot of men come into the movement all puffed up. They think they are the controller rather than Krishna. They naturally take credit for their actions and try to one-up the other devotees. But

this isn't a Krishna-conscious attitude. One can't be Krishna-conscious until they surrender to the idea that they are not the controller. . . . For some men, this need to surrender to Krishna fully is a source of problems (San Diego 1984).

Some men who join ISKCON initially struggle a great deal in their attempt to adjust to the social world found within the movement. These men find the requirement of surrendering to the authority of the guru, to community leaders, and to the larger needs of the devotee community a severe test of their commitment. Surrender, in this sense, is simply not compatible with the values and attitudes held by most men in modern society. The values and the lifestyle found within ISKCON can be a source of attraction to men feeling marginal and isolated from the society, but these very same qualities can also become a roadblock for some men's membership, because of the need to let go of previous attitudes and ways of being, which were adaptive in the larger society.

## Gender, Public Places, and Differential Recruitment

Having discussed the importance of social networks to the recruitment process, I now want to consider the importance of public places and their role in the processes by which both men and women are recruited into ISKCON. First, I will explore the nature of public life as it differently affects the sexes. Then, I will relate the interactional contingencies embedded in public settings to the processes of movement recruitment.

As Goffman has so richly described, public places are fraught with potential dangers. For all intents and purposes, a sense of vulnerability is a natural part of public settings for all who participate in them—men or women.

Wherever an individual is or goes he must bring his body along with him. That means that whatever harm bodies can do, or be vulnerable to, goes along too. As for vulnerabilities, their source allows us to distinguish two kinds. First, impersonal risks, seen as lodged in a setting and not specifically intended for the recipient: physical risks—fire, falling objects, accidental collision, etc.; medical risks due to contagion, poisons, etc.; contamination of body by smell and grime. Second, social risks, those seen as a product of a malefactor's intention. Here central matters are physical assault, robbery, sexual molestation, kidnapping, blocking of passage, breaching of conversational preserves, verbal insult delivered in conversation already established, importunement. Whomsoever an individual is in the presence of, he makes them vulnerable in these ways and they make him vulnerable similarly (1977:327).

While it is clear that public life in general can pose a threat for all who take part in it, the degree of vulnerability is felt very differently by the sexes. Because of women's social and biological status within society, they face more potential for hassling and assault than men do. The troublesome contingencies present in public places tend to be both more numerous and more intense for women than for men (Goffman 1977). Indeed, women are often the targets of interactional improprieties and physical assault, usually at the hands of men. As one investigator of the public lives of men and women comments, "a woman's public life is greatly different from a man's and this difference comes in part from the manner in which she is treated by men" (Brooks Gardner 1981:333). While, theoretically, men can be sexually assaulted, as a rule it is women who are raped and sexually attacked by men. More routinely, women are subjected to street remarks and other verbal insults from men as they travel in public places. This kind of a situation rarely confronts a man, because such public remarks are for the most part sexual in content:

In urban areas women, especially youthful ones, are subject to a free and evaluative commentary by men that is the lot of neither youthful men nor the prerogative of women to deliver if they so choose. This commentary does not deal solely with their appearance, though that is a common subject and a ready resource for them (Brooks Gardner 1981:333).

As this statement dramatizes, women tend to be perceived by men as open and available for interaction in public places. This very perception of availability makes women more subject to the problematic properties of public life than their male counterparts.

Because of the potential dangers associated with public places, people make use of a variety of interactional practices to limit the possibilities of contact with unknown persons. People also use certain strategies in public to clue those present around them that they are not a threat. One such strategy involves the use of what Goffman refers to as the norm of civil inattention:

What seems to be involved is that one gives to another enough visual notice to demonstrate that one appreciates that the other is present (and that one admits openly to having seen him), while at the next moment withdrawing one's attention from him so as to express that he does not constitute a target of special curiosity or design (Goffman 1963:84).

Because the risks of public life are greater for women than for men, they develop specific interactional practices in an effort to avoid social discourse with strangers. Women, for example, often avoid certain public settings altogether—most women would not venture into an unknown bar alone or go to a park that has a reputation for being dangerous, perhaps especially at specific times; the streets may be safe during the day, but become fraught with potential dangers at night. Beyond such avoidance strategies, however, there are other interactional practices used by women to present the appearance that they are "out of contact" (Goffman 1963) and are thereby simply unavailable for interaction.

Women [also] report donning sunglasses so that men have less access to their reactions; adopting what they feel are 'tough' and 'business like' walks; avoiding what they feel is either 'provocative' or too casual dress; and refraining from smiling while maintaining a serious, even 'grim,' facial expression (Brooks Gardner 1981:345).

Because of the different levels of vulnerability experienced by the different sexes in public places, it seems logical to assume that these settings would be less profitable domains for a movement's efforts to recruit women. The fact that ISKCON has fared relatively poorly in recruiting women in public places on the face of it appears to confirm this proposition. Further evidence, however, is provided by observations of the interactions between Krishna devotees and members of the public.

## *ISKCON's Recruitment in Public Places*

Having discussed the general dynamics of public life as they differentially affect the sexes, I want now to look specifically at the interactional processes that ISKCON members use in order to contact people in public for purposes of preaching and distributing religious texts. Using data derived from structured observations of ISKCON members' attempts to distribute religious texts in the Los Angeles International Airport,[6] I want to begin exploring the interactional strategies and related outcomes associated with efforts of the Krishna devotees to contact people in public places.

The findings reported in table 5.2 show the efforts made by ISKCON

Table 5.2.
Gender of Persons Contacted in Public Places by the Gender of the ISKCON Devotee Initiating Contact

| Gender of ISKCON devotee initiating contact | Males | Females | Families/couples | Total |
|---|---|---|---|---|
| Male devotee | 69% | 27% | 4% | 100%(49) |
| Female devotee | 80% | 4% | 17% | 101%(54) |
| Mean percent | 75% | 15% | 11% | 101%(103) |

members to contact members of the public in the Los Angeles International Airport. While male devotees attempted to contact women passing through the airport terminal more often than their female counterparts did, all in all, men still were the favored targets of all the devotees' efforts. As the data indicate, three out of every four persons contacted were men. In addition, on those occasions in which the devotees approached a family or a couple, the contact was directed at the man rather than at his partner.

While one might reasonably argue that these findings are simply an artifact resulting from the greater proportion of men present in the airport terminal than women—which is the case—my observations of the devotees' efforts to make such contacts suggest that other factors were also operating. On a number of occasions, the devotees overlooked women who were readily available for contact in favor of trying to contact a man who was further away.[7]

Although the devotees clearly preferred contacts with men, the question still remains as to how successful they were in establishing ongoing interactions with the people they contacted. Without an opportunity to discuss the philosophy of Krishna Consciousness and the movement in general with the people they meet, the devotees' contacts actually mean little in terms of recruitment. Potential recruits must learn about the movement and about the ways it might prove appealing to them, on whatever grounds, if recruitment is to occur. Table 5.3 shows the devotees' degree of success in establishing face-to-face interactions with the people they contacted in the airport terminal. As the findings indicate, ISKCON members were able to establish interaction with people contacted in less than half of all the cases observed.

As the data further suggest, cross-sexed contacts yielded quite different results. When men devotees contacted women in the airport terminal, their efforts met with little success. In all, three-fourths of the women contacted by devotee men refused to interact with them, except perhaps to brush them off in passing.[8] A typical example is provided by this recorded interaction between a young male devotee and a middle-aged woman entering one of the terminals:

A woman of perhaps 45, white, and attractively attired stepped off the escalator and walked toward the right, to the gates marked 60–65. Before she got too far, however, a male devotee stepped up to her and asked, 'Excuse me, are you from LA or out of town?' The woman replied (looking down at the book in the devotee's hand), 'No. No. I've got no time for that.' The devotee followed her a few steps, trying to give her a small paperback book. He tried to put it in her hand, but she refused it. She walked hurriedly away, trying to act as if she were unaware of the devotee's continuing attempts to stop her.

On the other hand, the devotee women experienced considerably greater success in their efforts to establish face-to-face contact with men. In well over half the cases observed, devotee women were able to establish ongoing interactions with the men they contacted. When approached by a woman in public, men feel little threat and perhaps even a sense of obligation to attend to the communications of the woman. Because women rarely breach the rules of civil inattention in public settings, men may even feel intrigued by the advances of an unknown woman. One man, for example, who met the devotees in the Los Angeles Airport before joining ISKCON several days later, explained his interest in the woman who approached him in the terminal:

I was walking through the airport; I had just flown in from San Francisco, when this woman comes up to me. I didn't know what she was about or anything, but I stopped to listen. She started telling me about Krishna, showing me some pictures and stuff. I didn't understand what she was saying really, but there was something about her I liked. I bought the book and when she asked me to come to dinner, I thought, well, why not. I don't know anybody in LA and here is this nice lady asking me to dinner already (Los Angeles 1979).

As this account suggests, women ISKCON members have an interactional advantage when dealing with men in public places. In recogni-

Table 5.3.
Gender of Persons Contacted in Public Places and the Interactional Outcome by the Gender of the ISKCON Devotee Initiating Contact

| Gender of ISKCON devotee initiating contact | MEN | | | WOMEN | | |
|---|---|---|---|---|---|---|
| | Refused interaction | Face-to-face interaction | Total | Refused interaction | Face-to-face interaction | Total |
| Male devotee | 56%(20) | 44%(16) | 100%(36) | 76%(10) | 24%(3) | 100%(13) |
| Female devotee | 41%(21) | 59%(30) | 100%(51) | 33% (1) | 66%(2) | 100% (3)* |
| Mean percent | 48%(41) | 52%(46) | 100%(87) | 69%(11) | 31%(5) | 100%(16) |

*This low frequency of contact between female devotees and women passing by in the airport terminal itself points to the relatively greater prospects for women devotees establishing contact with men in public places. Given the availability of men in an airport and the greater likelihood of establishing interactions with men, devotee women make few attempts at contacting those women who are present.

tion of this, ISKCON relies on the efforts of its women to distribute religious texts and to preach to members of the public. Our survey revealed that one-fourth of the women surveyed took part in *sankirtana*, while somewhat fewer (19 percent) of the men participated. More telling, however, is the fact that women are known throughout the movement as the most productive book distributors. This success is generally attributed to their status as women and to the ways in which they are able to use their gender to play on the interests of men. As one male book distributor explained:

> EBR: Aren't women known to be the best distributors?
> DEVOTEE: Yes, but you know why that is?
> EBR: Why is that?
> DEVOTEE: Come on, let's face it, their bodies are an asset. They aren't pure devotees, they just use their female bodies to attract men. It's as simple as that (Denver 1980).

A former temple president—and a current ISKCON member —describes one strategy used by women performing *sankirtana*:

> They [women] do sort of have natural advantages. They can approach people and initiate conversations more easily. It never became, or it seldom became super overt, the use of sexuality. The use of feminity I would say perhaps. You know, standing a little too close. It never became overt flaunting of their sexuality. You know in America there is like twelve inches [between people] before it's seen as an invasion of the other person's space. So the [devotee women] would stand a little bit in. A little provocative. Nothing you could really put your finger on, but nevertheless people could get the [sexual] vibes (Philadelphia 1982).

This same devotee describes another strategy used on him by a devotee woman when he was approached in an airport and describes his reaction to it:

I had this experience once where I was coming back from a conference. I had grown my hair out some . . . Anyway, I was coming through the airport and this [devotee] girl came up to me and grabs my hand and says something like: 'We are giving these buttons to all the handsome men.' She starts to talk, but I say: 'Hare Krishna.' She must have turned eighteen shades of red. She was looking for a scarf to pull over her head [laughs]. It was a horrible thing. I mean here she realizes that she is dealing with a devotee and everything changes. It really blew my mind that she could be like that and then realizing it was a devotee had another whole set of rules (Philadelphia 1982).

But while men tend to be the favored targets of the devotees' efforts at making contacts in public—on interactional grounds—they are even more attractive as targets because of recent changes in the practice of *sankirtana*. Public places since the mid-seventies have become important to ISKCON more for financial reasons than for reasons of recruitment. Since men constitute a majority in airport settings, and because they tend to be more promising customers than women (men are both more approachable and tend to hold larger sums of money on them) the devotees consciously seek out contacts with men in these settings. But regardless of the devotees' motives for working this way in public places—be they for financial or for preaching purposes—by targeting men more often than women, ISKCON increases the likelihood that men rather than women will be recruited from these locations. Although clearly the vast majority of the people contacted by the devotees in public never seriously consider exploring the Krishna movement, some do decide to visit a local temple, and in some cases these people do become ISKCON members. Because the large majority of persons contacted in public are men, and because women tend to avoid public places and contacts with strangers, it stands to reason that these settings would yield more male recruits to ISKCON than female ones.

## Conclusion

Since the days of Aristotle, men have been portrayed as the powerful ones in society because of their dominance of the public realm. Women, on the other hand, have generally lived their lives confined to the private, apolitical realm of the family and household (see Elshtain 1974; Sapiro 1983). Throughout most of human history, this gender-based split in the social realm has shaped the roles played by men and women in society and has shaped thereby their everyday experience.

In this chapter I have discussed and analyzed the micro-structural processes by which men and women come to join the Hare Krishna movement. The findings suggest that men and women for the most part are recruited into the movement through different influence structures: women are more often recruited through social network ties, while men most often initiate the recruitment process after making contact with ISKCON members in public places. These recruitment structures, in a larger sense, speak to the differences between the sexes with regard to their participation in and experience of contemporary culture.

My discussion also suggests how membership in a society like Hare Krishna—precisely because of its emphasis on traditionalist sex roles—provides one solution to the problem of marginality faced by women in modern society. The Krishna lifestyle for the most part confines women to the private sphere at the expense of the public. To the eyes of an outsider, this may appear to stand as no more than sexism, but such a viewpoint overlooks the deeper sexism in the dominant culture in which women are more and more required to take part in the public sphere (i.e., mostly, the work place) while at the same time men are failing to become integrated into the private realm of family and household. For ISKCON's men, the movement's communal lifestyle and the *Gemeinschaft* ways of life it embodies inevitably does involve men in the private sphere of social life to a greater degree than is found in the larger society. In fact, a large part of the membership process for men involves being socialized into the private realm, that part of social life commonly associated with the female world.

# 6
# The Growth of Hare Krishna in America

This chapter and the ones to follow focus on the growth and development of the Hare Krishna movement in America. This chapter analyzes the growth and expansion of ISKCON over time and the various factors that have influenced the movement's ability to expand its ranks. In the following chapters, my discussion and analysis of ISKCON's development will center on a number of organizational changes and crises that arose in the middle and late seventies and the strategies used by ISKCON's leaders and members to avert the movement's decline.

In chapter three, I detailed the major sociological approaches to the issue of differential recruitment and suggested the ways in which each independently illuminates aspects of ISKCON's growth in America. In this chapter, I want to move beyond this essentially static treatment of recruitment by analyzing the interaction between a number of internal and external factors that have influenced ISKCON's growth and expansion. I focus on the interrelationship between recruitment strategies, ideology, movement structure, and external social forces as they have influenced ISKCON's history in America.

## Recruitment to Hare Krishna: The Nature of the Contact Process

The interactional processes that result in people making contact with a social movement are not randomly occurring events. Rather, movement organizations devise strategies by which their adherents can make contact with those people who might be generally sympathetic to the movement's goals and ideology. These strategies are most often seen by students of social movements as emanating from the movement's ideology (Freeman 1979; Garner 1972; Wilson 1973). But Snow *et al.* have recently suggested that a movement's recruitment strategies are strongly influenced by its overall organizational structure:

> Movements requiring exclusive participation by their members in movement activities will attract members primarily from public places rather than from among extramovement interpersonal associations and networks. Movements which do not require exclusive participation by their members in movement activities will attract members primarily from extramovement interpersonal associations and networks, rather than from public places (Propositions 3A and 3B) (1980:796).

But investigators favoring these lines of argument have neglected the ways in which external social forces constrain a movement's recruitment strategies. Research has not explored the ways in which external environmental factors are capable of shaping a movement's ideology and structural form, thus indirectly structuring the recruitment strategies it employs to promote its growth.

While contacts with a movement that have been initiated through social network ties have played a prominent role in the expansion of a number of new religious movements (Bibby and Brinkerhoff 1974; Gerlach and Hine 1970; Harrison 1974; Snow *et al.* 1980; Stark and Bainbridge 1980),[1] recruitment to the Krishna movement has been noted as an exception. Judah's (1974) study of the San Francisco ISKCON community in the early seventies found that people recruited into Krishna Consciousness most often made their initial contacts with the movement in public encounters with Krishna devotees. While two-thirds of the devotees sampled in that study (N-63) first made contact with the movement in public places, only three percent had initiated contact through pre-established social ties with friends or family members who had previously joined ISKCON. Snow *et al.* (1980) provide further evidence of the predominance of public places as settings for ISKCON's recruitment efforts; of twenty-five Krishna devotees interviewed in Los Angeles and Dallas, only one had been recruited into the movement by a former acquaintance.

The patterns of ISKCON recruitment strategies reported in table 6.1 contrast with those reported by Judah (1974) and Snow *et al.* (1980). Both social network ties and contacts in public places have served as important avenues by which the movement has sustained its growth. Nearly half of the devotee respondents reported having made contact with ISKCON and/or Krishna Consciousness through a social tie with friends or relatives who were either ISKCON members or who were movement sympathizers. A somewhat smaller number of the devotees initially made contact with ISKCON in public places.[2] These findings also reveal historical changes in recruitment processes. Approximately one-third of the people joining the movement prior to 1971 first learned about ISKCON from a friend or family member who had previously joined. Devotee network influences declined in importance after 1971, but became a major source of recruits again after 1977. The importance of social networks was maintained during this period, however. Between 1972 and 1978, nonmember networks increasingly became the major avenue by which contacts were initiated with Krishna Consciousness.

Recruitment patterns also varied widely according to location as

Table 6.1.
Mode of Recruitment by Year of Entry

| Year entered ISKCON | Devotee networks[a] | Nonmember networks[b] | Public places | Other[c] | Total |
|---|---|---|---|---|---|
| 1967–1971 | 29%. | 7% | 54% | 10% | 100% (40) |
| 1972–1974 | 16% | 33% | 38% | 13% | 100% (44) |
| 1975–1976 | 18% | 26% | 46% | 10% | 100% (50) |
| 1977–1978 | 23% | 40% | 31% | 6% | 100% (35) |
| 1979–1980 | 30% | 12% | 40% | 19% | 101% (43) |
| MEAN PERCENT | (23%) | (23%) | (42%) | (12%) | (100%)(212) |

[a]Devotee networks are contacts leading to membership initiated through social ties with persons who are already ISKCON members.
[b]Nonmember networks are contacts initiated with movement sympathizers that lead to persons taking up membership with ISKCON.
[c]Contacts coded as "other" include being picked up hitchhiking by ISKCON members, visiting a Krishna community for a school project, and meeting the devotees at an antinuke rally. Since only 6% of the devotee respondents indicated that they had initiated contact with the movement on their own (i.e., attended a Sunday Feast at a local temple or read ISKCON's literature) I have grouped them in the "other" category.

well as over time, as is suggested in table 6.2. The Los Angeles community, in particular, and several other ISKCON communities expanded for the most part through social network ties, while other movement communities have had greater success recruiting in public places.[3] These variations suggest that the movement's recruitment strategies are determined locally and not by either ideology or organizational structure.

*determined locally*

In the remainder of this chapter, I want to address the historical changes and community differences that account for ISKCON's varying patterns of recruitment. My analysis highlights the sensitivity of the movement's leaders and members to the recruitment avenues that are available in each of the movement's local settings. ISKCON's growth and expansion as a movement shows the role opportunism plays in recruitment for social movements.

*•oppurtunism*

## The Socio-spatial Dimensions of ISKCON's Recruitment Strategies

The Hare Krishna movement began modestly in New York City in 1965. Srila Prabhupada, or the Swami as he was known to his followers in those early days, came to New York from Calcutta to fulfill the instructions of his spiritual master to spread Krishna Consciousness to the western world. He came to America with no organizational backing and without a group of followers on hand who might help him in his efforts to preach and to begin his Hare Krishna movement. After first attempting to gain a following among the elderly on New York's West Side, Prabhupada quickly turned his proselytizing efforts to the young people living on the Bowery on the Lower East Side. As one of his early followers explained:

I think most of the teachers from India up to that time had older followers, and sometimes wealthy widows would provide a source of income. But Swamiji changed right away to the younger people. The next thing that happened was that Bill Epstein and others be-

Table 6.2.
Mode of Recruitment by Community Where the Devotees Joined ISKCON

| Community | Devotee networks | Nonmember networks | Public places | Other | Total |
|---|---|---|---|---|---|
| Los Angeles | 40% | 33% | 20% | 7% | 100% (30) |
| New York | 28% | 14% | 42% | 16% | 100% (43) |
| San Francisco* | 13% | 0% | 88% | 0% | 101% (8) |
| Denver | 13% | 9% | 65% | 13% | 100% (23) |
| Boston | 21% | 16% | 47% | 16% | 100% (19) |
| Other ISKCON communities in U.S. | 14% | 39% | 39% | 9% | 101% (65) |
| ISKCON communities in foreign countries | 31% | 15% | 39% | 15% | 100% (26) |
| MEAN PERCENT | (23%) | (23%) | (42%) | (12%) | 100%(214) |

*Despite the small number of respondents in the present survey who joined ISKCON in San Francisco, these data generally correspond with those collected by Judah (1974:162).

gan talking about how it would be better for the Swami to come downtown to the Lower East Side. Things were really happening down there, and somehow they weren't happening uptown (Goswami 1980:66).

Word of the Swami spread primarily among the musicians and the bohemian crowd that lived in or frequented the Bowery area (Goswami 1980:72). Their interests in Prabhupada and Krishna Consciousness were often far from being philosophical—many were only interested in fitting Krishna Consciousness into their own lifestyles:

Persons were coming to see what Prabhupada was doing so they could incorporate it into their own ways. Some who were into drugs saw what Prabhupada was doing in those terms. Others like myself were more impersonalist (in their philosophy) and were looking to see what the Swami was saying in terms of this. I mean a lot of people came because of the music. People came for a lot of different reasons, but not because they understood what Prabhupada was doing and what the philosophy was about. I didn't know what Prabhupada was about. I mean we understood about one-millionth of what Prabhupada was saying (from a personal interview with an early New York follower of Prabhupada, Los Angeles 1979).

In these early days, Prabhupada recognized that those becoming interested in his movement were not interested in forsaking their lifestyles to become Krishna-conscious. He did not try to restrict their activities, and he did not insist that his followers give up meat, intoxicants, illicit sex, or gambling. Nor did he require them to live with him in his temple. The majority of his followers continued to live and work in the surrounding community and helped support the temple through their earnings. Only a few of the most downtrodden ever took up residence with Prabhupada at the temple, and next to none of them stayed on to become his disciples (see Goswami 1980:124–125). ISKCON at that time had few spiritual practices or programs that in any way restricted the Bohemian lifestyle of Prabhupada's followers:

You have to remember that [in these early days in New York] there was only the chanting, *kirtanas,* the Swami, and *prasadam* [spiritual food]. That was all, it was a simple process, not complicated and culturally involved, like it is now (from a personal interview with an early New York follower of Prabhupada, Los Angeles 1979).

Because of the structural openness of ISKCON in those first days in New York and the availability of social networks as a means of disseminating information about the movement, we would expect that social ties would serve as the primary means by which Prabhupada was able to gain new followers. Indeed, during Prabhupada's first year in New York City, he initiated nineteen disciples; of the fourteen about whom information is available (Goswami 1980), eight met Prabhupada through network ties. Only six had encountered Prabhupada or his disciples on the street or in nearby Thompkins Park, where the devotees would sometimes go to chant the names of Krishna. Public chanting as a recruitment strategy was not well developed at the time. Only infrequently would the devotees venture out into public areas to chant and engage the public in discussions about Krishna.

ISKCON underwent radical changes after it moved its headquarters in 1967 to the emerging hippie community in the Haight-Ashbury district of San Francisco. Prabhupada decided to relocate into this area for the express purpose of attracting new followers to his Krishna Consciousness movement.

During the first week of the new year, a letter arrived from Mukunda [one of Prabhupada's first disciples in New York]. He had rented a storefront in the heart of the Haight-Ashbury district, on Frederick Street. 'We are busy converting it into a temple now,' he wrote. And Prabhupada announced: 'I shall go immediately.' Mukunda had told of a 'Gathering of the Tribes' in San Francisco's Haight-Ashbury. Thousands of hippies were migrating then from all over the country, to the very neighborhood where Mukunda had rented the storefront. It was a youth renaissance much bigger than what was going on in New York City (Goswami 1980:270).

The Haight-Ashbury section of San Francisco was a fertile environment for ISKCON's recruitment efforts; during its first two years there, an estimated 150 to 200 persons became converts (Johnson 1970:4).
The location of the temple brought potential recruits quite literally to the devotees' doorstep.

> The large scale dislocation accompanying the migration of young people to the Haight-Ashbury created a large, continually walking gathering of unattached persons. Several members noted that they had first discovered the Krishna Consciousness movement by accident — by walking by the temple or hearing the mantra performed in the park . . . The immediate area around the temple was characterized by extensive foot-traffic compared to other sections of the city. Below the large 'Hare Krishna' sign on the outside of the temple was a smaller placard which stated: 'Stay High All the Time, Discover Eternal Bliss' (Johnson 1970:13).

Cavan similarly observed that the Haight-Ashbury was crowded with unattached countercultural youth during the late sixties, people taking part in the hippie practice of "just being," that is, just meandering "through the day, caught up in no particular thing and in the company of no particular person" (1972:94).
With public places providing such an abundance of potential recruits, chanting parties were sent into the streets of the Haight-Ashbury district and to nearby Berkeley to spread Prabhupada's Krishna Consciousness movement. These encounters between the devotees and hippies were central to the movement's expansion during this early period.
While public places served as a rich avenue of recruitment, social network ties yielded relatively few adherents to Prabhupada's movement in San Francisco. Because Prabhupada's first disciples had only recently relocated from New York City, and since the majority of

those being recruited in the Haight-Ashbury district likewise had few social ties to the community, the devotees had little choice but to recruit from among the youth present in public locations. The Unification Church experienced similar problems in trying to recruit through social networks when the Moonies first moved from Oregon to San Francisco in the early sixties.

In San Francisco it [the church] was unable to grow for a considerable time because its members were strangers lacking social ties to potential recruits. Indeed, some new recruits continued to come out of the original Eugene network. Only when the cult found ways to connect with other newcomers to San Francisco and develop serious relationships with them did recruitment resume. But in relying on befriending lonely newcomers, the Moonies were unable to grow rapidly. New members did not open new social networks through which the cult could spread (Stark and Bainbridge 1980:1379).

Unlike the Moonies, ISKCON had a readily available source of potential recruits when it moved to San Francisco. Instead of waiting to establish social relations within the community, the devotees took to recruiting from among the countercultural youth who were seen daily on the streets outside the temple. This was an option not available to the Moonies several years earlier.

But while the social environment in San Francisco encouraged recruitments in public places, it also helped to shape the emerging structural arrangements being set up within ISKCON. Up until the time when Prabhupada expanded ISKCON's influence into San Francisco, the structure of the movement had been fluid and open to the surrounding worldly influences of New York City. Indeed, it was this relative openness that helped spark ISKCON's initial growth, prior to its move to San Francisco. Only after that move did a more closed, communal structure develop. In contrast to the situation in New York, many of the young people joining ISKCON in San Francisco had only recently migrated to the area and were without stable or permanent residences in the area. Because of the lack of living situations for these hippie recruits, ISKCON's communal structure emerged as a way to hold the young countercultural youth to Krishna Consciousness.

## Expansion and Adaptation

ISKCON's San Francisco organization served as a model for the large numbers of devotees who were deployed to other cities across America to establish Krishna temples and recruit members. And even though a closed communal structure emerged in every ISKCON community, that structure was modified to meet local opportunities for recruitment. For example, the socio-spatial environment encountered by ISKCON when it moved into Los Angeles in 1968 was quite different from the one found in Haight-Ashbury. Instead of locating itself in Hollywood or in the Venice Beach area, where the countercultural youth of Los Angeles could be found in large numbers, ISKCON established its community in a middle-class residential area. This environment afforded few opportunities for the devotees to confront people, and especially youth, on the streets around the temple. Even though chanting parties were sent out into the community, they had little success in persuading people to come to the temple and participate in the Krishna lifestyle. Because public places proved so unproductive, the community in Los Angeles focused its recruitment efforts on the friends and families of people already in the movement. In contrast to the recruits in San Francisco, most of those recruited in Los Angeles were from the local area. They were well connected into ongoing social relationships and the devotees made use of these ties to disseminate information about the movement and recruit new members.

Even with local variations in ISKCON's structure, the Krishna lifestyle in itself afforded few opportunities for its members to maintain contacts with the outside society. The isolation of the communities was accelerated in the early seventies, as ISKCON came under attack by deprogrammers and other opponents of the cults. The social ties of members with people outside the movement came increasingly to be seen as potential sources of trouble, rather than as possible avenues of recruitment (Rochford 1976). During this period, and up until Prabhupada's death in 1977, ISKCON was more closed to the outside society than at any other time in its North American history. The decline of the counterculture made public place recruitments ever less likely, and social ties began to seem more of a threat than a source of recruits; ISKCON's growth was sustained largely by the proselytizing of movement sympathizers.

## Movement Sympathizers in the Recruitment Process

As a movement becomes more closed structurally, its members concern themselves exclusively with internal movement activities, and recruitment through pre-established social ties becomes more difficult. If adherents are cut off from their previous social relationships, the movement must disseminate information about its mission through other channels. Snow *et al.* (1980:796) argue that movements like Hare Krishna, which demand a total commitment from its members, are "structurally compelled" to recruit new members in public places. While this may be true for the core adherents who live within the group, a larger body of movement supporters also contribute to the recruitment process. Table 6.1 shows that as ISKCON became increasingly closed to the larger society, it relied on the efforts of movement sympathizers to promote its cause and encourage potential recruits to seek out ISKCON. While devotees continued to have some success in recruiting in public places, the relative importance of movement sympathizers in the recruitment process grew significantly.

Little or no research has been done on the role that movement sympathizers play in the recruitment process. Snow *et al.* (1980) have discussed why movement sympathizers do not participate in movement activities (i.e, they lack time enough to participate), but they did not consider the role of sympathizers in influencing others to participate.

Yet many ISKCON devotees first learned about Krishna Consciousness and/or ISKCON through a friend or family relation who, while not a member of ISKCON, was nevertheless knowledgeable and sympathetic toward the movement and/or its philosophy. For example, consider the accounts of two devotees who described how they first made contact with ISKCON:

> My father received a book from a devotee in the airport and brought it home. He told me to read it and try chanting Hare Krishna. He brought me to various temples and was also interested in Krishna Consciousness (Questionnaire 1980).

> I studied religious studies with a noted religious scholar who is actively involved with ISKCON. I also had student friends in his courses who were likewise familiar with the philosophy and/or had been to an ISKCON temple (Questionnaire 1980).

Other devotees have reported that, even though they first made contact with the movement in a public place, it was only after being introduced to the movement by a nondevotee friend that they came to seriously consider joining ISKCON:

> I first saw the devotees chant at city hall in 1968 and I took an invitation card [to the Sunday feast]. The next Sunday I went to the feast. I didn't like it much, but through the years I didn't mind the devotees as much and would sometimes look at their literature. In 1971 a friend took me twice to the temple and I enjoyed the food and friendship very much. I joined right after that (Questionnaire 1980).

> I encountered the devotees on the street a few times, but was very *unimpressed*. Later some friends of mine took to chanting [not involved in ISKCON] and influenced me. Six months later I joined the movement (Questionnaire 1980).

While most sympathizers have no direct ties to ISKCON, others who contribute to the recruitment process do. People are sometimes recruited into Krishna Consciousness only after making contact with a former ISKCON devotee.

> One blooped devotee [former ISKCON member] came and got a job where I was working as an electronics technician. He introduced me to Krishna. He took me to the feast a number of times and encouraged me to chant and be more serious about becoming Krishna-conscious. He had a family, a wife and four kids, and I was very attracted to them because of their higher consciousness and activities (Questionnaire 1980).

> My friend, who was originally a devotee for three years, left ISKCON because he had lost faith. After spending six months away from the movement, he completely regained his faith and spent a lot of time and energy, with set determination, to make me understand the philosophy and believe in Krishna. It was the courage of his convictions that originally convinced me (Questionnaire 1980).

Nonmember networks can be important to the recruitment process in direct ways as well. Several devotees have reported that they first came to the Krishna community only at the urging of a friend or spouse who had also joined. In some instances, the nondevotee initiating the contact can best be understood as a movement sympathizer. Other cases are not so clearcut:

> I married a man who had previous contact with the devotees and who wanted to become a devotee himself. We joined together one year later (Questionnaire 1980).

> My friend took me for dinner at the temple and we both became involved. As it turned out, we joined together and will probably be married (Questionnaire 1980).

As these accounts suggest, potential recruits can come into contact with a movement in other ways than by means of direct contacts with core adherents. As a movement grows and becomes more visible within society, indirect means of contacting it can become increasingly important to its growth. Also, as adherents leave the movement, they may become vehicles for others to come into contact with the movement's ideology and lifestyle.

## Recent Changes in ISKCON's Recruitment

As a movement grows and develops within a cultural setting, its relationship with the surrounding society undergoes certain changes. In the extreme case, a movement may become institutionalized and thereby cease to be a social movement at all (Messinger 1955; Turner and Killian 1972; Wilson 1973; Zald 1970). Usually, changes in a movement's patterns of action are less dramatic and affect only certain ideological and structural features of the movement.

By the mid-seventies, ISKCON was facing decline as a social movement. Few recruits were being attracted, and Srila Prabhupada's death in 1977 and its resulting politicization of ISKCON resulted in an exodus of many long-time devotees from the movement. In response to these developments, ISKCON's ideology and organizational structure underwent important changes; specifically, many ISKCON communities opened up their communal structures and became more inclusive in their membership criteria. (These developments are discussed in chapters 7–10.)

The ISKCON communities' renewed openness to the surrounding society has taken several forms. First of all, relationships with non-devotees outside the Krishna community have become more common. One-fourth of the devotees surveyed reported that they have close friendships with persons outside the movement. Second, as indicated in table 6.3, 30 percent of the devotees surveyed thought that the community they were presently living in was now "more open to outside

Table 6.3.
Percentage of Devotees Who See Their Community as More or Less Open to Outside Worldly Influences*

| Community | More open to outside influence | Less open to outside influence | Neither | Total |
|---|---|---|---|---|
| Los Angeles | 53% | 0% | 47% | 100% (45) |
| New York | 27% | 9% | 64% | 100% (44) |
| Boston | 31% | 8% | 62% | 101% (13) |
| Chicago | 28% | 11% | 61% | 100% (18) |
| Denver | 7% | 3% | 90% | 100% (29) |
| Port Royal (farm community) | 15% | 23% | 62% | 100% (13) |
| MEAN PERCENT | (30%) | (7%) | (63%) | (100%)(162) |

*Includes devotees who have been in the movement for more than one year.

worldly influences" than it was during their early days in ISKCON. Only seven percent felt that the community in which they were now residing was currently less open to outside influences than it had been. Third, in those communities where social networks have served as a rich source of recruits (e.g., in Los Angeles and New York) devotees are both more involved in nondevotee relationships and see their communities as more open than formerly to outside influences.

Since 1976, the Los Angeles ISKCON community has been the most open to social and commercial influences from the surrounding urban environment. Automobiles, televisions, furniture, newspapers, and weekly news magazines have become commonplace within the community. An attempt in 1980 by the leadership to purge the community of these objects, especially televison sets, was largely unsuccessful. A number of Los Angeles devotees hold jobs outside the ISKCON community and an increasing number of devotees are living on the outskirts of the community where they are less under the control of the leaders.

In keeping with Los Angeles' image throughout the movement, devotees in other ISKCON communities refer to it as "Loose Angeles," implying that devotees there are too involved in the activities of the dominant society ("Maya") and are therefore not adhering to the dictates of Krishna Consciousness. The temple president of one of the ISKCON communities in Texas tried to account for the large fringe community of former or marginal ISKCON devotees in Los Angeles by pointing to the lack of preaching in that community:

There is a definite reason for the growth of the fringe community in L.A. The fact is that the householders [married devotees] who are living out there simply have it too easy. They are too comfortable. There is no emphasis on going out and preaching, distributing Prabhupada's books. This movement is based upon preaching. Without maintaining the proper preaching attitude, one loses touch with their Krishna Consciousness and falls into the fringe. Let them emphasize the preaching, the way they do in other ISKCON communities, and all this nonsense will go away. That is the essence of this movement (Chicago 1980).

The structural openness of the Los Angeles community in recent years has resulted in increased recruitment through devotee network ties. As indicated in table 6.4, devotee networks have become more important than movement sympathizers in producing new recruits in Los Angeles.[4]

This emphasis on network recruitment seems likely to grow stronger because of ISKCON's recent decision to try to build a new congregation of less committed members and of East Indian "life members," whose commitments to Krishna Consciousness and ISKCON can vary from primarily providing financial support to more or less regular participation. This strategy, aimed at recruiting part-time devotees,[5] was summed up by a devotee who has spent nine years in the movement:

If [potential recruits] can only accept five percent, fine then we should encourage them, so that they can accept more, make more progress. If a man drinks a beer, but has some feeling for Krishna Consciousness, then we should attempt to increase his feeling, not discourage him because he drinks. In the past, we would have criticized; now that we have matured, we see the need to encourage part-time devotees. We now need to build up our congregational devotees, encourage them. In this way we can spread Krishna Consciousness (Denver 1980).

Table 6.4.
Mode of Recruitment by Year Entered ISKCON for the Los Angeles Community

| Year entered ISKCON | Devotee networks | Nonmember networks | Public places | Other | Total |
|---|---|---|---|---|---|
| 1969–1971 | 33% | · 0% | 69% | 0% | (100%) (3) |
| 1972–1976 | 27% | 47% | 13% | 13% | (100%)(15) |
| 1977–1980 | 58% | 25% | 17% | 0% | (100%)(12) |
| | | | | | (30) |

A number of young persons are becoming part-time members of ISKCON. There are also a growing number of "life members," usually immigrants from India, who contribute financially toward ISKCON's support. In Los Angeles, the local Indian community uses the ISKCON temple to worship and they take part in the vegetarian feast. Their involvement is for the most part limited to participating in these Sunday services.

Thus as the boundaries between ISKCON and the dominant social structures have been broken down, recruitment through social networks has once again become possible—as it was during ISKCON's early days in New York City. ISKCON's communities are continuing to open up structurally, and as public recruitment declines because of the demise of countercultural clusters like Haight-Ashbury, we expect recruitment to occur increasingly through pre-established social ties.

## Conclusion

No social movement emerges with a fully developed ideology, a complete set of goals, or a stable organizational structure (Turner and Killian 1972). These evolve as the movement develops and expands within a cultural setting. From tenuous beginnings in New York, ISKCON's ideology and communal structure began to take shape as the movement began to attract committed adherents in Haight-Ashbury. But neither the movement's religious beliefs and practices nor its lifestyle really determined its recruitment strategies as it spread throughout the United States in the 1970s. Instead, the success of ISKCON's communities came to depend on the ability of its devotees to adapt their recruitment strategies to specific local socio-spatial environments. In order to take advantage of local lines of access, ISKCON's communities modified the movement's structures and ideology. Analysis of ISKCON's expansion suggests that there is no fixed linear relationship between ideology and structure, on the one hand, and the recruitment strategies devised by a social movement to assure its growth, on the other.

But the patterns of growth and expansion of the Hare Krishna movement raise two additional questions about building up and recruiting members for social movements. First, these patterns suggest that opportunism lies at the heart of some world-transforming movements' efforts to recruit new members to their cause. These movements seek social change as a result of recruiting and converting the masses to their values and way of life (Bromley and Shupe 1979). Leaders and members alike face considerable pressure to recruit more people into the movement. But despite the importance put on recruitment within these world-transforming movements, external constraints limit their capacities to win new converts. All world-transforming movements by their very nature challenge the values of the prevailing social order. Growing public awareness of these movements' objectives often generates a public outcry that restricts their access to legitimate channels for promoting their cause and recruiting new adherents. If the movement is seen by the public as peculiar or perhaps even as threatening, as is the case with ISKCON, lines of access may be further curtailed (Turner and Killian 1972). The dilemma this mistrust poses for world-transforming movements seems to necessitate their becoming opportunistic. While my findings and analysis demonstrate ISKCON's opportunism, similar patterns have been demonstrated in other world-transforming movements, such as the Unification Church (Bromley and Shupe 1979; Lofland 1966), the Children of God (Davis 1981), and Nichiren Shoshu (Snow 1976, 1979).

Second, my analysis of ISKCON's growth and expansion has identified the potentially critical role played by movement sympathizers in movement recruitment. This study suggests that movement sympathizers can be instrumental in the growth of exclusive movements. Because of the intense and total commitment demanded of members in exclusive movements, many who do come into contact with the movement remain outside the organization, despite the attraction of its ideology for them. Conversely, in the case of less demanding and inclusive movements such as Nichiren Shoshu (Snow 1976), people with an equally strong degree of sympathy would probably be granted formal membership. As a result of such different membership criteria, I suspect that member networks are more important for the expansion of inclusive movements, while nonmember networks are more critical for exclusive movements. Furthermore, as an exclusive movement becomes structurally more open to the outside society and therefore more inclusive in its membership, the role played by member network ties in recruiting will increase.

# 7
# Airports and Public Places

Since the early 1970s, deviant religious groups have gained widespread notoriety in the United States and all over the world. The growth and expansion of these new religions—popularly defined as cults—has led to a vociferous public outcry. A major reason for this negative reaction involves the recruitment strategies and information-spreading efforts of these cults. Charges of brainwashing and attempts by anticultists to deprogram members of deviant religions reflect the intensity of the controversy these cults have engendered. While scholars have studied the recruitment strategies and information-diffusion efforts of such deviant groups as the Unification Church (Bromley and Shupe 1979; Lofland 1966), the Children of God (Davis and Richardson 1976; Davis 1981), and Hare Krishna (Judah 1974; Rochford 1982), there has been no investigation to date which addresses the public outcry generated toward the new religions and the ways in which this reaction has influenced their choice of strategies and overall patterns of development in the United States or elsewhere. To promote social change in accordance with its ideological prescriptions, every social movement must act on the society in which it operates. If a movement wants to disseminate its message and mobilize the resources required to reach its goals (i.e., people, power, and money), leaders and members alike must develop outward-reaching strategies directed toward these ends. In reaching out, however, a movement's actions become subject to public scrutiny and evaluation. Public interest and response—whether favorable, neutral, or hostile—in turn affect the growth and survival of the movement. As a number of investigators of social movements have noted, the public's definition of and response to a social movement can have a variety of consequences for its development. The public's response can influence the resource mobilization opportunities available to a movement, its choice of recruitment strategies, the kind of opposition it encounters, the nature of its goals and values, and its overall prospects for survival and prosperity (McCarthy and Zald 1974; Snow 1979; Turner and Killian 1972; Zald and Ash 1966).

In this chapter, I examine ISKCON's emerging resource mobilization strategies in light of the American public's changing attitudes toward the Hare Krishna movement. I then analyze how ISKCON's strategies and public image have in turn influenced its overall patterns of development in America during the 1970s. I demonstrate this relationship by describing and analyzing an activity known within ISKCON as *sankirtana*: originally a practice by which Krishna devotees went out into public places to chant, distribute literature, recruit new members, and solicit donations but which by the mid-seventies had begun to take on a more monetary character. This chapter is divided into three sections. The first part presents a natural history of ISKCON's use of public places during the seventies. The second part details the changes in ISKCON's public place strategies that began in 1973. The third part describes and analyzes the ways in which the public backlash toward ISKCON influenced both its choice of recruitment strategies and its overall history as a social movement during the 1970s.

# A History of ISKCON's Use of Public Places

Public places have been crucially important in the development of ISKCON in the United States. They have been important for the movement's recruitment efforts and for raising financial support for ISKCON's communities. My devotee survey revealed that 42 percent of ISKCON's members in the United States were recruited through public place contacts with movement members. The distribution of literature and other forms of public solicitation (seeking donations and selling various consumer goods) in public places have financially supported ISKCON's expansionary efforts.[1]

Beginning in 1968, Srila Prabhupada instituted the practice *Hare Nam*[2] as a means of preaching Krishna Consciousness, recruiting members, and raising money in public settings. Until 1972, ISKCON's communities were almost completely supported by groups of devotees venturing out into the streets and other public places to distribute literature and seek donations from the public. As one long-time ISKCON member explained:

When I joined the movement in '71, the whole temple went out each day. There were twelve to fifteen people at that time. We chanted in the street from eleven in the morning until six in the evening. Half the group chanted and half stood on the corners, with *dhotis* and *telac* on, extending a BTG [*Back to Godhead* magazine] out saying [to people passing by] 'Take one.' And each devotee would come home with $8, $10. Average income to the temple each day was between $50 and $75. But our rent was only $400 a month, so it was enough (Philadelphia 1982).

The strategy of combining the movement's missionary goals with collecting money became standard ISKCON policy throughout the 1970s. In 1971, ISKCON established the Bhaktivedanta Book Trust in Los Angeles to publish Prabhupada's translations and commentaries on the

*Bhagavad Gita, Srimad Bhagavatam,* and other Vedic scriptures.
With his teachings now in print, Prabhupada instructed his disciples to
distribute his books in volume.[3] Between 1972 and 1974, ISKCON
members distributed the movement's literature primarily in shopping
malls and parking lots across Canada and the United States. While
these locations proved productive for ISKCON's distribution of literature, a major change took place in 1974 that had a revolutionary impact on the future of ISKCON's book distribution.

Under constitutional protections provided by the First Amendment
(*Murdock* v. *Pennsylvania,* 1942)[4] ISKCON shifted its *sankirtana* efforts from the streets and parking lots into airports, national parks, and
state fairs.[5] When these public locations were opened to *sankirtana,*
ISKCON's literature distribution increased dramatically, between 1974
and 1976. As table 7.1 indicates, *sankirtana* devotees in 1976 distributed over eighteen thousand hardback books per week throughout
Canada and the United States. At the Los Angeles International Airport alone, devotees were distributing as many as five thousand to six
thousand each week in 1976. Literature distribution doubled each year
between 1974 and 1976, then declined modestly until 1979, when it
began to fall off significantly.

Economically, the growth in book distribution resulted in a financial
boom for the movement. ISKCON members received an average of four
to five dollars as a donation for each of the large books they distributed to members of the public. With a cost to the movement of approximately $2.50 per book, ISKCON made considerable profit from the
large volume of books distributed. If we take the conservative figure
of four dollars received for each book, ISKCON grossed over $13 mil-
lion between 1974 and 1978 just on hardback books alone.[6]

As a result of the financial prosperity brought about by this growth
in book distribution, ISKCON purchased half a dozen new and larger
temples in 1975 and 1976. The decision to acquire larger temples was
based on the assumption that the movement's ranks would continue to
grow and that book distribution would continue to expand as it had in
these years. By 1975, however, ISKCON's recruitment numbers had al-

Table 7.1.
Average Amound of ISKCON Literature Distributed Weekly In the United States and Canada by Year*

| Year | # Weeks | Large books | Medium books | Small books | (Total) | Communities reporting (average) |
|---|---|---|---|---|---|---|
| 1974 | (36) | 1,748 | 6,830 | 19,570 | (28,148) | (12) |
| 1975 | (45) | 3,434 | 5,759 | 40,750 | (49,943) | (18) |
| 1976 | (32) | 18,406 | 8,555 | 118,724 | (145,685) | (24) |
| 1977 | (42) | 23,393 | 5,203 | 93,693 | (122,294) | (25) |
| 1978 | (51) | 28,976 | 4,014 | 91,813 | (124,803) | (26) |
| 1979 | (52) | 20,442 | 6,634 | 75,640 | (102,715) | (21) |
| 1980 | (19) | 11,985 | 1,724 | 19,921 | (33,630) | (18) |
| 1981 | (26) | 10,456 | 5,692 | 35,594 | (51,743) | (18) |
| 1982 | (41) | 11,852 | 22,273 | 24,534 | (58,659) | (20) |

*These data are compiled from ISKCON's weekly Sankirtana Newsletter, which began in 1974. The figures reported by each of ISKCON's communities are deemed to be generally reliable by my sources within the movement. Gross exaggerations by any community would become apparent when the claimed number of books distributed failed to match the actual number ordered from the Bhaktivedanta Book Trust in Los Angeles. Since book distribution is very competive between ISKCON communities, it is unlikely that the leadership in Los Angeles would fail routinely to monitor the figures reported by other ISKCON communities. I have computed weekly figures because the Sankirtana Newsletter was not published consistently during the 1974–1982 period.

ready begun to decline,[7] and in 1977 book distribution began to level off as well.

It was in the midst of the apparent affluence of the movement in 1975 and 1976 that the seeds of ISKCON's coming decline were being planted. The mass distribution of books brought large sums of money into the organization, but this did not come about because the public was becoming more receptive to Krishna Consciousness. On the contrary, the rapid growth in literature distribution reflected ISKCON members' use of a variety of interactional strategies meant to increase the volume of literature distributed and to maximize the financial return from each book. These changes ultimately altered the very structure and purpose of *sankirtana* and brought the movement into conflict with the public. From the public's perspective, *sankirtana* was seen as motivated more by financial concerns than by religious principles.

## *From Preaching to Selling: Micro-structural Changes in Sankirtana*

As early as 1973, a number of changes were already underway in ISKCON's *sankirtana* practices. Initially, these changes appeared to reflect no more than ISKCON's continuing search for more effective missionary work. By the end of the seventies, however, ISKCON's *sankirtana* practices were becoming ever more financial in character.[8] A devotee who joined ISKCON in 1971 provided a description of the changes that took place:

> Even in the early seventies Prabhupada was saying 'Just a magazine [*Back to Godhead*]. If they can give a quarter, fine.' So you would preach to them [people met in the street] and then ask 'Could you just give a quarter donation?' And if they didn't give it to you [we] just let them go. It was no big deal then . . . . We didn't want to pressure anyone, we just wanted to give them a taste of Krishna (Los Angeles 1978).

But, as this devotee further explained, *sankirtana* had undergone a fundamental change by the mid-seventies:

> While there was some trouble with devotees being aggressive [in their *sankirtana* efforts], up until '74 and '75 it was limited and excusable really. If there were any problems it was just the immaturity of the devotees and it came off that way. But then you saw the aggressive sort of thing. Finances became important. Everything became conscious, organized. You could see there was a change. Not just goofy mistakes like before. They were organized (Los Angeles 1978).

While this insider's account is suggestive, it ultimately says little about the interactional dynamics underlying the changes that took place in *sankirtana*. In the following discussion, I will look at four interactional changes in *sankirtana* that reflect ISKCON's changing uses of public settings.

*Changes in the Targets of the Devotees'*
*Contact Attempts*

With the decline of the counterculture in the early seventies, public places became less productive locations for recruitment purposes. The youth of the counterculture were no longer available in large numbers in communities such as the Haight-Ashbury district in San Francisco and the Bowery on the Lower East Side of New York. With the demise of public places for purposes of recruitment, ISKCON shifted its public efforts mostly into airports to take advantage of the better prospects they offered for distributing the movement's literature. With this shift, ISKCON members began seeking out a range of social groups in these public places that would not have gained much attention previously.

Systematic observation of the devotees' book distribution efforts at the Los Angeles International Airport in 1980 revealed that devotees generally sought out people who would have little or no prospect of becoming ISKCON members, or who would not even be sympathetic to the movement's message. This conclusion is based upon observations of 103 attempted contacts between devotees and members of the public. These contacts fell into several categories.

First, devotee distributors often attempted to make contact with older people. Forty-five percent of the people they contacted were over the age of thirty-five (based on age estimates by the author). A substantial number of these people were fifty years of age or older. Because ISKCON can accurately be considered an age-graded association, which favors participation and interest by the young, it seems unlikely that people over the age of thirty could be considered serious candidates for preaching and recruitment. The devotees surveyed revealed that the average age of ISKCON members when they joined was twenty-one. Only eight percent of the devotees sampled had been over the age of thirty at the time they joined. Moreover, the average age of current members is twenty-seven.

Second, one-third of the people contacted by the devotees were Orientals, including many Japanese. While in some measure this high frequency of attempts at contacts with oriental people is an artifact of the ISKCON distributors's proximity to a Japanese airline, the devotees did choose to take up their positions in this area out of a range of other possibilities in the airport terminal. Only one oriental person was among the devotees surveyed (excluding members originally from India). One reason why oriental people might be preferred targets for the devotees is suggested by the finding that they were both more likely to stop and talk with the devotees upon contact, and they were also more likely to purchase a book than other social groups contacted.

Third, the vast majority of the persons contacted by ISKCON members were men. Three-fourths of all contacts initiated by the devotees were with men. Since airports tend to have a higher proportion of men than women, one might suppose that men were the favored targets because of their sheer numbers. It seems, however, that other reasons were involved. Observation revealed that even women who passed close to devotees were generally overlooked in favor of contacting a man. As discussed in chapter five, men make better prospects for contact and interaction because of the dynamics of male-female encounters. In addition, men, in general, tend to hold larger sums of money on them than women do and therefore they make better (that is, more profitable) targets for ISKCON solicitations.

## *Changes in the Devotees' Presentations of Self*

As any door-to-door salesman can tell, making a sale to a stranger who has not expressed an interest in a particular product is a difficult task. When the salesman is a member of a religious group that is defined by the public as peculiar, strange, or perhaps even threatening, this job becomes even more problematic. While for traditional religious organizations and for a number of the Christian-based new religions (e.g., the Unification Church and the Children of God), such selling can be accomplished rather easily, managing their identity presents a unique problem for ISKCON members because they have taken on the identity equipment (Goffman 1963) of a traditional Eastern culture. To help overcome the stigma attached to their appearance, ISKCON members have devised a number of strategies to disguise their identities during *sankirtana*. In 1973, ISKCON members began wearing conventional clothes to conceal their identity as Hare Krishna devotees (shirts, pants and wigs for the men and dresses for the women).

Something new has been added to the Hare Krishna movement: the toupee. Numerous male members are wearing hairpieces on their shaved pates these days while they are distributing literature. And both sexes are shedding the orange saffron robes in favor of more traditional dress in public. 'We sort of freak out people with our normal appearance,' said Krishna member John Robertson, 27. 'Our culture is so aesthetic that people get upset when they see anything religious' (*Los Angeles Times*, March 19, 1976).

ISKCON members also tried to neutralize their identities as Krishna adherents in other ways. Beginning in 1975, *sankirtana* devotees began to alter their appearances in more extreme ways in an effort to upgrade their respectability in the eyes of the public. I encountered one in this way. I was walking down Westwood Boulevard [in Los Angeles] one afternoon, when a Santa stopped me on the street and offered me a candycane.

> SANTA: Ho, ho, ho. Have you been a good boy this year? Responding that I had indeed, the Santa asked, Would you give a donation to help needy people throughout the world?
> EBR: What kind of help?
> SANTA: (As he raised his money bucket to reveal some small pictures on the side) Book publishing, education, and food distribution.

> At this point I recognize the pictures and the organization ISKCON written on the side.

> EBR: Oh that's a nice thing to be doing.

> As I reached into my pocket for some change, the Santa held the bucket up high to expose numerous dollar bills.

> After I had put the money into the bucket, the Santa handed me a *Back to Godhead* magazine and said:

> SANTA: I am part of a movement that is seeking to alter people's consciousness, through yoga and meditation (Los Angeles 1975).[9]

By taking on roles that the public can interpret as respectable and harmless, the devotees gain special license to accost persons in public settings. In Goffman's (1963) terms, the devotees project a public image that allows them to be seen as opening persons, thereby facilitating their *sankirtana* efforts.

*Changes in the Structure and
Content of Sankirtana*

Beginning in 1975, ISKCON devotees began employing *sankirtana* tactics that were meant to maximize the financial returns from literature distributed. The following interaction between the author and a male ISKCON member at the Los Angeles International Airport in 1981, shows the ways in which preaching had become secondary to the goal of raising money:

DEVOTEE: Sir! Sir! Where are you flying today?

EBR: Oh, I'm just here to pick someone up who's flying in.

DEVOTEE: Look what we have for you. We have already given away hundreds today. Everyone is getting one and here is yours (and he hands me a copy of the *Bhagavad Gita*).

EBR: Thanks, I appreciate that. This will give me something to read while I wait. (I start to move away, but he opens another text exposing pictures of art work.)

DEVOTEE: Uh, we do ask for a donation to cover the cost of publishing. Give a donation.

EBR: Sure, how much do you want?

DEVOTEE: As much as you can. If you give ten dollars that would ·really help.

EBR: (Reaching for my wallet) I can't give ten. How about a couple of dollars? (I open my wallet and pull out two one dollar bills, but in so doing I expose a ten dollar bill.)

DEVOTEE: (Looking over my shoulder) Would you mind exchanging that ten dollar bill for some ones? I have a lot of ones.

EBR: Sure (Giving him the ten).

DEVOTEE: (He reaches into his pocket and pulls out a handful of bills, none of which are one dollar bills. He has nothing but fives and tens and grabs one of the fives.) Could you give five?

EBR: No, I'm a student. I don't have much money. How about four.

The devotee reaches into the other pocket, pulls out a number of one dollar bills, and then gives me six one dollar bills.

In this interaction, the devotee made use of a practice known as the change-up. Having gotten agreement to pay for the book, the devotee then tried to obtain a large bill. With the bill in hand, he then was able to bargain further for a higher price.

More systematic evidence of this profit-seeking motive is provided by a study conducted by the Portland Airport authorities in 1976. Of the 154 persons interviewed[10] who had been contacted by ISKCON members in the airport terminal, fifty-two percent stated that they had not been aware that the person they had encountered was a member of any religious organization. Also, a number of these airport patrons who had been aware that the person they had contacted represented a religious group had no idea that the group was ISKCON; many of them reported that they thought the money was to be used for a Christian charity. More telling is the finding that eighty-nine percent of these respondents reported that the ISKCON member who had contacted them had made no effort whatsoever to discuss religious principles of any sort (Port Authority Study on the Activities of Hare Krishna Members 1976).

## Changes in the Objects Distributed in Public Places

A major change took place in ISKCON's use of public places beginning in 1977. When book distribution began to level off during that year, many ISKCON communities began to face economic difficulties. As literature distribution continued to decline over the next five years, ISKCON faced growing serious financial problems. To help bring money into the movement's communities, ISKCON members began to sell a variety of consumer goods in public settings. In contrast to book distribution, during which individual devotees could take it on themselves to preach, the practice of *picking*, as it is referred to by the devotees, affords little or no opportunity to carry out any missionary activities.

*Picking* is a form of public solicitation that involves seeking straight donations on behalf of a worthy cause (e.g., to feed needy people) or selling nonreligious products to strangers in such locations as rock concerts, shopping centers, roadside rest areas, and in California at the

Department of Motor Vehicles. Items sold to the public include: candles, record albums, candy, cookies, prints of art work, American-flag lapel pins, and buttons (supporting various sport teams and recording artists). When involved in *picking*, devotees wear conventional clothing to disguise their identity as Hare Krishna converts.[11]

Between 1977 and 1979, the devotees sometimes distributed literature when *picking*. After that, this practice became less common and was actively discouraged by the leaders in many ISKCON communities because the distribution of literature often interfered with making a sale. A male devotee, who *picked* at rock concerts on the East Coast in 1980 in order to help finance the many building projects going on at ISKCON's West Virginia farm community, explained why the devotees in his area stopped giving out Krishna books when selling records:

We had to stop giving out books at rock concerts. People would realize that we were devotees and they would just tear them up anyway. I mean these are sex-and drug-crazed people. There is no point in giving them Krishna like that. They won't read the book anyway (Cleveland 1980).

The inability to preach Krishna Consciousness often created considerable distress for *sankirtana* devotees. A devotee woman from the Los Angeles ISKCON community contrasted her feelings about book distribution and *picking* in a 1980 interview:

EBR: When you distribute books does it feel like a different kind of thing than doing records?

DEVOTEE: I do books and records. When you're doing the books it's different because you are giving them Krishna. But you see, a lot of times when you're doing records you can't give them a book. A lot of times they won't take them. Right now I am fried out on doing these records. . . . I want to go and preach to people. I actually want to tell them about Krishna. I'm a devotee. I want to spread Krishna Consciousness, not sell records (Los Angeles 1980).

The decision of ISKCON's leaders to favor *picking* at the expense of book distribution effectively blocked putting forward the movement's missionary goals in public places. *Picking* involves selling commodities to a public who has no commitment, or even potential commitment, to Prabhupada's mission of spreading Krishna Consciousness. This form of public solicitation works quite differently from book distribution because it involves no presumption that the buyer has any interest in ISKCON or in the philosophy of the movement.[12]

## Strategy, Public Definition, and Decline

As a number of investigators of social movements have noted, the developmental pattern of any movement is neither fixed nor solely determined by its goals and ideology (Snow 1979; Turner and Killian 1972; Zald and Ash 1966). Instead, the history of a movement is strongly influenced by the dynamic interplay between its values, goals, and strategies, on the one hand, and the way these are defined and reacted to by the public, on the other.

In the early seventies, the recruitment tactics and information-spreading efforts of the new religions became a public issue in the United States. A countermovement of anticultists emerged, bent on discrediting the cults and shaping public opinion against them. The anti-cult movement sought to influence the public's view of the new religions through the media, through conventional church organizations, through chambers of commerce, civic groups, and through an extensive lobbying campaign directed at state and federal legislators (Shupe and Bromley 1979, 1980). Bromley and Shupe describe the anti-cult ideology and how it was used to legitimize the tactics of those opposing the cults:

> Conversion to new religions was explained in terms of brainwashing, drugging or spot hypnosis; this explanation effectively reduced 'converts' to 'victims.' The remainder of the anti-cult ideology provided the rational for such manipulative and abusive

practices. Leaders of new religions were portrayed as authoritarians and charlatans who exploited their young followers for power and profit. Thus, these groups were not religious at all but merely self-aggrandisement schemes masquerading as religions to avoid taxation and criminal prosecution. Since conversion was neither voluntary nor to a legitimate religion, even forcible removal hardly represented a serious infringement of constitutional rights or personal freedom (1982:4).

While the claims of the anti-cultists have proved largely unfounded (Bromley and Shupe 1981), the anti-cult movement was largely successful in mobilizing what had been an innocent bystander public into a struggle against the cults. By the mid-seventies, the cults had become a publicly defined social problem. As a result, ISKCON and the other new religions came to be viewed by the public as threatening.[13]

Because of this strong public opposition, ISKCON's mobilization strategies were greatly narrowed; the movement had few choices and chose to pursue covert and illegitimate tactics to help assure its survival. The choices were particularly limited in ISKCON's case because its exclusive communal structure and sectarian beliefs further restricted the financial strategies that otherwise might have been available (e.g., outside employment). To have chosen this employment alternative would have involved changes in the movement's exclusive structural arrangements, which would have in turn risked the commitment of its membership, because, as a result of worldly influences, they would then be subjected to influences pulling them away from the group. Most critically, working outside the devotee community might well have resulted in members forming social ties with nondevotee co-workers, which might have acted as countervailing ties, threatening members' commitment to ISKCON and Krishna Consciousness. Because of the limited strategies available, ISKCON began to stress the financial side of *sankirtana* at the expense of missionary activities. As book distribution began to level off and then decline after 1977, ISKCON's public place strategies shifted once again. *Picking* became the dominant financial strategy.[14]

These changes in ISKCON's *sankirtana* practices during the middle and late seventies further shaped and rigidified the public's image of ISKCON as a deviant and threatening cult. By employing tactics that were viewed by the public as coercive, financially motivated, and lacking in religious content, ISKCON helped to mobilize public opinion against its beliefs and way of life. Literature distribution declined even more dramatically beginning in 1979, and many, if not most, ISKCON communities faced serious economic problems. The public became keenly aware of ISKCON devotees in airports and other public places and actively sought to avoid contact with them.[15] But more formal and systematic efforts were also instituted to control ISKCON's use of these settings. In the mid-1970s, airports, state fairs, and other public facilities throughout the United States began to legally challenge ISKCON's *sankirtana* practices. The authorities argued that ISKCON was using tactics that were more financial than religious and therefore that the movement should be denied First Amendment privileges. Despite a wealth of legal precedents in its favor, ISKCON faced a stiff challenge in protecting its free access to public settings. As the ISKCON member largely responsible for opening public settings to *sankirtana* explained in a 1983 interview, the movement's tactics became the grounds for legal attempts to limit ISKCON's access to these settings:

> While it was initially easy to open these various public places to *sankirtana*, suddenly everything began to change. When we [ISKCON] came back to fight time, place, and manner regulations, we had a hard time. They [airports, etc.] would say: 'Look what you are doing. You are using the change-up on people and other practices of this sort simply to get money from them. We don't think First Amendment rights are at issue.' So they would get the judge thinking that we were involved in fraud. As a result, we could no longer assert *pure* First Amendment rights (Philadelphia 1983).

Initially, the courts reacted only by imposing limitations on ISKCON's use of public settings. These included restrictions on where

ISKCON members could distribute literature in a particular public facility, on how many devotees could distribute it at any one time, and/or placing time limitations on *sankirtana*. In addition, in the late seventies, state fairs in several states won legal rulings confining ISKCON members to booths, thereby limiting the devotees' access to fair patrons (*ISKCON* v. *Barber, Young, and Garlick*, 1980; *ISKCON* v. *Evans*, 1977; *ISKCON* v. *State Fair of Texas*, 1978).

Several state courts, beginning in 1977 and 1978, began hearing lawsuits aimed at denying ISKCON's right to engage at all in public place solicitation. Airports in Los Angeles, Seattle, Chicago, and other locations initiated litigation meant to deny ISKCON access to airport facilities. Public zoos and a number of state and county fairs from California to New York brought legal actions aimed at ending *sankirtana*. Finally, in 1978, O'Hare International Airport in Chicago was closed to *sankirtana*. As one ISKCON leader explained in 1981, the public reaction that had been generated by the movement's *sankirtana* practices was largely responsible:

> While book distribution went up and up between 1974 and 1977, the public reaction was also building. And then bam, there was a chain reaction: O'Hare [airport in Chicago] went down and there was litigation to get us out of other airports and public places. . . . The airport managers used to discuss with each other at their conventions: 'How do we get the Hare Krishnas out?' (Philadelphia 1982).

In 1981, the U.S. Supreme Court ruled (*Heffron* v. *ISKCON*, 1981) that ISKCON members did not have the legal right to distribute literature and solicit donations at state fairs throughout the country. Because of this decision and a number of other legal rulings that either restricted or prohibited *sankirtana*, ISKCON discontinued or limited literature distribution in a number of public settings, particularly airports.

Even as ISKCON faced being discredited by the anti-cult movement, the public, and the courts, it also began to face criticism from within. A growing number of ISKCON members began openly to question the movement's *sankirtana* practices, to the extent that ISKCON's legitimacy as an instrument for putting forward the cause of Krishna Consciousness was challenged. As one long-time ISKCON member explained in a 1982 interview:

> One thing that you have to realize is that from the beginning to the end, the change-up and so forth were very controversial within the movement. Some devotees were sensitive to how the public would react and realized from experience that *karmies* [members of the public] weren't stupid. They were going to figure it out in due course of time and it was all going to come back on us. . . . Some leaders grossly underestimated the consciousness of the people who were coming into contact with the devotees. They seemed to think that people didn't realize that they were being manipulated . . . But some of us knew that sooner or later it was going to come down. It was a mistake to become unethical with the people (Philadelphia 1982).

The controversies surrounding the movement's money-gathering strategies led to an erosion of member commitment and to mounting internal conflicts, factionalism, and a growing number of defections. The loss of ISKCON credibility in the eyes of a part of its membership became a major force causing ISKCON's decline during the late seventies. While external challenges to the movement could be interpreted as no more than a deepening of the general persecution of ISKCON and the cults in general, internal challenges to the authority of the organization brought ISKCON to the edge of organizational crisis. As Zald and Ash (1966) argue, the decline and failure of a movement organization is often the result of strategies that place the organization's legitimacy in doubt from *within*. By altering the purpose of *sankirtana*, ISKCON's leaders unwittingly set off a process that led to their being discredited, which ultimately undermined the organization's legitimacy and helped to hasten the decline of Hare Krishna in America.[16]

## Conclusion

All 'social movements are involved in a continuous process of exchange with the socio-cultural environments in which they operate. If a movement is to reach its aims, it must mobilize the resources necessary to promote social change. Gaining these resources from society requires that a movement develop outward-reaching strategies. By doing this, however, a movement invites public evaluation and response, which may either facilitate or limit its achievements. As the public outcry against the cults' recruitment strategies and information-diffusion efforts grew during the 1970s, ISKCON was forced to adjust its money-gathering strategies in public settings. Lacking alternative ways of supporting itself, ISKCON began to favor the financial side of *sankirtana* at the expense of the movement's missionary goals. By doing so, however, ISKCON only further intensified the conflict between itself and the public. This conflict, in turn, caused a variety of social controls to be directed toward limiting ISKCON's practices in public settings. Largely as a result of these developments, ISKCON in North America faced decline and organizational crisis by the end of the decade.

# 8
# Change and Adaptation

*I*t is a truism that social movements and their organizational forms undergo change over the course of their histories (Michels 1962; Turner and Killian 1972; Weber 1968; Zald and Ash 1966). As suggested in chapter six, no social movement comes onto the scene with a fully articulated ideology, a complete set of objectives, or an established organizational structure. But neither do movements and their organizations reach what might be thought of as developmental endpoints, where their ideologies and structures can be considered more or less final.

The events affecting ISKCON during the 1970s had a major impact on the Krishna movement's development in America. By 1977 circumstances had culminated in ISKCON's rapid decline as a social movement and organization. Later that same year, Srila Prabhupada died, and the movement faced succession problems, which further aggravated the growing sense of crisis (to be discussed in the next chapter). Compounding these problems was the challenge coming both from within and from outside the movement regarding the strategies that had been developed by the leadership to deal with the organization's financial decline. The major protest centered on the changes made in *sankirtana* by ISKCON's leaders. The movement's critics interpreted these changes as evidence of a basic transformation in ISKCON's purpose in America: finances and maintenance concerns had come to replace the goal of spreading Prabhupada's Krishna Consciousness.

In this chapter, I will examine the strategies that ISKCON's leaders and members adopted to deal with the crisis of legitimacy that had emerged as a consequence of the movement's changing *sankirtana* policies. First, I want to discuss the ideological work (Berger 1981) done by both the leadership and the members, as each sought to adapt to change. I then want to examine the relation of ideology and religious belief in general to ISKCON's patterns of adaptation. In conclusion, I will evaluate current models of movement change and transformation in light of ISKCON's history in America during the 1970s.

## Ideological Work and Organizational Adaptation

If a movement organization is to hold its membership successfully and thereby maintain its efficacy as an instrument for social change, its values and goals must be articulated, understood, and ultimately internalized by its members. When a movement organization confronts circumstances that raise an apparent contradiction between its professed beliefs and the day-to-day practices of its members, ideological work must be done in order to repair the disjuncture between the beliefs and the daily realities of its members. To the extent that a movement organization is able to establish a link between its current practices and the sanctioned beliefs of the movement, it will be able to maintain its members' commitment and thereby its efficacy as an instrument for social change. Bennett Berger describes the nature and purpose of this ideological work:

Ideological work enables those engaged in intellectual combat to attempt to persuade their critics and their own constituents (more or less plausibly in different cases) that apparent discrepancies between preaching and practice are in fact illusory and can be successfully resolved (1981:181).

In the case of a declining religious movement like ISKCON, in which strategies used to deal with the decline appear logically to contradict aspects of ideology, it becomes critical that current objectives be seen and accepted by the members as spiritually and ideologically defensible. To the extent that the organization is able successfully to present an explanatory apparatus that sustains a definition of reality in accordance with the movement's ideology, thereby unmasking the false consciousness of its detractors, its capacity for survival is markedly improved. In short, the organization must be able to promote a reasonable explanation for its actions that removes doubts from the minds of at least a significant portion of its adherents, if the organization is to avert failure and disintegration. Berger and Luckmann describe the ideological work involved in maintaining such plausibility structures and their intended effects on members:

The plausibility structure is also the social base for the particular suspension of doubt without which the definition of reality in question cannot be maintained in consciousness. Here specific social sanctions against such reality disintegrating doubts have been internalized and are ongoingly reaffirmed. Ridicule is one such sanction. As long as he remains within the plausibility structure, the individual feels himself to be ridiculous whenever doubts about the reality concerned arise subjectively (1966;155).[1]

If member commitment is to be maintained, any changes in a movement organization's practices must be given the legitimacy of sacred ideas. Without such sanctions, the organization's plausibility structure would be open to doubt. To the extent that the leaders fail to align present practices with the movement's ideology, the organization's legitimacy as an instrument for change is discredited from within. Being discredited from within deepens the movement's decline, perhaps bringing on mass defections and the ultimate collapse of the organization (Zald and Ash 1966).

As will be discussed in the next section of this chapter, ISKCON experienced only partial success in aligning its new economic concerns, as they related to *sankirtana*, with the Krishna-conscious worldview. For now, however, I want to discuss and analyze the nature of the organization's ideological work; how it was carried out; and what factors influenced the success ISKCON experienced in ideologically legitimizing the strategies chosen to deal with the organization's decline. The primary thrust of ISKCON's ideological work involved efforts to legitimize the changing nature of *sankirtana* rather than other strategies developed to deal with decline, such as the development of a Krishna-conscious congregation. The development of such a congregation involved fundamental changes in the structure of ISKCON but, from the point of view of the average devotee, this change was seen as generally consistent with the movement's goal of spreading Krishna Consciousness throughout the world. *Sankirtana*, because it had traditionally served as the movement's major form of missionary work, presented a different problem and one that required leaders and members alike to take part in ideological work directed toward bringing current economic practices in line with the movement's overall mission.

The ideological work required of ISKCON's leaders to maintain the organization's plausibility structure involved two basic strategies: First, the leaders needed to present moral justifications for the changes made in *sankirtana* tactics, arguing that any changes that had taken place were insignificant with respect to the movement's overall mission. They argued that *sankirtana* continued to fulfill its traditional purposes of preaching and missionary activity despite everything. Second, and in contradiction to the first strategy, spiritual status within the ISKCON communities began to be evaluated largely in terms of a devotee's success in raising money for the benefit of the movement. In this sense, success in raising money through *sankirtana* became a ma-

jor criteria by which status within the devotee community was gained
or perhaps lost.

## Moral Justification as Ideological Work

The basic strategy employed by ISKCON's leaders to demonstrate the
link between its organizational practices with regard to *sankirtana* and
the overall beliefs of the movement involved the rhetoric of moral
justification. The content of the leader's ideological work stressed that
*sankirtana* had not, in fact, undergone any significant change, that
preaching continued to lie at the heart of this activity. When members
questioned the changes made in the practice of *sankirtana*, the leaders
attempted to shift the burden of blame away from the organization and
its policies. Consider, for example, the words of Western Guru spoken
at an early morning meeting in the Los Angeles community in the
summer of 1980. On this occasion, a member of the community challenged ISKCON's book distribution tactics in a question directed at
Western Guru:

> DEVOTEE: Isn't the movement's book distribution causing prob-
> lems for the movement? It has alienated the public and therefore it
> is more difficult to preach Prabhupada's message.
> WESTERN GURU: We have to be very very careful. Don't blame
> *sankirtana*, *the process of preaching*, of going out and giving to the
> people. Don't do that, it 's an excuse for why you won't do it. That
> has been done so many times. But if anyone tells you this, you can
> see right through it and understand that this devotee is looking for
> an excuse not to preach. Somehow or other this preaching has
> to go on. Don't think preaching ruins the movement (Los Ange-
> les 1980).

Another strategy of moral justification involved holding the society
and external ongoing sociocultural changes responsible for ISKCON's
declining emphasis on missionary activity. As one ISKCON devotee explained, there had in fact been little or no changes made in the every-

day spiritual practices of the movement's members. Any changes in
ISKCON's missionary activity were simply a reflection of societal
changes, changes which were clearly out of the hands of the movement and its leaders:

When the decline in book distribution came, we had to do so many
things to keep things going. This did not mean, however, that we
had in any way given up on the core values of Krishna Consciousness. Rather, this was simply a change brought on by the larger society. There wasn't any change among the leaders away from
preaching or the core values. The devotees continued chanting their
rounds. No one decided 'Now we will only follow two of the [reg-
ulative] principles.' While it is true that we were not able to fulfill
all of Prabhupada's goals, this doesn't mean that our values were
changed. They weren't (Philadelphia 1982).

But moral justification was also used in another way. Some ISKCON
leaders and members, while openly acknowledging that *sankirtana*
had indeed undergone changes meant to bring larger sums of money
into the organization, argued that these revenues indirectly contributed
to the movement's missionary goals and therefore that any changes
were legitimate and morally justified because of the ultimate use of the
money collected.

When ISKCON began the practice of *picking*, for example, the leadership in Los Angeles stressed that this form of enterprise would actually facilitate the movement's overall missionary objectives. As
one devotee who resided in the Los Angeles community during this
period explained:

DEVOTEE: The initial idea behind *picking*, as presented by the authorities, was that it would actually help our preaching.
EBR: How's that?
DEVOTEE: Well, devotees could go out and raise money, then,
based on how much they collected, they would calculate how many
books they could give away . . . . That was the rationale behind it .

. . . But the idea was that you could go up to people and talk to them, and if you saw where they could benefit, you just gave them a book. You know getting into the real preaching concept, not force, you were actually giving them a book. You could distribute kind of purely, you didn't have to hassle someone for it. So it sounded real appealing (Los Angeles 1978).

Another devotee who sold records and buttons at rock concerts on the East Coast in 1980 also legitimized *picking* in similar ideological terms:

We [the devotees] want to be sure they read the books. Devotees are distributing in so many ways, but who is actually reading the words of Srila Prabhupada? By *picking*, we can afford to give away the books and then the *karmies* will read them. So actually we are just supporting the preaching work that is going on (Cleveland 1980).

Although ISKCON's leaders attempted to legitimize the changes in *sankirtana* by arguing that these changes actually facilitated the movement's missionary goals, they also stressed the ways in which the money collected provided spiritual benefits to those contributing. Regardless of the devotees' tactics and motives, they argued that any person who contributed to ISKCON's cause stood to gain spiritually. As one devotee explained:

There is the idea within our beliefs that getting money from someone is actually spiritual in itself. And this wasn't a rationalization or any ideological adjustment that came later, to give a spiritual or scriptural basis to a new commitment on the movement's part, or to legitimate a new direction. That was there from the beginning . . . Prabhupada's idea was that the money is in the hands of the atheists and so we want to take some portion of it back for spiritual purposes and use it in Krishna's service. So this isn't something that was tagged on later, but it was there from the beginning (Philadelphia 1982).

The ideological work of a male devotee who *picks* to help support the movement's farm community in West Virginia went this way:

Let's face it, we are actually allowing these people to render some service [to Krishna]. I mean we are liberating *lakshmi* [money] from people who wouldn't buy a book or render some service. It's not that we are using the money for our own sense gratification. No, we are using it in God's service to glorify God. So we are actually benefiting these people, because we are allowing them to render some service by helping to build New Vrindaban (Cleveland 1980).

Two former ISKCON devotees explained how "stealing for Krishna" (speaking here of the change-up tactic used in book distribution) was justified for much the same reasons.

FIRST DEVOTEE: A lot of devotees have come up with the understanding that they can steal for Krishna. And actually if they feel this way sincerely, and do it for Krishna, then it is OK. It may not be OK to contemporary minds and ways of thinking, but it really counts in God's eyes.

SECOND DEVOTEE: Actually the potency behind it is where it's at . . .

FIRST DEVOTEE: I try to look at all these different activities as being all ISKCON's activities, even if they are wrong, and how they relate to the overall mission, because I accept it as all being bonafide (Los Angeles 1979).

Another devotee, who took part in the movement's annual Christmas marathon dressed as Santa Claus soliciting donations on the street, justified raising four hundred dollars in one day in the following terms:

The money that the people give, even if they do feel tricked, helps them spiritually. What would they do with the money anyway? They would spend it on some sense gratification, right? So we are actually rendering these people a special service, even though they may be so foolish that they can't recognize it (Los Angeles 1976).

But the spiritual benefits accruing to members of the public from these activities did not stop at their financial contributions to the movement. As one devotee explained, a person could benefit even if he or she failed to purchase the book from a devotee:

The attitude among the book distributors was to just get the book out. Prabhupada said that these books were so potent that if a person just touches it, if he just reads one word, if he just reads one line his life will be transformed. Regardless of the tactics being used, the books had such spiritual potency that they naturally benefited anyone who came into contact with them. This was the consciousness of the devotees out there distributing (Philadelphia 1982).

While the leaders in most of ISKCON's communities were required to do extensive ideological work to legitimize the changes in *sankirtana*, one community stands out from the others in terms of its ability to provide an adequate plausibility structure for these changes for its members. The unique mission of the New Vrindaban community, in West Virginia, provided a direct link between money making and the movement's missionary goals.

Under the direction Srila Prabhupada's first disciple in America, ISKCON's two-thousand-acre, two-hundred-plus devotee community in rural West Virginia has been in the process of building a traditional spiritual community for the past dozen years. This project has involved building traditional *Vaisnava* temples, restaurants, camp grounds, and other tourist attractions meant to bring in large numbers of the public. In 1980, Prabhupada's Palace was opened to the public and thousands of tourists have visited it each year. The community is presently building the first of several planned temples, which it hopes will attract even more visitors in years to come. The New Vrindaban community is of particular interest regarding ISKCON's ideological efforts to provide moral justification for the changing nature of *sankirtana*. This community perhaps more than any other has discontinued practicing *sankirtana* in its traditional form, yet it has apparently met with less overall criticism and loss of member commitment than the other communities. Devotees residing at New Vrindaban do little or no book distribution in public places. Revenues are derived almost exclusively from the *picking* efforts of the community's members as well as from a number of small business enterprises. But while this community has for all intents and purposes abandoned *sankirtana* as a form of missionary activity in public, it has not given up its commitment to preaching Krishna Consciousness. Preaching has simply taken on a different form. Prabhupada's Palace and the ongoing building projects at New Vrindaban stand as monuments, symbolic of this community's commitment to preaching Krishna Consciousness. The fact that thousands of people continue to visit these institutions each year is a testimony to the community's commitment to preaching and missionary work. New Vrindaban's success lies precisely in its ability to demonstrate to its members the direct link between money making and the movement's commitment to missionary activity. For devotees residing in other ISKCON communities in America, direct evidence of a continuing commitment to preaching was much harder to come by.

## Spiritual Differentiation and Ideological Work

As ISKCON came to favor the economic side of *sankirtana*, spiritual statuses within the devotee communities changed accordingly. Attracting potential converts to Krishna Consciousness ceased to be a major criteria by which spiritual status and advancement were judged. As organizational goals shifted away from recruitment and preaching to raising money to help meet the movement's growing financial needs, the bases for member stratification changed accordingly. As I reported in 1976, recruiting new members served traditionally as an important symbolic basis for differentiating members on moral or spiritual grounds.

Success in recruiting new members also served to enhance one's spirituality. Reference to the leader of the *bhakta* program as a 'first class devotee' is public recognition of his spirituality. . . . Proselytizing by all devotees is likewise interpreted as indicating spirituality. The goal of converting 'fallen souls' is the manifest function, but success in such efforts publically acknowledges one's own spirituality (Rochford 1976:25).

During the movement's early years in America when recruitment of new members was a major organizational goal, deference was extended to devotees who had success in this realm. By the late seventies, as ISKCON began to face serious financial difficulties, spiritual differentiation was changed accordingly. As one long-time devotee acknowledged:

Everyone in the temple knows who the best [book] distributors and *pickers* are. I mean it matters. In America it's that way. We're [the devotees] into competing. You see that among the devotees like anyone else (Denver 1980).

Another devotee, who left ISKCON in 1980 but who had worked as a *picker* in the Orient to raise money for the movement's projects in India, reported how the devotees used to react toward him and other members of his *picking* team:

DEVOTEE: It got to the point where, when you told devotees that you were with [name of the devotee organizing the team] they would say 'You were with that party? Boyyy!' They thought we were saints, scholars. People [the devotees] actually thought we were saints. I mean we were raising all that money for India and everyone felt we had to be saints.

EBR: But they didn't know the types of things you were doing to
get all that money?

DEVOTEE: Some did, but even they didn't say anything, 'cause
they needed the money (Los Angeles 1979).

Also reflecting the changing basis of spiritual status within the
movement was the decision in the late seventies to document not only
the number of books distributed by individual devotees in the weekly
*Sankirtana Report* but also the amount of money collected (referred to
as *lakshmi* points). Competition between devotees and ISKCON communities grew in intensity as *sankirtana* profits began to decline.
To encourage productivity in collecting money, devotees who had ac-
cumulated the highest number of *lakshmi* points were rewarded
each year by being sent to the movement's yearly festival in Maya-
pur, India.

Spiritual differentiation on the basis of economics was also made
evident in at least some ISKCON communities by the preferential treatment accorded *sankirtana* devotees. In Los Angeles, for example,
*sankirtana* devotees in 1980 ate separately from other community
members. This policy allowed *sankirtana* devotees to begin their work
earlier than other community members each day, but the purpose of
the policy was not limited to this consideration alone. *Sankirtana* devotees were routinely given *maha prasadam*, foodstuffs that are considered spiritually empowering because they have been directly offered to
Krishna during the morning *arati* ceremony. Because of its spirituality, this food is highly valued by all Krishna devotees. Routinely to
give one group of devotees this food to the exclusion of others is to
manifest the difference in status between *sankirtana* devotees and devotees who perform other duties on the movement's behalf. One former
devotee, who had resided in the Los Angeles community for several
years, commented that this decision provoked considerable dissension
within the community: "It was a bad decision. It just made for more
party feelings among the devotees" (Los Angeles 1979).

This account suggests that the group's spirituality came increasingly
to be fused with ISKCON's financial purposes: devotees who brought in

the greatest financial returns to the organization were recognized within the movement as having high spiritual status. As ISKCON struggled with organizational decline, the basis of status within the devotees' stratification system came to reflect organizational needs.

## *Ideological Work and Member Adaptation*

While virtually any movement organization subject to the vicissitudes of historical change engages in ideological revision in order to maintain or perhaps re-establish the link between its organizational practices and the beliefs and ideology of the members, the success or failure of this work ultimately depends on the members. If a substantial number of the members internalize the ideological work of the organization's leaders, then the movement's potential for survival is increased. On the other hand, if the ideological work of the leaders is seen as no more than self-serving, member commitment becomes problematic and the organization may be discredited. This negative reaction by the membership may in turn put the organization's continued existence in jeopardy.

Ideological work directed toward the maintenance of plausibility structures is not exclusively the domain of a movement's leaders, however. Members too have a stake in the organization and its continuation, even if they object to the decisions and policies of the leaders. While some members do uncritically internalize the ideological work of the organization, others, those who continue to harbor doubts, may engage in ideological work of their own in an effort to maintain their commitment to the movement's goals and purposes, if not to the organization per se. In other words, members may reject the ideological work done by the organization's leaders and nevertheless remain committed to the movement on personal ideological grounds. Finally, some members may come to view the strategies and policies of the organization's leadership as having gone beyond any possibility of legitimacy. These members come to view the leaders' ideological work as no more than a sham based on self-deception and the self-serving manipulation of the members' interests. For these members, defection from the organization becomes the strategy of choice.

It is just this range of adaptive patterns that I want to explore and analyze. I will discuss three adaptive styles employed by ISKCON's members in the face of changing circumstances and the leaders' efforts both to deal with change and to legitimize the policies they developed. The adaptive strategies to be discussed are: 1) organizational adaptation; 2) spiritual adaptation; and, 3) defection.

*Organizational Adaptation*

The majority of ISKCON's members were virtually unaffected by ISKCON's decline and the new strategies used by the leadership to deal with it. While most devotees recognized that *sankirtana* had undergone a shift in emphasis toward money making, they did not interpret this change as reflecting a fundamental change in the movement's mission. Because belief is more the "natural attitude" (Schutz, 1971) than nonbelief, most of ISKCON's members simply accepted the ideological work of the organization and its leaders.[2] As one long-time devotee who has served as temple president in one of ISKCON's communities explained:

> I have worked with literally hundreds of devotees and I can say that for them as a class they are very idealistic. Their sense of what they are doing when they are distributing books, even if there is a significant financial element involved, is always that we're giving the spirit soul [members of the public] a book. From their point of view, it never became strictly a financial transaction. They see themselves as preaching, as benefiting the spirit soul (Philadelphia 1982).

But even though some of ISKCON's members uncritically accepted the ideological work of the leaders, others came to view ISKCON's altered circumstances as ultimately inconclusive. As Bennett Berger suggests, "'selling out,' 'struggling,' and 'accommodating,' are seldom unambiguously self evident while they are occurring" (1981:22). Because of their uncertainty as to whether ISKCON had in fact given up its missionary goals, the strategy of some devotees was "a wait-and-see attitude." These members argued that no reliable assessment of ISKCON's present pattern of development could be made, because only the future would show the meaning of the present. In this sense, some of ISKCON's members used a strategy analogous to what Garfinkel, following Mannheim, refers to as "the documentary method of interpretation":

> It frequently happens that in order for the investigator [whether a professional sociologist or a lay person interested in his/her practical affairs] to decide what he is now looking at he must wait for future developments, only to find that these futures in turn are informed by *their* history and future. By waiting to see what will have happened, he learns what it was that he previously saw (1967:77).

For those ISKCON devotees making use of the documentary method of interpretation, any analysis of the changes associated with ISKCON's decline must necessarily wait until further events have clarified the meaning of that time. They argued that all analyses that had concluded that ISKCON had been transformed into a power- or maintenance-oriented movement necessarily relied on inadequate or incomplete history. Moreover, they argued that if it was the recalcitrant nature of external circumstance that had contributed to ISKCON's decline, as well as to the strategies developed by the leadership to deal with it, then changing social conditions in the future could lead to a re-establishment of the movement's missionary zeal. The use of the documentary method is clearly shown in the analysis of one ISKCON member who comments on the movement's past and future prospects:

> If there has been any decline in preaching, that doesn't mean that our purpose has changed. We are just *unable for the time being to*

*execute our purpose.* My purpose hasn't changed nor has the movement's. For example, any business in the material world has its up
and downs. But you don't necessarily sell the business because you
suffer a low period. Rather you develop a new product line or whatever is needed to keep things going. You hang on during the rough
period until things become more receptive. That's what ISKCON did
during the 1978 to 1980 period. Our preaching was down, but we
continued to push forward until things got a little easier. It was a
period of decline, but nothing really changed. We were never content with that, but what could we do? Now as we move into the
'80s we can already see that things are changing. There has been an
upsurgence in book distribution in the past year [1982] and that en-
thusiasm is there once again throughout the movement [emphasis
added] (Philadelphia 1982).

*Spiritual Adaptation*

A second adaptive strategy involved rejecting the ideological work of
the organization in favor of more individually-based forms of spiritual
legitimacy. Spiritual adaptors viewed the changes in *sankirtana* as
lacking any source of legitimacy and therefore they rejected the ideological work of ISKCON's leaders. Consider for example the comments
made in 1980 by four devotees from three ISKCON communities:

My commitment to ISKCON has decreased because of the fact that
the devotees and the leaders are not seeing or realizing the importance of distributing Srila Prabhupada's books, selling a bunch of
garbage, not taking the order of the spiritual master seriously (Chicago 1980).

We are not following the directives of the spiritual master [to distribute books]. That is a sin of the third degree. Prabhupada said
that our business should be to distribute his books, yet some leaders
are choosing to, momentarily perhaps, disregard this. By not following, we will suffer in the end (Los Angeles 1980).

There is too much desire to conquer the *karmies* [the nondevotees]. Book distribution for years has reflected this. It isn't any longer based on love and compassion. We are going out there [in public] but we are going out with the consciousness of Mafia hitmen. We should try to make the movement more loving, personal, and compassionate as it was in the early days (Port Royal, Pennsylvania 1980).

*Sankirtana* techniques preclude ecstatic pure preaching and chanting and numerous festivals. Ensuing bad reputation makes it more difficult in public. Devotees have greatly lost the preaching spirit (other than collecting money) and there is a schizoid mentality both in the individual [devotee] and amongst various interest groups of the devotees (Los Angeles 1980*)*.

But even while rejecting the ideological work of ISKCON's leaders, these spiritual adaptors were still able to promote their own plausibility structures in order to remain ISKCON members. The content of spiritual adaptors' ideological work tended to emphasize their devotion to Srila Prabhupada and their spiritual commitment to Krishna Consciousness as a reason for remaining within ISKCON. They reasoned that, despite its faults, ISKCON provided a better alternative than moving back into the larger society, where following a strict Krishna-conscious lifestyle would be difficult at best. A devotee woman from Los Angeles explained in 1980 why she continued to be an ISKCON member, despite fundamental disagreements with the leaders' *sankirtana* policies:

DEVOTEE: From the very beginning I was against the changes that [Western Guru] was making in *sankirtana*. It was obvious that the public was beginning to turn against us and we just couldn't preach like we had in the past. I felt deeply disappointed at the shortsightedness of the leaders. Here we were making all this money, but what good was it, when in the end no one would have any feeling toward the devotees, toward Krishna Consciousness. . . .

EBR: But why did you stay?

DEVOTEE: I thought seriously about leaving the movement, or moving to another [ISKCON] community, but in the end I valued my commitment to Prabhupada to spread Krishna Consciousness. I mean I had a spiritual commitment that was much bigger than ISKCON. But I also knew that by leaving the movement [ISKCON] I would go out from under the protection of the devotees, of Krishna, and that I would find myself in *maya*. I didn't want that, so I decided to dedicate myself to Prabhupada and Krishna and not get agitated by ISKCON (Los Angeles 1980).

Another women from Los Angeles reported on her efforts to make the leaders aware of the ways in which changing *sankirtana* tactics was undermining the movement's preaching mission and how, in the end, she adapted to the situation:

In expressing some of these deep feelings and realizations, I met with opposition from authorities and had to proceed along 'independently' in positive experimentation. It's getting a bit better more recently. The reasons are: my faith in Srila Prabhupada's desire for pure book distribution; my faith that Krishna Consciousness need not be improperly and superficially presented; my desire to show a pure alternative by going out as a devotee [*sari, dhoti, tilaka*), chanting, distributing profuse free literature, setting up Krishna Consciousness display booths, participation in college programs, purely preaching and trying to cultivate all interested people to become devotees and regular donors (Los Angeles 1980).

As the above statements suggest, many ISKCON members did view the changes in *sankirtana* as representing a fundamental shift away from Prabhupada's mission of preaching Krishna Consciousness and recruiting new members. Despite this conclusion, however, they chose to remain ISKCON members, largely because of their spiritual commitments to Krishna Consciousness and Prabhupada.[3] The strategy of these spiritual adaptors rested on a process of differentiation whereby

ISKCON was cognitively separated from Krishna Consciousness. Throughout ISKCON's history in America, ISKCON, Prabhupada, and Krishna Consciousness had been viewed and openly spoken of as one and the same by the devotees. With the changes in *sankirtana* and the perceived shift in goals away from missionary activity in the late seventies, some ISKCON members began to differentiate between the organization ISKCON and Prabhupada's Krishna Consciousness movement. Spiritual adaptors considered themselves to be devotees of Krishna Consciousness and Prabhupada first and to be members of ISKCON second. Their continued membership in ISKCON was not a matter of commitment to the organization as much as it was a reflection of their deep spiritual commitment to the spiritual master and to the body of Krishna beliefs.[4]

But while some of ISKCON's members employed a strategy of differentiation to adapt to the movement's apparent shifts in purpose, others felt that their spiritual goals could only be served apart from ISKCON altogether. To these devotees, defection provided the most reasonable choice of action.

*Defection*

While the clear majority of ISKCON's members chose to continue in their affiliation with the movement, others found the changes in *sankirtana* and the efforts of the leaders to legitimize these changes unjustified and morally indefensible. To these devotees, voluntary disassociation or defection from ISKCON provided the basis for their reaction to change. An unknown but not insignificant number of Prabhupada devotees left ISKCON because they believed ISKCON's leaders had forsaken the mission of their spiritual master to preach Krishna Consciousness. The following statements from devotees who defected from the movement in Los Angeles suggest the link between their defections and ISKCON's *sankirtana* policies:

EBR: Do you feel there is a problem in the current concept behind book distribution?

Sure, why do you think most of us left ISKCON. ISKCON made a serious mistake when it turned *sankirtana* into making money. I mean the tactics of the devotees distributing the books changed. This caused [the movement] a lot of harm in terms of its public image. If they need money why can't they all go out and work; that's what we did in the early days. Why can't they go out and work now (Los Angeles 1979).

All I want to do is straight Krishna Consciousness. When I was in ISKCON I wanted to see this happening. My problem was [from the authorities' point of view] that I used to talk badly, not badly, but finding some faults with the situations that existed in ISKCON. I felt there was this thing—preaching—that wasn't happening, that should be happening. And finally I decided, what am I doing? I don't need anybody's permission to preach. I don't have to go to them [the leaders]. I mean I already have permission to preach from Krishna. He said to go out and tell everyone you can to chant Hare Krishna. I mean what's important is that this preaching takes place. That's all. If I can see that it's happening, then why do I care about ISKCON or anything else (Los Angeles 1979).

They [the current leadership] can't agree to distribute [Prabhupada's] books. Prabhupada said to distribute books. That's a simple question. Some of the leaders are doing it and others are saying 'No. I don't need to do what my spiritual master wants me to do.' They are changing things. Why? Because I am going to distribute candles, 'cause I want more money. To me there is no interpretation, period. That's just like saying 'Thou shall not kill,' then interpret it, so now it means 'thou shall not kill humans' . . . . In the end, I realized what matters, what the final bottom line is, it's my relationship with my spiritual master. Everybody else's trip, that's just their trip. My relationship with Prabhupada is the life and soul of my Krishna Consciousness, not ISKCON (Los Angeles 1979).

The problem, as I see it, is that the authorities are making decisions based on what is good for them. What will be good for me. Instead of what will be good for Prabhupada, or what will be good for Krishna. That's how they should be making decisions, but they're not (Los Angeles 1979).

From the perspective of the devotees who chose to defect from ISKCON in the late seventies because of what they saw as the declining emphasis being placed on preaching and missionary activity, the ideological work of the leaders could be understood as no more than self-serving rationalizations. The ideological work of the devotees who defected emphasized their conviction that changing social circumstances should *not* serve as a basis for altering the movement's mission of spreading Krishna Consciousness. Whether they themselves were actually purists or not, the content of their ideological work emphasized that the Krishna beliefs and Prabhupada's mission in general should not bend to circumstances or otherwise accommodate themselves to the recalcitrant nature of the social environment. In this way, at least some of those devotees who chose to defect from the organization showed themselves to be idealists, unable to reconcile the differences between the organization's practices and the Krishna beliefs given them by their spiritual master, Srila Prabhupada.[5]

## *Value Indeterminism as a Basis for Ideological Work*

By nature, ideology becomes flexible when it is placed in the hands of believers. Even systems of belief that appear outwardly or formally to be completely rigid are ultimately used to serve the interests of the group and its individual members. Often this means bending or perhaps loosely interpreting ideology to meet the requirements imposed by external circumstances. Social science sometimes involves unmasking the "true" motives behind peoples' behavior by pointing out inconsistencies between their ideologies and their everyday practices; in fact, such discrepancies are more the norm than the exception (Berger, 1981)[6] While to the outside observer, ISKCON's history in America seems to manifest large changes and an overall transformation in its purposes, to the insider these same changes may be interpreted as being largely consistent with the movement's ideological goals and purposes. Social scientists as well as lay analysts of social life are often readily able to find the inconsistencies in the behavior of others, yet remain virtually blind to similar inconsistencies in their own lives or in the causes they support. As one Krishna devotee paraphrasing from the Bible once told me: "People all too often tend to be acutely aware of the splinter in the eye of their fellow man, yet blind to the log that protrudes from their own" (San Diego 1984).

To a degree, the success or failure of any movement organization rests squarely on the adaptability of its ideology to changing circumstances. The leaders of such a movement organization must be in a position to take advantage of social conditions and to garner resources as they become available from the social environment. Conversely, such leaders must also have the latitude to deal with circumstances that pose a potential threat to the organization, its members, and the respective goals and purposes of each. But such flexibility, of course, must have limits. Even though leaders must be allowed to interpret ideology loosely in order to deal with reality, they do not have total freedom to disregard ideology or to reformulate it in a self-serving way. Rather, leaders and members must pursue the organization's needs with an eye to the broad moral parameters imposed by the group's ideology. For leaders to ignore these moral boundaries brings the risk of being severely discredited from within, and could bring about the possible failure of the movement organization.

While ISKCON and its leaders did face being discredited in the eyes of some of its members in the late seventies, the Krishna organization was able nevertheless to hold onto the commitments of a large majority of its members. I want now to suggest that one major factor working to facilitate the success of ISKCON's ideological work lies in the inherent flexibility and generally indeterminate nature of the Krishna belief system when it is applied to the organization. In essence, Krishna Consciousness, like many ideological systems, can be considered as largely value determinate with regards to the demands placed on members, but largely indeterminate with regards to the policies and practices of the movement organization. As Kanter (1972) suggests, value indeterminism increases the survival potential of any social movement or utopian community by allowing leaders to pursue organizational strategies meant to further the goals and objectives of the group without compromising the values that structure members' everyday lives. Value indeterminism aids organizational flexibility during periods when a movement must deal with an external environment that is continually changing, but from which it must mobilize needed resources to insure its survival (Kanter 1972:154). Value indeterminism, therefore, becomes a strategy used by the organization to deal with tensions caused by having to make exchanges with a society it largely rejects.

When Srila Prabhupada first came to America in 1965, he accommodated various aspects of his *Vaisnava* beliefs to the society around him in order to gain a following and begin his Krishna Consciousness movement. As I discussed in chapter six, Prabhupada tailored his Krishna beliefs to local social conditions in an effort to expand his movement within the American context. As one devotee explained, Prabhupada understood the need to adjust the Krishna ideology to circumstances, though not to the degree of transforming the essence and distinctiveness of the belief system:

Prabhupada lightened up on a number of traditional vedic concepts in order to further his preaching efforts in the West: one being the relationship between men and women in the movement and the overall role of women more generally. What some of the Indians think of us, boyyy. We have women on the altar, women preaching, women living in the temple. Sheer heresy from an Indian's point of view. But Prabhupada wanted us to see the more important principles and adjust or adapt the more minor ones to the parent culture that he was trying to get established in. So you find that kind of flexibility in the history of our movement. Which is not to say that Prabhupada was going to let America change him and his beliefs. A lot of Swamis who came to this country in the sixties actually watered down the spiritual process to gain a large following.

Look at T.M. and Muktiananda. Prabhupada never went to that extreme. He knew how to sacrifice the minor principle without losing the essence (Philadelphia 1982).

By differentiating the value expectations of the leadership from those of the rank and file, ISKCON gained latitude to deal in a strategic fashion with the outside society. In this way, value indeterminism as a policy facilitated the ideological work of the organization and helped to head off the possibility of widespread disaffection from within. For the majority of devotees, the movement continued as it always had, and their daily religious practices were largely unaffected by policy changes. To this extent, the ideological work of the organization was successful.

## Models of Change and ISKCON's History in America

ISKCON's history in America raises several larger theoretical issues relating to movement change and transformation. By the beginning of the 1980s, ISKCON to all appearances had begun to change in structure and ideology toward becoming a denominational form of religion. These changes were further solidified following Srila Prabhupada's death in November of 1977 when his charisma was replaced by a largely bureaucratic structure. By the end of the seventies, ISKCON had become accommodative in its value orientations, increasingly inclusive in its structural arrangements, heterogenous in its membership, and increasingly concerned with power, control, and organizational maintenance.

The traditional approach used to analyze movement change has been the institutionalization model. Both in the study of social movements in general and in the study of specifically religious groups and movements, this model stands as the dominant framework for analyzing movement change and transformation. The model's strength lies in its analysis of largely successful groups and movements. Groups that gain large numbers of members, economic prosperity, and power within the society tend to undergo changes in structure and ideology that lead to institutionalization. With increasing institutionalization, a movement tends to become more conservative in tone and suffers goal displacement and a growing preoccupation with organizational mainte- nance. Zald and Ash summarize the major features of the institutional- ization model in this way:

> This model, which stems from Weber and Michels, takes the fol- lowing line of analysis: As a MO [movement organization] attains an economic and social base in the society, as the original charis- matic leadership is replaced, a bureaucratic structure emerges and a general accommodation to the society occurs. The participants in this structure have a stake in preserving the organization, regardless of its ability to attain goals. Analytically there are three types of changes involved in this process; empirically they are fused . . . goal transformation, a shift to organizational maintenance, and oli- garchization (1966;327).

A movement is institutionalized when it has gained both internal stability and has been recognized as legitimate by the larger society. The movement is then viewed by members of the society as having a necessary function to perform. Instead of continuing to challenge vari- ous aspects of the larger culture, an institutionalized movement mod- ifies its beliefs and purposes to bring them into close alignment with the society's dominant ideology. Participation in the movement be- comes a basis for prestige and social recognition within the larger so- ciety. As the organization gains widespread respect, prestige within the group also serves as a ground for prestige in the society (Turner and Killian 1972).

Investigations of the developmental patterns of religious groups and movements have largely borrowed the assumptions and theoretical framework of the institutionalization model. The histories of religious movements have classically been analyzed within the church-sect ty- pology. Put simply, the sect and the church represent the two polar types of religious organizations. Sectarian religious groups that progress to the stage of institutionalization become denominations or churches. Again, an increasing group membership, a stable economic base, and expanding power in the society becomes the basis for denominationalism. As one investigator of sectarian movements has concluded:

> The tendency for sects to develop into denominations has sometimes been presented as an inevitable or probable linear progression—as though 'denomination' equals 'sect' plus passage of time, plus increased prosperity (Isichei 1967; 161).

More concretely, the changes involved in a sectarian movement becoming institutionalized as a religious denomination are defined by organizational and ideological changes of the following kinds[7]:

1. A sect is a religious group that rejects, or at least is indifferent toward, the value scheme of the prevailing social order; a church is a religious group that generally accepts community norms and values (Brewer 1952; Johnson 1963).

2. The sect renounces established religious institutions and presents utopian ideals to a select few; a church seeks to conserve traditional religions and accommodates its own ideals to the prevailing order in order to gain widespread acceptance (Brewer 1952; Pope 1942; Wilson 1959).

3. A sect gains little public acceptance, or at least the public is indifferent toward sectarian groups; a church gains a respectable level of acceptance within the society, even if it is only "tolerated" as an adjunct to other religious institutions (Bainbridge and Stark 1980; Johnson 1963; Turner and Killian 1972).

4. Personal charisma is often associated with a sect; office-holding and professional and centralized organizations are more often associated with a church (Hill 1973; Pope 1942; Weber 1968; Wilson 1959; Yinger 1970).

5. Poverty and communal sharing characterize economic relations

in a sect; wealth and formally organized means to raise necessary revenues mark a church (Brewer 1952; Pope 1942; Wilson 1959).

6. The sect is small and exclusively organized; a church is large, inclusive, and heterogeneous in its membership (Brewer 1952; Wilson 1959; Yinger 1957).

On the basis of the above criteria, it is tempting to argue that ISKCON during the seventies moved progressively toward institutionalization as a denomination. One observer of the Krishna movement in America has in fact already suggested that ISKCON is well on its way to becoming a church or denominational structure (Ellwood 1983). I want to suggest that the features of denominationalism apparently present within ISKCON do not point to denominationalism, at least not in the ways suggested by the church-sect typology. Furthermore, ISKCON in all probability will remain unable to attain denominationalism in the forseeable future because of one serious limiting factor—its public definition as a threatening movement.

As has been suggested, the underlying assumption of the church-sect model of change is that mounting success and social acceptance are the major factors operating in the process of sectarian groups becoming denominations. By contrast, ISKCON's development in America suggests that *declining* religious movements may also move toward denominationalism as a strategy to avoid organizational failure. Only as ISKCON's decline deepened in the middle to late seventies did the organization become more inclusive in its structure and more accommodating in its value orientations in an effort to bring critical resources—people and money—into the organization. Accompanying these trends was the overall tendency for the movement to accentuate its power orientations in an effort to gain some level of control over its hostile environment. These developments, if interpreted uncritically according to the church-sect model, would lead to the logical conclusion that ISKCON was moving away from its sectarian way of life toward denominationalism. Such an interpretation may well be true, but the underlying reasons and causes of this development have little to do with the normal processes associated with the shift from sect to church. I would argue in fact that ISKCON was *not* consciously attempting to move toward a denominational form of organization, but was instead simply employing certain protective strategies (e.g., becoming structurally more open to the outside, inclusive in its membership, and maintenance-oriented at the expense of missionary objectives). If we move beyond the movement's specific policies for dealing with the outside society for the sake of garnering needed financial resources, it is clear that the sectarian lifestyle and practices of the devotees remained largely intact. Using the strategy of deliberate value indeterminism, ISKCON was able to deal with the outside society in terms of power and control, but at the same time was able to insure that its sectarian way of life remained largely unchanged for its own members. While the strategies developed by the movement's leaders to deal with its economic decline were not universally accepted by all ISKCON members (there was internal disaffection and there were defections), by and large, ISKCON's strategies did afford the movement survival into the eighties.[8]

The conclusion that ISKCON is progressing toward denominationalism also overlooks one other important consideration. Denominationalism implies some level of public acceptance. No sectarian movement can hope to become a denomination without at least a minimum of public acceptance as "a tolerated adjunct to other religious institutions" in the society (Turner and Killian 1972). Because of the virulent nature and intensity of the public's definition of and responses to ISKCON, it seems most unlikely that denominationalism could have ever been a conscious goal of the organization during the middle to late seventies. If denominationalism had in fact been a real goal, ISKCON's leaders would have chosen strategies with an eye toward gaining public acceptance, instead of having chosen strategies directed toward raising the money necessitated by the organization's decline. As we have discussed, these very strategies (principally those pertaining to *sankirtana*) became in fact a significant factor in producing the negative public backlash toward the movement during the seventies.

Two other issues of theoretical interest should also be raised in relation to ISKCON's patterns of adaptation to change during the seventies in America: First, the institutionalization approach tends to view organizational change as a matter of kind rather than degree: Sects become denominations, value-oriented movements become power and maintenance movements, charisma is replaced by bureaucratic rule, and so on. Movement change as analyzed within this framework is understood in a linear and ultimately rigid and static fashion. Because this approach to movement change tends to focus heavily on the role of internal processes (e.g., leadership change and crisis, accommodation of movement beliefs) to the relative exclusion of external factors, it tends to overlook the ways in which changing external social circumstances in a movement's environment can push a movement off on a different path of development or perhaps allow for its return to previous modes of adaptation. A more dynamic view of movement change, which incorporates the influences of both internal and external social forces operating on a movement, allows for the possibility that the goals, ideology, and organizational structure of a movement are forever in the flux of adaptation and change. In a sense, the present structure and goals of any movement stand as no more than temporary oscillations in its developing history. Because environmental forces continually impinge on a movement, change is an ongoing process. Goals and objectives that appear to be abandoned at one point in time may show up again in the future and take a central place in the organization's program of action. Or, alternatively, a movement may set off on a new course of development, which may promote new goals at the expense of traditional objectives.

Second, my discussion of ISKCON's patterns of adaptation to change also points to the differences in and tensions between insiders' analyses of the social circumstances affecting a movement and the analyses of outsiders, both social scientists and bystanders who take an active interest in the activities of the movement. As Bryan Wilson suggests, the view of the social sciences—because of their outsider status and analytic interests—often stands in a problematic relationship to members' understandings of the circumstances acting on the movement.

Thus, the religionist and the sociologist might disagree about what
constitutes 'failure' for a given movement, but the sociologist will
necessarily judge performance in social terms, with regard to number, endurance, maintenance of individual commitment, persistence
or attainment of a movement's original goals. Where it is possible,
he will appraise performance in terms of criteria that a movement
has—perhaps in its early days— laid down as indicating success;
for, whatever their transcendental goals may be, movements necessarily make promises about their social goals. In using these criteria, I make no value judgments about the worthiness of any movement, nor can it be inferred that social evidences of failure
necessarily imply failure at a spiritual or transcendental level. We
may observe that movements oscillate in their self-interpretation,
emphasizing quality when numbers are low, and quantity when
growth is occurring, when new buildings are being opened, and
mass rallies are being staged (1983:2).

As Wilson suggests, what constitutes success for any movement always remains an open question and a matter of contention. Social scientists, using their tools of measurement, tend to view success largely
in quantitative terms; movement members often use criteria that are
both more qualitative and more shifting because of the influence of
changing social circumstances on the movement. The institutionalization approach implicitly assumes that members of movement organizations define their success in terms roughly similar to those of an outside analyst: that increasing prosperity and greater overall acceptance
by the society in which it operates provide the benchmark of success
for such a movement. In fact, these indicators may just as easily
be defined as measures of failure by members of sectarian movements who desire to uphold their traditionalist ways of life (Isichei
1967; Robertson 1967). The goal of many sectarian movements is
to maintain their distinctive ways of life without succumbing to the inevitable pressures to accommodate their values and practices to the
larger society.

# 9
# The End of Charisma

The death of the charismatic leader forms a critical juncture in the life of any group, community, or social movement. Some groups simply fade away with the death of charisma, never to be heard from again. As Kanter (1972) describes, even utopian communities that have proven successful often face extinction after the death of their charismatic founder. Other groups that do manage to survive the loss of charisma nevertheless often face deep and continuing sources of internal conflict, conflict that may result in factionalism and splintering (See Gamson 1975; Wallis 1977; Wilson 1961; Zald and Ash 1966). Yet still other groups seem to be somehow less subject to the internal conflicts so often associated with the death of charisma.

Srila Prabhupada's death in the fall of 1977 in Vrndavana, India, was a major turning point for ISKCON's development in America and all over the world. Over the next several years, ISKCON faced continuing and often bitter sources of internal conflict. Prabhupada's death left ISKCON with no one legitimate heir or power structure to lead the movement. There existed a number of competing groups that sought to legitimize their authority within the emergent reorganizational structure. In this chapter, I describe the changes that occurred within ISKCON following Prabhupada's death. Analytically, my discussion centers on internal conflict, factionalism, and schism.

## Prabhupada's Death and the Reorganization of ISKCON

The succession problems that emerged following Prabhupada's death resulted from the political uncertainties that then prevailed regarding who had the ultimate authority in the movement to make policy and to direct the movement's future. Like some other charismatic leaders, Srila Prabhupada had established a governing body in 1970 to help oversee the administrative affairs of his movement. It was assumed that the Governing Body Commission (GBC) would naturally retain the power to govern the movement following Prabhupada's death. While the GBC certainly did retain a measure of power in the reorganized ISKCON, its overall authority to direct the movement's future came into conflict with another group of leaders, the new gurus.

In the months preceding his death, Srila Prabhupada had appointed eleven of his closest disciples to act as initiating gurus for ISKCON. The appointment of the gurus was based upon two communications between Prabhupada and several of his disciples in the summer of 1977.[1] The gurus were to be responsible for continuing Prabhupada's movement all over the world by initiating new disciples into Krishna Consciousness. The basis for the guru system had been established at the movement's yearly Mayapura festival in India in March of 1978. Each of the newly appointed gurus was responsible for initiating new disciples into the movement in some specific area or zone in the world. The initiated disciples would then recognize their guru as their spiritual master in the same way that Prabhupada's disciples saw him as their ultimate spiritual authority. Through this arrangement, the time-honored disciplic succession would continue: the new disciples of the current gurus would become grand disciples of Srila Prabhupada, who in turn would connect them to previous *acaryas* going back to Lord Krishna Himself.

The eleven gurus shared the responsibility for governing ISKCON with the fourteen GBC members. These twenty-five men comprised the major decision-making body within ISKCON following Prabhupada's death. This structure joining gurus and other non-*acarya* leaders, all serving together on the GBC, proved to be a major source of conflict in the years to follow. The question of who had ultimate power within ISKCON—individual gurus or the collective GBC—was debated time and time again following the reorganization of the movement. As early as March of 1978, as ISKCON's leaders were in the midst of reorganizing the movement, the issues of power and control as these related to the gurus and to the GBC was raised by Prabhupada's closest and most respected Godbrother, Maharaja Swami:

The majority (on the GBC) are non-*acarya* [non-guru]. According to my opinion, that will create a difficulty. In our system, both autocracy and democracy cannot go together. But ours is an autocratic thing, extremely autocratic. Guru is all-in-all. Our submission to guru is unconditional. This is a great difficulty. Submission to guru is unconditional. So when I [as a disciple] see that my guru's powers are being pressed by other *Vaisnavas,* it will create disturbance in the mind of the *sisya* [disciple], to grow his *sraddha,* faith, absolute faith. . . . But whenever he [the guru] initiates, he is absolute in the eyes of his disciple; and the *sisya* will not tolerate that any other *Vaisnava* will come to disturb the absolute position of my guru. . . . It is better that the members of the governing body be gurus. They are all *acaryas*. The assembly of *acaryas* will consult with one another (from a transcribed discussion between Maharaja Swami and ISKCON leaders, India 1978).

The centrality of the guru to the movement's religious system clouded the whole question of authority following Prabhupada's death.

In the years following, much of the conflict within the movement resulted from the continuous struggle being waged by several of the
gurus and their new disciples against the collective power of the GBC
and Prabhupada's disciples. The earliest signs of the succession problems to follow were not, however, directly related to the power struggle between the GBC and the gurus. Rather, economic problems, which
had begun prior to Prabhupada's death, provided the first source of
tension between ISKCON's leaders as they pursued different strategies
to meet the financial needs of their respective zones.

## Succession, Decline, and the Early Growth of Factionalism

The first year following Prabhupada's death was taken up primarily
with the problems associated with ISKCON's economic decline. The
financial crisis and the measures taken by the leadership to deal with it
provoked considerable controversy within ISKCON. The de-emphasis
on book distribution in favor of *picking* and the conflict that caused
were important factors in later challenges to the leadership, because
this conflict organized many of Srila Prabhupada's disciples into challenging groups.

   The first major conflict, which arose in the Los Angeles ISKCON
community, involved differences with regard to economic policy. In
the months just prior to Prabhupada's death, a group of devotees who
were businessmen or who were otherwise interested in the economic
future of the movement began what was called the Bhaktivedanta Fellowship. Many of the twenty-five or so devotees who participated in
this group were long-time ISKCON members. The Fellowship initially
was very much attached to ISKCON, as it tried to develop economic
policies that could help resolve the ongoing financial crisis and draw
up financial plans for the future. One member of this group described
the Fellowship's purpose in the following terms: "It was kind of like a
rotary club of *Vaisnava* businessmen who were concerned with the
movement's financial future (Los Angeles 1980).

Within a matter of months, however, the Fellowship became increasingly political, because it sought to have its policies implemented. Because it developed economic strategies that stressed business, the group faced open opposition from the leadership of the Los Angeles community. Although book distribution began to decline in late 1977, the leadership continued to see the movement's financial future in terms of book distribution. In attempting to push forward its economic policies, the Fellowship became involved in a political struggle, which in the end led to the demise of the group. As one ex-ISKCON member who had participated in the Bhaktivedanta Fellowship commented:

> We wanted to remain attached to ISKCON in some way, but of course we were doomed, because nothing as nice as the Fellowship could ever survive under the firey glances of the Swamis [ISKCON's new gurus]. So it all smouldered away and burnt to a crisp and that was the end of that (Los Angeles 1980).

This confrontation led many members of the Fellowship to leave ISKCON. Some left on their own, feeling that the judgments of the leadership had been mistaken. Others were ultimately forced out of the movement, after having been dismissed from their movement jobs and not having been offered any other employment. One devotee, who had worked in a movement business in Los Angeles, explained what happened to him after the break up of the Fellowship and the loss of his job:

> EBR: So when they cut you out of your job, what did they say? Did they offer you another job?
> DEVOTEE: No, they just said: 'You don't have a job anymore.'
> EBR: But what did they want you to do?
> DEVOTEE: That's what I wanted to find out. I asked to see [Western Guru]. I had my name put on the list to see him. So week after week he never responded. So I got the hint. I just stopped coming around [the community] because I was hurt. What do you expect? (Los Angeles 1979)

With the beginning of the guru system, another development took place involving economics and book distribution that also served to create factionalism within ISKCON. Because ISKCON had been reorganized into zones, each of which was more or less autonomous under the leadership of a specific guru, different economic policies emerged. This resulted in different emphases being placed on book distribution in different zones. Several of the gurus chose temporarily to discontinue book distribution altogether in favor of *picking*. Others continued to distribute books at least to some degree, but also sent devotees out to sell candles, records, and other products to help support the communities in their zone. The New Vrindaban community in West Virginia, for example, favored *picking* as the means to support itself. Book distribution in public places there became almost nonexistent. This policy led a number of Prabhupada disciples from this zone to seek out other ISKCON communities, where they could continue to distribute the literature of their spiritual master. One devotee, from a community controlled by the guru who heads New Vrindaban, explained to me why he was considering changing zones in 1980:

Some devotees are into collecting money, *lakshmi*, but I just want to do books. I have gone out doing records, but I just don't like it. It's such a drain. I don't feel any bliss. Krishna Consciousness is supposed to be full of bliss and knowledge, and if one of these is missing, I'm not satisfied. I can't do just anything. I have to get some satisfaction. That's why I want to distribute books. It's a preaching thing which I can feel blissful about (Cleveland 1980).

A second early source of factionalism in the movement involved a growing economic competition between zones. Traveling *sankirtana* parties, selling records and other commodities, began crossing boundaries into other zones in an effort to raise money for the communities in their area. It became commonplace for devotees from across America to converge on a major sporting event or rock concert and compete with one another to sell buttons, records, and other such products. When the Pope visited America in 1979, traveling *sankirtana* teams from virtually every zone throughout the country followed his travels, selling buttons to the public with the Pope's picture on them (*Fresno Bee*, June 27, 1980).

The gurus competed for financial resources; they also competed in some instances for the services of devotees residing in other zones. In several instances, devotees with special talents were lured by the leaders in one zone away from another zone with promises of better work opportunities and/or living conditions for themselves and their families.

Finally, some ISKCON members in Los Angeles charged that competition between the new gurus was one cause of the growing financial problems faced by the Bhaktivedanta Book Trust in the late seventies. Apparently, several ISKCON communities in one zone refused to pay for books they had purchased, thereby putting the Los Angeles community in financial difficulties. Some devotees have charged that this nonpayment was decided upon deliberately, as a way of limiting the power of the guru from the western zone. In other zones, book distribution was purposely deemphasized for the same reason.

## Succession and the Crisis of Leadership: The Guru Controversies

In the months immediately following Prabhupada's death, a number of controversies arose in quick succession regarding the spiritual and organizational powers of the new gurus. Beginning in 1978 and continuing up until 1982, ISKCON faced a series of guru controversies that threatened to splinter the organization entirely. Initially the crises emerged from within ISKCON itself. Later ISKCON came under attack from other sources: most significantly, from an increasingly well-organized group of ex-ISKCON members. Shortly after the guru system was established in the spring of 1978, the first controversy surrounding the gurus arose. One of the appointed gurus, who at the time was living in the movement's community in Bombay, India, but who would later come to oversee a zone in America, demanded that devotees residing in the Bombay community extend to him all the priviledges of guruship. He sought from these disciples in Bombay the same level of worship that Prabhupada had received from his disciples. He demanded that a larger *vyasasana* (a chair that is placed in the temple for the spiritual master) replace the smaller one then present in the temple. He also demanded that his disciples offer him *Guru Puja* (worship of the spiritual master) during the morning services in the temple. He sought to legitimize his requests for such worship by citing the need of his disciples to acquire the necessary degree of faith in their guru in order to make spiritual advancements. These actions by the guru from Bombay produced considerable ill feeling among Prabhupada's disciples residing in the Bombay community. Many felt that he was trying to equate himself with Prabhupada by instituting such forms of worship for himself.

This initial controversy also raised the more general issue of what role the new gurus should play vis-à-vis their own disciples and their fellow Godbrothers and Godsisters. Was it required that the gurus' disciples extend to them the same level of worship they had offered to Prabhupada? Wouldn't such worship ultimately detract from the overall importance of Prabhupada? The following discussion between two devotees who left ISKCON in 1979 suggests the feelings many of Prabhupada's disciples had toward the level of worship being extended to the new gurus by their disciples:

> FIRST DEVOTEE: One thing I think is kind of strange is the amount of worship the [current] gurus are allowing. It took us so many years to develop this, the familiarity, to offer such intimate worship. Then you see them all receiving *arati* during *Guru Puja*.
>
> SECOND DEVOTEE: When it was done with Prabhupada, it was understood that this was born out of a process. Now they have just accepted it as part of the thing. The original feelings [in the early days] were that he [Prabhupada] didn't ask for such worship. You gave it to the spiritual master because of the strong feelings you had for him. We wanted to do it and he understood that we needed to do it, so we could advance more. I remember I was there the

first time and you could just see the humility in Prabhupada's face (Los Angeles 1980).

In a major confrontation that took place at the movement's yearly meeting in Mayapura, India, in 1979, it was decided by the G B C that the new gurus should have essentially the same relationship with their disciples as Prabhupada had had with his. The gurus should have *vyasasanas* in each temple in their zones and receive worship each morning from their disciples, just as Prabhupada's disciples worshipped him. As one devotee recounts:

> At the Mayapura meeting in '79, the gurus argued that they should be worshipped for the good of their disciples' faith. Those who opposed the idea were roundly defeated. But it left a lot of wounded feelings. Like one more victory like that and [the movement] is done for. It was a smash at the opposition without any recognition that the other side may have had a case (Philadelphia 1982).

This G B C decision proved important in a much larger way than simply settling the issue of guru worship and the role to be played by the new gurus with regard to their disciples. From this point forward, the issue of who was to have ultimate authority within I S K C O N—the new gurus or the G B C—would frame all the controversies surrounding the gurus. This initial decision by the G B C and many subsequent ones led many of Prabhupada's disciples to the conclusion that the new gurus were systematically minimizing Prabhupada's position as well as their own by undermining the G B C's power to set policy for the movement. As one devotee explained: "Prabhupada's disciples felt that Prabhupada was acting through the collective body of the G B C. The G B C was the manifestation of Prabhupada. These decisions by the gurus began to make things very unclear" (Philadelphia 1982).

The controversies surrounding the new gurus escalated in 1980 as three of the eleven gurus were sanctioned by the G B C. Three of these controversies involved questions relating to the proper spiritual and organization roles of the new gurus within I S K C O N. Another involved an incident that received national publicity and proved to be a major blow to ISKCON's already deteriorating public image.

## The First Guru Crisis

In March of 1980, the Berkeley police, in the course of an investigation of the possible involvement of some ISKCON members in another criminal case, uncovered "an arsenal of weapons at the sect's ranch in Lake County," California (*Los Angeles Times*, March 16, 1980). Later that month, police searched a warehouse owned by the Berkeley ISKCON community and found a large amount of ammunition there (*New York Times*, June 9, 1980). Initially, Northwest Guru, who resided at the Berkeley ISKCON community, was arrested, but the charges were later dropped.

The apparent involvement of one of ISKCON's gurus in stockpiling weapons caused considerable debate in the movement about how the movement should deal with Northwest Guru. Many devotees and members of the GBC argued that he should immediately be excommunicated from the movement. Others argued that he should be kept within the movement, to guard against the further harm he might cause to ISKCON should he be pushed out. Still others argued that no one ultimately had any authority over Northwest Guru because he was a guru and was therefore beyond reproach. As one ISKCON leader explained in 1982, there was considerable disagreement among GBC members but, in the end, they chose to take away his guruship for one year:

> Their judgement [GBC] was really a matter of *Vaisnava* compassion and sympathy. He is our Godbrother. He has done so much service for ISKCON. Show him mercy. Show him compassion. Somehow keep him in the fold, so he won't go off the deep end. And then the other factor is, if you keep him in, we can keep him under the direction of the GBC and he won't go off. But then others felt he has already damaged our movement so much—get him out . . . . In the end, they decided to take away his guruship for one year . . . . But

the GBC was divided as to whether he should be ex-communicated immediately or not. Even to this day, there are deliberations. Some say they should have cut him, but they decided to give him another chance. There was just so much controversy you just can't believe it (Philadelphia 1982).

Following on the heels of the gun controversy, the second guru crisis of 1980 arose. This one involved two points of controversy, one old and one new.

*The Second Guru Crisis*

The second ISKCON guru who came to be sanctioned by the GBC was the spiritual leader of a zone outside America. The initial incident concerning Foreign Guru proved to be just the beginning of many controversies that would surround him over the course of the next two years. The initial problem involving Foreign Guru was very different from the controversy involving Northwest Guru. Foreign Guru began to display certain kinds of behavior that were bizarre and out of character.

> There was Foreign Guru and the weird stuff, the singing and all that . . . I mean he was simply shrieking. Shrieking during *kirtan* [singing and dancing in the temple]. He had tears flowing down his face and falling off his *vyasasana* . . . He would come down in the morning [for the morning worship services] and give *Bhagavatam* class, but then begin a *kirtan* that just gradually became more and more bizarre. It would go on all day; for hours and hours. From six in the morning to four or five in the afternoon (Philadelphia 1982).

Foreign Guru, in defense of his behavior, claimed to be experiencing the kind of ecstatic symptoms characteristic of a self-realized devotee.[2] The interpretation put on his behavior by the GBC and their advisor Maharaja Swami was quite different. Having been consulted by the GBC, Maharaja Swami put an interpretation on Foreign Guru's behavior that cast doubt on his spiritual sincerity:

The other day [name of devotee] came to find out whether all the crying and singing and laughing of Foreign Guru whether they were genuine feelings or not; whether they were genuine symptoms of ecstacy or not. So I said 'No.' First I gave the spiritual injunction . . . that crying is merely to get name and fame. . . . Lastly I pointed out that your spiritual master [Srila Prabhupada] did not manifest these symptoms in public, then why is he trying to go above your guru? (From a transcribed discussion between Maharaja Swami and the then president of the Los Angeles ISKCON community, India, August 1980).

The GBC, following the precedent established by the actions taken against Northwest Guru, suspended Foreign Guru for a one-year period. The GBC also required him to take *sannyasa*[3] because they felt that his bizarre behavior was the result of "emotionalism" caused by his renewing his relationship with his wife. The GBC had also heard from a number of sources that Foreign Guru had been breaking one of the movement's regulative principles by taking drugs.

### The Third Guru Crisis

The third controversy involving ISKCON's new gurus centered on two different issues: book distribution policies and the spiritual superiority and preeminence claimed by the guru from Bombay.

In reaction to growing criticism by devotees within his zone in America to the use of the change-up and other such money-making tactics being used by book distributors, Bombay Guru discontinued *sankirtana* and instructed the devotees under his jurisdiction to seek outside employment. He believed that the money earned in this manner would have the effect of taking the financial pressure off *sankirtana* and would allow preaching again to become the primary motivation for book distribution. While this rather bold change in policy stirred considerable controversy among ISKCON's leaders, it was Bombay Guru's further insistence that the Prabhupada disciples in his zone treat him in the same way as they treated ISKCON's founding *acarya* that created a major controversy.

In the spring of 1980, Bombay Guru began preaching to the devotees in his zone that he was the true intermediary to Srila Prabhupada. Bombay Guru not only expected his own disciples to recognize him as *acarya*, but also wanted his fellow Godbrothers and Godsisters likewise to embrace him as their spiritual leader. As one devotee explained:

He began to say that now that Prabhupada is gone, I am the way to Prabhupada. And he began pressuring his Godbrothers to see him as their guru also. Pay obeisances when they see him as if he was their guru . . . He was representing himself as the interpreter of everything. Now you had to go to Prabhupada through him, at least for the devotees within his zone (Philadelphia 1982).

The GBC responded by stripping Bombay Guru of his guruship for a one-year period. During this time, he was forbidden to initiate any new disciples or to carry out any of the other responsibilities associated with his being guru of his zone.[4]

Even though the GBC decisions to strip three gurus of their spiritual authority appeared on the surface to signify that this body had the ultimate upper hand in governing ISKCON, the issue of who had real control—the gurus or the GBC—was in fact clouded. Following the sanctions imposed by the GBC against Bombay Guru and Northwest Guru, the latter sought the counsel of Prabhupada's Godbrother in India, Maharaja Swami, questioning the GBC's actions. Both of the gurus felt that they had been wrongfully sanctioned and that the GBC had no legitimate right to strip them of their guruships. Maharaja Swami agreed with their position and sided with them against the GBC. In so doing, he affirmed the supremacy of the gurus over the GBC. Maharaja Swami's attitude toward the position of the gurus and his disagreement with the GBC's actions against the gurus is suggested by the following statement he made to the then president of the Los Angeles ISKCON community just after the sanctions were imposed:

This has been a very serious mistake. It can be considered to be a death blow. . . . This has been a very bold step. This has been an interference into the *Srota Pantha* [Line of Gurus]. I think that such a bold step should not have been taken. To challenge the decision of the spiritual master and give a verdict against his will . . . [and] to remove the nominated *acaryas* of Prabhupada so soon . . . is almost suicidal, almost suicidal. It has challenged the very nomination of Prabhupada (India, August 1980).

After gaining the support of Maharaja Swami, Bombay Guru and Northwest Guru met with the chairman of the G B C. They protested the G B C actions that had stripped them of their guruships and presented Maharaja Swami's support for their position. Shortly thereafter, the G B C convened a meeting and overruled the sanctions, allowing both gurus to return to their zones and resume all the duties associated with their guruships. This ruling by the G B C intensified the questioning throughout the movement over who had power and authority to rule I S K C O N—the collective G B C or the gurus.

## The Fourth Guru Crisis

The last guru controversy of 1980 was essentially a reaction by one of the eleven gurus to the previous guru controversies. The guru from the western zone in America sought to have the spiritual role of the new gurus redefined theologically. It was his view that because the gurus had shown themselves to be fallible and therefore not pure in their Krishna Consciousness, which their guru status required, the formal role of the gurus should be altered. In particular, he believed that the gurus were not worthy of the level of worship they had been receiving from their disciples. He wanted that level of worship to be reserved for Srila Prabhupada, the true *acarya*. Western Guru argued that the new gurus should serve only as Prabhupada's representatives. The gurus would initiate disciples into Krishna Consciousness on Prabhupada's behalf, instead of on their own behalf. The then president of the Los Angeles I S K C O N community summarized the thoughts of Western Guru and his desire to recognize only Srila Prabhupada as the true *acarya* in a 1980 conversation with Maharaja Swami:

> Western Guru is saying that I am somewhere between a neophyte and intermediate level devotee . . . I am like the *madhyama-adhi-kari* guru [intermediate level guru], but I am giving my disciples the *uttama-adhikari* guru [the highest level guru] of Srila Prabhupada . . . So they have the *uttama* connection [through me] (India 1980).

Western Guru believed that the proper role of the new gurus should be to link their disciples directly to Srila Prabhupada. Acceptance of this interpretation of the role of the new ISKCON gurus would have limited dramatically the independent authority of the gurus. In a symbolic gesture, Western Guru had his *vyasasana* removed from the temples in his zone and discontinued *Guru Puja*. Despite the fact that this proposal had the support of many of Prabhupada's disciples, the GBC, under pressure from the other ten ISKCON gurus, overruled Western Guru's proposals to restructure the guru system.

## The Impact of the Guru Controversies on the Political Structure of ISKCON

While each particular guru crisis of 1980 seemed to reaffirm in the end the overall authority of the new gurus, a major change in ISKCON policy resulted from these controversies. Under the pressure of growing criticism by Prabhupada's disciples of the guru system, the GBC—the gurus and other GBC members alike—decided in the spring of 1981 to define more clearly the overall authority of ISKCON's gurus. The GBC chose to limit the independent authority of the gurus by requiring them to recognize the collective GBC as the ultimate and final authority within ISKCON. Individual gurus would no longer be allowed to claim power independent of the GBC. While each guru would retain final authority over his disciples, he was now required to work through the

GBC on any issue that involved ISKCON as a whole. Moreover, the gurus were to be held accountable to the GBC for any future sanctions to be imposed against them. In short, as a matter of policy, the gurus were to be subject to the authority of the GBC and could no longer claim to be beyond the control of this governing body. As one long-time ISKCON member explained, this decision pleased Prabhupada's disciples because it provided them with a power base, which they had lost when the prominance of the new gurus had risen:

> When three gurus in one year had to be censured there was suddenly this realization. The GBC simply had to be in the position to judge the gurus, whether they are up to standard or not. And a lot of Prabhupada disciples felt, well, Prabhupada is back in the movement! (Philadelphia 1982).[5]

## Succession and Challenges to Legitimacy

The guru controversies of 1980 caused a series of threats to ISKCON's survival to arise. An unknown but apparently significant number of ISKCON members defected from the movement as a consequence of these leadership crises; other devotees began to organize themselves to protest the movement's reorganizational policies—in particular the guru system. Instead of simply questioning the spiritual and organizational abilities of specific gurus, however, the dissident elements within ISKCON and the growing contingent of ex-members overtly challenged both the legitimacy of the guru system and Prabhupada's supposed appointment of the gurus to their positions. Virtually without exception, those protesting against the guru system were disciples of Srila Prabhupada who felt that Prabhupada's role as spiritual leader of the movement had been weakened by the policies initiated by the new gurus. It must also be mentioned that an organizational structure that recognized the gurus as the primary source of authority within ISKCON left Prabhupada's disciples little or no power to influence the policies of the movement.

The mobilization of Prabhupada's disciples against the policies of the new gurus began soon after the guru system was put into place. Many devotees had been reluctant from the beginning to accept the legitimacy or the claimed spiritual status of the new gurus, because prior to their elevation they had had equal standing with them. Many of Prabhupada's disciples found it difficult to take seriously the claim that their Godbrothers, whom they often knew rather intimately, were now "realized souls," pure in their Krishna Consciousness, and capable of teaching others the path to self-realization. As two long-time Prabhupada disciples explained:

> In the beginning [when the gurus were appointed] there was your old friend so and so, who was now a guru and being worshipped, sitting in his *vyasasana* being worshipped. It was difficult to take . . . I mean all of a sudden they are glorifying this guy as guru. But I kept thinking that I knew this guy when he did this and this (Los Angeles 1978).

> There were some overcompensating tendencies at first that some of the Godbrothers were put off by. To establish the institution of guru put a lot of Godbrothers off. In the beginning there was a lack of clarity. Now my friend, who I have grown up with [in Krishna Consciousness] is guru. People are bowing down to him, offering him *Guru Puja*. Now he is the representative of God. How do I relate to him now? (Philadelphia 1982)

The guru controversies of 1980 further strengthened the view of many Prabhupada disciples that the new gurus were not worthy of their guru status. The strength of this attitude throughout the movement influenced Western Guru's attempt to restructure the role of ISKCON's new gurus. When his efforts failed, Prabhupada's disciples in Los Angeles and elsewhere throughout the movement began openly to question the guru system. Many previously faithful disciples of Prabhupada began seriously to reconsider their membership in ISKCON. As one devotee who weathered the crises of this period explained:

When I think back to that time I think of a period when a lot of people were disturbed and confused. I've always been kind of a loyalist. . . . While I have always been serious about remaining an ISKCON devotee, at that particular time I began to have very scary thoughts. This movement may become something I simply can't be a part of. There are serious problems, and maybe some mistakes are being made that are so serious that they will ruin the movement and the movement won't be what it was intended to be. There were a lot of serious, thoughtful, conscientious, sincere Prabhupada disciples who were thinking like that and feeling a great difficulty. . . . It was a difficult time and large numbers of devotees were seriously questioning major new policies. It was a difficult time and many devotees left [ISKCON] (Philadelphia 1982).

While some devotees chose to defect from ISKCON during this period, many others faced serious questions of commitment. Their faith in ISKCON had been shaken by the movement's succession problems.

With Srila Prabhupada's disappearance, my commitment fluctuates, depending on how strictly Prabhupada's orders are being carried out by ISKCON (Questionnaire 1980).

Srila Prabhupada's leaving the planet and the lack of cooperation among the devotees affects my commitment. There seems to be a tendency to forget the urgency of trying to make everyone God-conscious (Questionnaire 1980).

Table 9.1 summarizes the reasons given by Prabhupada's disciples and the disciples of the new gurus for the spiritual crises that led them to consider leaving ISKCON. These data highlight the overall impact of organizational factors on the commitment of Srila Prabhupada's disciples. In all, 43 percent of the reasons given by Prabhupada's disciples for their loss of commitment were organizational in nature (i.e., differences with ISKCON policy, differences with local movement authorities, and differences over book distribution policies). Conversely, the

Table 9.1.

Reasons for Spiritual Crises of Disciples of Prabhupada and New Gurus

| | Breaking principles | Lost faith in philosophy | Differences with ISKCON policies | Differences with local authorities | Book distribution policies | Work-related problems | Personal problems | Lack of adequate financial support | Other[a] | Total |
|---|---|---|---|---|---|---|---|---|---|---|
| Prabhupada's disciples[b] | 17% | 6% | 12% | 21% | 10% | 13% | 12% | 3% | 7% | 101%(120) |
| Disciples of the new gurus[c] | 14% | 13% | 6% | 8% | 6% | 12% | 6% | 7% | 28% | 100% (61) |
| MEAN PERCENT | 15% | 9% | 9% | 16% | 8% | 13% | 9% | 5% | 16% | 100%(181) |

[a]Most of the responses in this category involve the desire to break the regulative principles.

[b]The total number of Prabhupada disciples reporting spiritual crises amounted to 56 out of 127 surveyed. Therefore, on the average, each of Prabhupada's disciples gave approximately two reasons for considering leaving ISKCON.

[c]The total number of disciples of the new ISKCON gurus reporting spiritual crises was 39 out of 86 surveyed. Therefore, on the average, each of these disciples gave approximately two reasons for considering leaving ISKCON.

disciples of the new gurus more often reported problems living up to the movement's religious philosophy and way of life as the reasons for their having considered leaving ISKCON.[6]

The loss of commitment on the part of many Prabhupada disciples led them to act politically to bring about change within ISKCON. A number of ex-members of ISKCON and dissident devotees who had remained within ISKCON joined forces to push for change. Although most of the protest against ISKCON and the gurus was centered in Los Angeles and along the West Coast, there were pockets of protest in many other ISKCON communities throughout America. The protest took many shapes — from informal discussion groups within ISKCON to organized challenging groups whose goal was to overthrow the leadership. These groups openly challenged the authority of the gurus to rule ISKCON. They argued that the improprieties of the new gurus proved that their appointments were no more than a conspiracy to grab power following Prabhupada's death.

In the middle of the guru crises, many of Prabhupada's disciples who had remained within ISKCON met collectively in informal friendship groups to discuss the fate of the movement. As one devotee explained, these informal discussion groups provided the only real forum available for discussion of the movement's problems:

> The thing was that these things were never openly discussed in an open forum. They were discussed in small groups of devotees. No one [in the morning] *Bhagavatam* class said '*Prabhus*, the movement is in real crisis, let's all think about it.' . . . Most Prabhupada disciples at least thought about it and many discussed ISKCON's problems openly in small groups (Philadelphia 1982).

Because of the potential threat posed by Prabhupada's disciples, the leadership in at least some ISKCON communities attempted to prevent challenging groups from forming by limiting opportunities for formally organized meetings. In Los Angeles, for example, where protest against the new gurus was perhaps the strongest to be found in any ISKCON community, the leadership actively attempted to undermine the mounting protest. A letter was written by a group of Prabhupada disciples to Western Guru in 1981 that reflects the level of conflict going on there:

> Part of the necessary adjustment [that needs to be made] is that the right to assembly by the *Vaisnavas* should be acknowledged, rather than condemned. There should be no stigma against such assemblies, such as 'black-balling,' character assassination, fear of various types of retribution, etc. Even the meateaters who established the U.S. constitution recognized the right to assembly. Are we to say that the *Vaisnava* kingdom should be less magnanimous than the kingdom established by meateaters? Concerning another matter, we request that your close associates not spread inciting emotions amongst your disciples. This is certainly avoidable, as it can be explained to them that the Godbrothers are meeting to seek solutions to problems in the community in cooperation with the authorities, not to overthrow them (Los Angeles 1981).

The threat to ISKCON's new leaders became even more serious when a group of present and former ISKCON members began openly to campaign against the gurus. They claimed that the appointment of the gurus was a myth. Because of the sanctioning of three gurus in one year, this group argued that it was not possible that Prabhupada could have appointed such incapable men to the position of guru. Prabhupada was a pure devotee and incapable of mistake.

> If Srila Prabhupada actually recognized anyone as *acarya*, he would have made that very clear and specific for us. We should have faith in him that he would have done that for us on such an essential consideration. He simply could have said: 'So, you, such and such, have reached complete perfection in Krishna Consciousness. All of my disciples should now recognize you as the next *acarya* in the line of the disciplic succession.' Prabhupada has left us no such record. . . . If we conclude that Srila Prabhupada recognized the self-acclaimed *acaryas*, and if we are free enough from

delusion to see how they have contradicted and deviated from the authorized injunctions of *shastra* [scripture] since that time, both in their statements and behavior, we will find ourselves in a quandary. This would mean that we would also have to conclude that Srila Prabhupada did not have the power to recognize a self-realized soul and that he made a serious mistake in recognizing imperfect disciples as gurus. That is not possible ("When You Hear Someone Say," unpublished document of a group of ex-members of ISKCON challenging ISKCON's gurus 1980).

Under the leadership of one long-time disciple of Srila Prabhupada, dissident elements began actively to challenge what they referred to as the "appointment myth." Literally hundreds of pages of literature criticizing the new gurus were produced and circulated throughout ISKCON's communities. During the fall of 1980 in Los Angeles, strategy meetings were held in the homes of ex-members of ISKCON to discuss ways by which the new leaders might be stripped of their guruships. These meetings were attended by dozens of ex-members and dissident devotees residing within the Los Angeles ISKCON community. The general tone of this group's attack on ISKCON is suggested by the following passage taken from their literature.

Any sane man will be able to see that UPA-ISKCON[7] has severely deviated from the truths which Srila Prabhupada gave all of us. Any sane man will be clearly able to see that the very foundation of the contentions of UPA-ISKCON is based on misconception, misinterpretation, misrepresentation, and adulteration. . . . The great falldowns which have been steadily taking place in UPA-ISKCON are not products of some innocent misunderstanding. They could not have reached to the dimension which they have if that were the case. They became the predominate energy less than six months after the departure of Srila Prabhupada. These great falldowns have now become virtually the only energy of UPA-ISKCON. When somebody becomes fixed in the pride of his own infallibility of purpose and claims to be spiritual master, such a person becomes the greatest cheater in human society . . . He becomes more and more inclined to misuse the philosophy of 'the end justifies the means.' (unpublished document of group of former ISKCON devotees 1980).

Both the challenges levelled at the guru system and ISKCON's response to them were framed within an ideological or theological context. The dissidents presented a wealth of evidence from Prabhupada's books to bolster their argument that a guru is never appointed. The evidence most commonly cited by this group was a statement made by Srila Prabhupada concerning the movement's next leaders:

All of my disciples will take the legacy. If you want, you can also take it. Sacrifice everything. I, one, may soon pass away. But there are hundreds and this movement will increase. It is not that I give order, 'Here is the next leader.' Anyone who follows the previous leadership is the leader. . . . All of my disciples are leaders—as much as they follow purely. Leader means one who is first-class disciple. *Evam parampara praptam.* One who is following perfectly (*Back to Godhead,* vol. 13: quoted in "The Spiritual Master Never Deviates" 1980).

Searching the movement's scriptures, those challenging ISKCON's leaders found nothing to support the claim that a guru can be appointed. Rather, a guru is recognized by his spiritual qualifications. Spiritual charisma, not bureaucratic appointment, is the basis for being a guru. The true *acarya,* it was thought, would emerge from among Prabhupada's disciples over the course of time. Until such a saintly individual should come forth, the challengers argued that the initiations of all disciples by the gurus into Krishna Consciousness should cease. This position implied that all Prabhupada's disciples should be seen as having the same opportunity to ascend to the position of guru, based upon the qualifications of spiritual purity and self-realization.

Nobody was recognized by Srila Prabhupada as having attained perfection in Krishna Consciousness. If he did recognize someone, he did not choose to inform all of his disciples of it. He would not have had to inform them. The bonafide spiritual master manifests according to the infallible direction of the Supreme Personality of Godhead, and he is self-effulgent ("Guru is Never Appointed" 1980).

In response to growing protest against the new gurus, the GBC issued a report in August 1980 to address the question.

> Some persons, citing many scriptural references describing the qualities of the *maha-bhagavata* [qualified guru], have questioned whether any ISKCON *acarya* exhibits these qualities. And they have further concluded that the ISKCON *acaryas* cannot fully live up to the requirements of a regular guru in devotional service. This criticism is speculative. . . . But aside from that, the whole line of reasoning is fallacious and the argument inapplicable. It starts with a speculative opinion and backs it up with quotes from Srila Prabhupada's books; but by this method one could 'prove' all kinds of things (Governing Body Commission Report 1980:2).

The GBC report went on to defend ISKCON against the attacks of the dissidents. It cautioned against the growing reality of schism and reminded ISKCON members of their obligation to follow Prabhupada's instructions and to accept the reorganization structure that had been established:

> By saying that Srila Prabhupada's disciples are not or cannot become advanced devotees of the highest order casts doubt upon Srila Prabhupada and our previous *acaryas* . . . It is one of the greatest services that we can do for ISKCON enemies and Kali's agents to publicize that our gurus following Srila Prabhupada are by definition second and third class devotees, unable to deliver a fallen soul to the highest position of *bhakti*. The *sahajiya* enemies of our *sampradaya* [society] already are having their agents spread rumors in the USA and other parts of the world that people should go else-

where for getting highest understanding of devotional service. . . .
Every time some unauthorized statement disturbing the actual
teachings of the *guru-parampara* is broadcast, this plays into
the hands of ISKCON's enemies (Governing Body Commission Report 1980).

## The Threat From India: Defection, Schism, and the Unification of ISKCON

Without question, the most serious crisis faced by ISKCON after Srila
Prabhupada's death and the reorganization of the movement occurred
in the spring of 1982, when one of the new gurus defected from the
organization taking dozens of his disciples with him to join forces with
Prabhupada's Godbrother, Maharaja Swami. At the time of his departure, Foreign Guru vowed to establish his own communities in those
cities around the world where ISKCON was already located and thereby
openly compete with ISKCON. As the regional secretary for one of
the gurus on the East Coast explained, the threat was considered
very serious:

> There was the split. And that was the biggest threat to date of what
> you could call a genuine splinter, a breaking off. It was the first de-
> fection of a guru and he had marshalled his forces and it looked
> like they were really going to give ISKCON a fight (Philadel-
> phia 1982).

The defection of Foreign Guru and the resulting crisis for ISKCON
must be understood as the culmination of a long series of events that
had involved Prabhupada's Godbrother, Maharaja Swami. During the
first two years following Prabhupada's death, Maharaja had been considered a valued advisor by ISKCON's new leaders. Beginning in 1980,
however, Maharaja Swami became the central figure around whom
those challenging ISKCON's new leaders rallied. While the Maharaja
challenge threatened to pull ISKCON apart in 1982, in the end it became

the major factor helping to unite ISKCON, and that unity helped resolve the succession crises that had plagued the movement for the preceding four years. It is to the events leading up to the defection of Foreign Guru and the subsequent resolution of the succession crises to which I now turn.

In the months prior to Prabhupada's death, as plans were being laid for the reorganization of ISKCON, Srila Prabhupada instructed his leading disciples to seek out the counsel of his trusted Godbrother, Maharaja Swami, as they faced the inevitable problems resulting from his departure. As one senior devotee stated, the role that Maharaja played in the movement's affairs reflected Prabhupada's wishes:

> Prabhupada left some instructions 'When I am gone you can go to him for advice on etiquette.' There were so many details to be worked out. For instance we had to find out what to do when Prabhupada disappeared: How to properly entomb him in the *samadhi*, so many things. So Prabhupada said that you can go to him for advice (Philadelphia 1982).

Maharaja Swami's involvement in ISKCON began in the spring of 1978, when members of the GBC sought his advice on the role of the new gurus within the reorganized ISKCON. The nature of the relationship between the GBC and the gurus was of special concern to them. In particular, they needed to determine who would have greater authority under the new structure—the collective GBC or the individual gurus? As the devotee quoted above explained:

> In 1978 the GBC went to Maharaja for advice as to what to do about the gurus and he gave them a perspective which was tainted by his own point of view. This later led to the problem of seeing the guru as higher and independent from the GBC. For after all, he was somewhat antiinstitutional. So for him the guru was independent and absolute. And he shouldn't be seen by his disciples as subordinate to anything. So that was sort of suddenly embodied in the early views that everyone had of the gurus (Philadelphia 1982).

Maharaja became a major figure in the guru controversies that emerged in 1980. At each juncture of decision, he acted to reaffirm the ultimate predominance of the gurus over the policies and decisions of the GBC. Even though the GBC had imposed sanctions against three of the gurus in 1980, the authority of this body was later severely undermined when it was forced on two occasions to rescind the suspensions it had imposed. The GBC's political clout was further tested when at least two of the gurus raised the possibility that they and their disciples would break away from ISKCON, if the GBC was going to make decisions pressuring them into conformity with its unwanted regulations. For example, the GBC was hesitant to impose sanctions against one of the gurus for developing a new style of worshipping Prabhupada at the new palace in New Vrindaban because of fears that he would break his affiliation with ISKCON. Maharaja Swami's philosophy supporting the ultimate authority of the guru over the GBC played a major role in provoking the political uncertainties of this period. As one devotee explained:

The debate about who was in charge—the GBC or the guru—went back and forth. First it was the guru who was on top and the GBC was sort of out of it . . . It was just so unclear. The issue was that the guru had absolute authority over his disciples. Yet, is he answerable to the GBC body? So there was the question: Is the guru absolute, or relatively absolute, or is he relative? (Philadelphia 1982).

In siding with the gurus against the GBC, Maharaja, perhaps unwittingly at first, became a political symbol for a growing number of devotees who had begun overtly to challenge the policies upon which ISKCON's reorganization rested. Maharaja came to be seen as an alternative authority to ISKCON and a number of long-time ISKCON members joined forces with him in his ashram in Navadvipa, India. As one ISKCON leader explained:

He was seen as an alternative absolute authority. They could build the movement under his guidance and they could leave ISKCON rationalizing that ISKCON was no longer fulfilling Prabhupada's goals. Only the real goals of ISKCON and Prabhupada could be fulfilled under the leadership of Maharaja Swami. And that's what happened. And there was the potential for it to take root. And in fact it was (Philadelphia 1982).

Several of the fifteen to twenty ISKCON members who first joined forces with Maharaja in 1980 were devotees who had lost power politically when ISKCON reorganized.[8] The first major figure to leave ISKCON and become involved with Maharaja was Jiva Swami, an ISKCON *sannyasi* and the recently deposed president of the Los Angeles ISKCON community. As one devotee commented, Jiva Swami's departure from ISKCON and the departure of several of the other dissidents who joined Maharaja's mission were politically motivated:

Jiva Swami was always a maverick within ISKCON. He was perceived by people as politically ambitious. He really wanted to be a guru. He was wetting his pants in great eagerness to become a guru. . . . It was clear to see that several of the men who took initiation from Maharaja were ambitious and resentful that they couldn't thread their way up the political ladder [in ISKCON]. They simply wanted to be gurus and they were feeling that the existing gurus were going to limit the number, keep it to an elite eleven and not open it up (Philadelphia 1982).

In a move that demonstrated overtly to ISKCON's leaders the potential threat he posed, Maharaja Swami initiated several of the dissident ISKCON members into the order of *sannyasa*.

The overt threat that he posed was literally initiating them [dissident ISKCON members] as *sannyasi*. Granted, he is not answerable to the GBC, but out of courtesy he should have consulted with them first. And then other Godbrothers of Prabhupada began coming forward and saying that he had broken etiquette by doing this. So it escalated like that. Everyone was becoming more and more apprehensive (Philadelphia 1982).

While only a small number of devotees actually joined Maharaja's ashram, there were dozens of others who supported the idea of his being brought into ISKCON as one of the initiating gurus. The high level of support for Maharaja Swami within the movement began to express itself in ways that continued to cause trouble for ISKCON's leaders:

DEVOTEE: Then evidence came out of different developments around the world where Maharaja Swami's tapes [of his lectures on Krishna Consciousness] were being played, his picture was being put on the altar [in ISKCON temples] and different things like that, which indicated that there were little pockets where he was getting in.

EBR: This is happening in Foreign Guru's zone?

DEVOTEE: Yes, in South Africa and in England. A little in Detroit. In Northwest Guru's zone and of course out on the West Coast with Jiva Swami. So there were these different influences (Philadelphia 1982).

In a major development, Jiva Swami in the summer of 1980 made the first formal effort to have Maharaja Swami recognized as one of ISKCON's initiating gurus. At the GBC meeting held in Dallas that year to consider the proposals of Western Guru redefining the position of the new gurus, the GBC considered a proposal drafted by Jiva Swami to give formal recognition to Maharaja as an ISKCON guru. The GBC soundly rejected his proposal and it was then that Jiva Swami formally defected from ISKCON and established his own community of followers in San Jose, California.

Even though the defection of Jiva Swami created only minor problems for ISKCON, the developing relationship between Foreign Guru and Maharaja Swami did become an increasing source of concern for ISKCON's leaders. After having sanctions laid against him by the GBC and after having been instructed to take *sannyasa* in the spring of 1980, Foreign Guru, under pressure from his wife, decided after six months to give up his *sannyasa*. He first traveled to America to discuss his decision with two of his Godbrothers and fellow gurus. Both of these friends tried to convince him of the need to continue his *sannyasa,* but he returned to England unconvinced. Foreign Guru and his wife then traveled to India to tour the holy places and to speak with Maharaja Swami about his desire to give up his *sannyasa.* Maharaja Swami convinced Foreign Guru to continue his *sannyasa.* This meeting between Foreign Guru and Maharaja Swami forged the beginning of a relationship between the two that would later culminate in Foreign Guru's defection from ISKCON in order to become part of Maharaja's mission.

Soon after their meeting, Foreign Guru adopted Maharaja Swami as his *Siksa Guru.* Over time, he came to rely on Maharaja more and more as his spiritual authority and confidant. The strength of his relationship with Maharaja led Foreign Guru to petition the GBC to have Maharaja Swami brought into ISKCON as an initiating guru and a formal advisor to the GBC. Foreign Guru made it known to the GBC members and to others that either Maharaja would be brought formally into ISKCON or he and his disciples would break away and join forces with Maharaja Swami. The whole issue came to a head at ISKCON's yearly Mayapura meeting in India in the spring of 1982. Initially, the GBC was split on the issue. While three of the initiating gurus favored Maharaja's participation in ISKCON, most GBC members were against it. Considerable ill feeling had been generated by Maharaja Swami when he had acted to undercut the authority of the GBC by coming out in support of the gurus who had been punished and then had begun initiating dissident ISKCON devotees into his ashram. Also, there was evidence that Maharaja had been openly criticizing Srila Prabhupada, and some members feared that his becoming formally involved in ISKCON would only result in further criticism of ISKCON's founding *acarya:*

At first he [Maharaja] began to criticize the GBC and then gradually it escalated to include Prabhupada. That's when it became serious . . . . For example, there are occasional places in Srila Prabhupada's books where he says things critical of the *Gaudiya Math* [the organization founded by Prabhupada's spiritual master in India], that they didn't strictly follow Bhaktisiddhanta (both Prabhupada's and Maharaja's spiritual master). Maharaja wanted future editions of the books to have those passages expunged. It was just horrifying that we should now have to censor our spiritual master because he didn't like it. He also thought that Prabhupada was being worshipped too much [by ISKCON devotees] (Philadelphia 1982).

While the GBC remained stalemated on whether to bring Maharaja into ISKCON, the one hundred and twelve temple presidents and regional secretaries present in Mayapura met to consider the issue. One participant at that meeting described what happened this way:

All the temple presidents from around the world met and that's where you got a real consensus of the second echelon of leaders, how they were feeling. The presidents recommended [to the GBC] that if Foreign Guru was going to stay with ISKCON he would have to make his connection with Maharaja less and less. . . . There was a definite feeling against Maharaja coming in. This decision gave the GBC inspiration. This was taken as Krishna's direction. This is what the temple presidents want, leading devotees from all over the world. So then they got strength from that to make a stand not to allow Maharaja's influence in the movement to continue to spread. So Foreign Guru said 'OK that's it' (Philadelphia 1982).

When Foreign Guru defected from ISKCON with as many as one hundred of his disciples to join Maharaja, he openly threatened to fight ISKCON.

When Foreign Guru left, the threat was that they were going to start their own temples. To start a countermovement in the cities where ISKCON was. Everybody was real concerned. He said 'I am going to put an end to ISKCON in two years.' It was quite a threat (Philadelphia 1982).

Foreign Guru's defection, while it did pose a potentially serious threat to ISKCON, ultimately had an even greater force in helping to resolve the succession crises that had plagued the movement over the preceding four years. Foreign Guru's defection and his threats against ISKCON caused a renewed sense of solidarity and esprit de corps throughout the movement. Even though internal strains, which had resulted in mass defections, factionalism, and splintering, threatened to pull ISKCON apart in the years following Prabhupada's death, the threat posed by outside forces was what ultimately served to restore unity to the movement as a whole. Even devotees who had been ISKCON's most outspoken critics closed ranks to face the potential challenges ahead:

> So when Foreign Guru left, that's when everybody closed in; 'ISKCON all the way.' It was such a rally around the flag kind of thing. And a lot of people who had been very critical of the gurus, of ISKCON, and the GBC, their attitude changed. It was like a resurgence. It was like a boil coming to a head and all the poisons coming out (Philadelphia 1982).

The second major development that grew out of Foreign Guru's defection was the resolution of the power struggle between the GBC and the gurus. Following the guru controversies of 1980, the gurus formally agreed to recognize the GBC as the final authority within ISKCON. It was only after Foreign Guru's defection to Maharaja, however, that the gurus' fully recognized the critical necessity to adhere to this policy. As one ISKCON leader explained:

> In 1981, at the Mayapura meeting, it was put into writing that the GBC was the ultimate authority within ISKCON. At that time it was theoretically understood by everyone. But, in fact, it was the defection of Foreign Guru that really was the strong force for unity in the movement in that now it was clearly recognized that there was a need for a strong centralized administrative body that the gurus would work under. . . . So Foreign Guru's defection really cemented things—that the gurus had to be servants of the GBC. . . . In fact, it is clearly conceived by everyone now that the tendency to

think that the gurus were somehow beyond G B C control was a death knell for the movement (Philadelphia 1982).

In contrast to the political upheavals that disrupted the 1982 Mayapura meeting, the mood of the 1983 gathering was characterized by a sense of unity and a spirit of cooperation. In a telling symbolic gesture, the gurus at the 1983 meeting broke with past precedent and decided to forego the normal practice of each guru having his own *vyasasana* in the temple and being offered guru worship by his disciples. As one participant in these meetings said:

> Usually when the gurus come to Vrndavana there are *vyasasanas* placed out for all thirteen[9] of them. But this year, the gurus decided that it was just too cumbersome. They just didn't want to do it. . . . So, they just put cushions down [on the floor] for the gurus and for G B C members so they could sit among everyone. What that showed to me was a symbolic relaxation on the part of the gurus. They understand the new structure is in place and the threat on them and I S K C O N is basically over. In past years, there was a concerted effort by the gurus to establish that the real heart of I S K C O N was the gurus. Now they realize that their role as guru has not been diminished (Philadelphia 1983).

## Conclusion

The most immediate and crucial consequence of the end of charisma for a group or movement is the power vacuum that often results, which ushers in a struggle for control of the movement by various interest groups. The need to replace charisma with a new basis for authority affords an opportunity for a variety of individuals and groups who had previously held little or no power within the movement to try to gain control and to legitimize their interests within the new organizational structure. Conflict and factionalism come about because these various interest groups contend for the right to oversee the movement's future. It was just this kind of a power vacuum that characterized the succession controversies that arose following Srila Prabhupada's death in the fall of 1977.

The succession controversies that plagued ISKCON were empirically and theoretically unique, because two competing and ultimately conflicting structures of authority challenged each other for power and control of the movement (i.e. the charisma of the gurus versus the bureaucratic authority of the GBC). The established presence and legitimacy of the GBC provided a structure that might have allowed the routinization of charisma to have proceeded smoothly with little conflict and factionalism. This kind of bureaucratic structure was in fact crucial to the Christian Science movement after the death of its charismatic founder, Mary Baker Eddy. As Wilson notes: "A system of absolute personal authority of a leader was transformed into the absolute impersonal authority of a board" (1961:159). In contrast to the Christian Science movement, ISKCON's religious beliefs require that charismatic leadership be continued in the form of the gurus. To become Krishna-conscious requires that a devotee become initiated by a spiritual master. As Srila Prabhupada states in his commentaries on the *Bhagavad Gita*:

> The path of spiritual realization is undoubtedly difficult. The Lord therefore advises us to approach a bonafide spiritual master in the line of disciplic succession from the Lord Himself. . . . No one can be spiritually realized by manufacturing his own process, as is the fashion of foolish pretenders. . . . One has to approach a bonafide spiritual master to receive the knowledge. Such a spiritual master should be accepted in full surrender, and one should serve the spiritual master like a menial servant, without false prestige. Satisfaction of the self-realized spiritual master is the secret of advancement in spiritual life (1972:259–260).

Because of the centrality of the guru-disciple relationship in the movement's religious beliefs, provision had to be made for carrying forward the principle of disciplic succession (*Parampara*). ISKCON could not solve its succession problems by the rule of a committee (i.e., the GBC). Provision had to be made for carrying forward the Krishna religious system.

To avoid the kind of conflict that ultimately destroyed his own spiritual master's organization following Bhaktisiddhanta's death, Prabhupada chose to appoint ISKCON's gurus, rather than allow any one or more of his disciples to rise naturally or unnaturally to the status of guru. To help avoid factionalism and schism, Prabhupada bureaucratized charisma by appointing his spiritual successors. The authority of the gurus rested squarely on their ties to ISKCON, however, instead of on their own spiritual-charismatic qualities. Structurally, the gurus occupied an organizational position within ISKCON. Prabhupada's appointment of the gurus constituted an attempt to institutionalize charisma in order to preserve both the organization and the movement's religious system. As I have described, however, this institutionalization of charisma became problematic almost immediately following Prabhupada's death.

# 10
# The Future of Hare Krishna

This case study of ISKCON's growth and development in America suggests the full range of social forces that promote movement change and adaptation. In less than twenty years, the inspiration of one elderly man, traveling to America on his own from India, was transformed into a worldwide religious movement. Along the way, of course, ISKCON has faced a variety of problems and crises as it has sought to expand its influence in America and beyond. The road was not easy, but the movement continues on into the 1980s and promises to exist into the twenty-first century.

In this chapter, I want to bring ISKCON's history in America up to the present, simultaneously addressing the issue of the movement's prospects for the future. My task will be to align ISKCON's past with its present in an effort to project the future of Krishna Consciousness in America. The question that guides my inquiry is not whether Krishna

Consciousness will go forth into the next century, but in what form and under what circumstances it will do so. After nearly two decades in America, the movement has cultivated thousands of seriously committed devotees whose lives will continue to be dedicated to the spiritual goals and practices embodied within Krishna Consciousness.

Consistent with the analytic concerns of this study, my discussion of the Krishna movement's future will focus on a number of organizational issues that appear to be crucial to ISKCON's survival and potential success. Questions of particular interest include: Will the movement continue as a single formal organization (i.e., ISKCON) or will it fragment under the leadership of the new gurus, resulting in multiple movement organizations? If the movement avoids such fragmentation and continues as a single organization, will it shift its organizational goals and values toward becoming institutionalized as a church, or will the movement maintain its largely sectarian way of life in the years to come? I explore four factors that promise to have a continuing influence on ISKCON's future as a movement organization: (1) leadership; (2) recruitment and membership; (3) the relationship between financial resources and preaching; and (4) the possible impact of ISKCON's public definition on its future growth and expansion in America.

Playing the role of prophet is of course a risky business. Even spiritually empowered religious leaders often have what prove to be erroneous visions of the future, which may be accompanied by a loss of faith among their followers. While the risks are certainly not as great for the scholar turned prophet, nevertheless, scholarly futuristic projections can be just as incorrect and consequential. For example, consider these words of two early investigators of ISKCON regarding the movement's future:

> Perhaps the most important test of [ISKCON's] survival will be the reaction to an eventual crisis of leadership succession. Such a crisis is likely because of the absolute centrality to the movement of its seventy-eight year old spiritual master, A. C. Bhaktivedanta. On

his eventual 'passing from the lifecycle' Krishna Consciousness seems unlikely to survive in its present form (Johnson 1976:51).

The discipline the devotees follow for their spiritual requirements in their alternative style of life should impart reasonable stability to the Society. Its flourishing business enterprises will meet the material needs of the devotees. With capable management, these businesses should give every devotee the possibility of pursuing his goals of attaining Krishna Consciousness (Judah 1974:182).

These assessments of ISKCON's future were made in the early to middle seventies. While it is possible to understand the reasons for these two researchers' predictions, it appears for now that they have proven largely untrue. Beyond the question of accuracy is another issue of perhaps greater overall importance: How might the predictions of scholars influence a movement's course of development? In other words, are such scholarly assessments of a group's future merely neutral exercises in prophetic theorizing, or do they constitute a variable capable of promoting change? I fear the latter is the case, and it is with some trepidation that I proceed.

## Leadership

As discussed at length in chapter nine, ISKCON's reorganization following Srila Prabhupada's death resulted in two systems of authority competing for power. Although for the moment that conflict has been resolved, the possibility remains that one or more gurus could break from ISKCON and establish his own separate community. The expulsion of Northwest Guru from ISKCON in the summer of 1983 points to the continuing tension between the power and authority of individual gurus and the collective decision-making body—the GBC. In defiance of the GBC, Northwest Guru initiated several devotees residing in his zone into the order of *sannyasa*. All such appointments normally require GBC approval. Northwest Guru refused to confer with the GBC, insisting that his authority as guru was independent of ISKCON's governing body. After years of controversy that had surrounded Northwest Guru, the GBC finally decided to expel him from ISKCON.

Even though such conflicts among ISKCON's leaders are not inevitable, the existence of two structurally distinct sources of authority operating within the movement will keep alive the potential for factionalism and schism. Because of the importance of the guru-disciple relationship to the movement's religious system, any political conflict between one or more of the gurus and the collective body of the GBC could result in a major schism which could cause literally hundreds of disciples to leave ISKCON along with their spiritual leaders. Should the movement splinter along these lines, ISKCON would likely face considerable decline, if not outright organizational failure. Other movement organizations could grow up around individual gurus, but the structures, organization, ideologies, and goals of such groups could well differ so much that Krishna Consciousness could come to take a variety of forms in America and worldwide.

Another factor likely to affect ISKCON's political future as an organization involves the declining number of Prabhupada disciples remaining within ISKCON. Recent estimates suggest that there were approximately one thousand Prabhupada disciples in ISKCON in 1983, out of nearly five thousand he initiated. Though the number of Prabhupada's disciples leaving ISKCON has dramatically declined since the mass defections of the 1978–1980 period, Prabhupada's disciples nevertheless continue to lose power as their ranks get smaller, relative to the increasing numbers of disciples of ISKCON's thirteen gurus. Unless the GBC remains the dominant governing institution within ISKCON, Prabhupada's disciples may well lose whatever political influence they presently hold. Should the balance of power shift again toward the authority of the gurus, Prabhupada's disciples may well become a powerless group within the organization, unable to significantly influence ISKCON's future. If this happens, another wave of defections by Prabhupada's disciples could be expected. Because Prabhupada's disciples have a larger stake in maintaining ISKCON than the disciples of the present gurus do, their declining power promises to be a destabilizing factor, which may increase the likelihood of the group splintering, threatening ISKCON's vitality as a movement organization.

## Recruitment and Membership

One ongoing change, which promises to alter ISKCON structurally and ideologically in the future, involves the movement's changing membership profile. On the one hand, ISKCON is experiencing an expansion in its congregational members, yet, on the other hand, the number of its full-time core adherents is continuing to decline in America. As suggested in chapter six, ISKCON began to cultivate a new constituency of part-time members in the mid-seventies, one comprised of loosely committed youths and immigrants from India and their families. Although ISKCON continues to attract a limited number of fully committed core members in America, it is likely that in the future they will comprise only a minority of the movement's membership. This ongoing change in the movement's membership profile is likely to result in continuous structural and ideological change. As one ISKCON leader explained, the development of a congregation is likely to result in ISKCON becoming more inclusive and open to the surrounding society, thereby allowing it to become a broad-based religious movement.

> Our long term plan is to develop a congregation. . . . We see now that a person who shows a little interest may have to be cultivated a whole lifetime before he becomes a member. We have that broadness of vision now. So in the core you have full-time devotees who maintain the four regs [regulative principles], and chant sixteen rounds [each day]. Then, expanding out, you have lesser degrees of commitment and involvement, and our preaching should be aimed all the way out. . . . You have to keep your standards and preach to these people all the time, but at the same time not drive them away for not living up to them. We are just trying to work a larger field

now, with the sensitivity that it is there. If our movement is genuinely world-transforming, then it's not going to happen that everyone in the whole world will join our temples and move in. Its going to have to be a broader social movement (Philadelphia 1982).

ISKCON's efforts to attract new members during the eighties is likely to yield a substantial number of congregational members, in particular, Indian people. Since the late seventies, ISKCON has actively sought the support and participation of Indian people in urban areas such as Detroit, Los Angeles, Chicago, and New York. In less than a decade, thousands of Indian "life members" have joined ISKCON's ranks. A growing proportion of the Indian population in America is looking to ISKCON as a link to their own spiritual and cultural traditions. They come to ISKCON's communities to worship the deities and to educate their children in Krishna Consciousness. ISKCON has responded by developing various programs for its Indian members, ranging from social gatherings to the provision of religious training for their children. As one devotee explained, the movement expects to attract an increasing number of Indian followers in the coming decades:

The Indians are looking for a way to live in America and still remain Hindu and we are the only ones who have got it. . . . There is going to be a day when there will be a real *Vaisnava* revival among the Indians in this country. It will really catch on among the Indians, they will become devotees and we will get a good slice of them (Philadelphia 1982).

As the number of Indian members increases within ISKCON, perhaps ultimately to become the majority, we might expect them to take on positions of spiritual and political leadership within the movement. Since the late seventies, several ISKCON communities (e.g., Chicago and Detroit) have had Indian men serve as temple presidents. Should the present trend continue, it is possible that ISKCON, as Rodney Stark has suggested, will be transformed into an ethnic church (1982:14). Such a development would profoundly alter ISKCON, ultimately moving it as a movement away from its initial purposes and objectives. In an ironic twist, white American *Vaisnavas* may come to serve as spiritual teachers for a larger body of Indian members and their families.

The expansion in the numbers of ISKCON's Indian members may indirectly affect the movement in still other ways. Although some Indian people have become initiates of the new gurus and some of their children may in the future choose to become committed disciples, past experience suggests that most Indians will not commit themselves in this way. The commitment of the Indian people is less clearly to ISKCON per se and more clearly to the religious traditions that the movement represents and makes available to them. ISKCON's Indian supporters are therefore unlikely to develop any strong sense of commitment to ISKCON as an organization or to the movement's spiritual leaders. In the future, this lack of commitment and therefore the lack of a real basis for organizational control may lead to conflict, particularly if ISKCON's Indian members ultimately come to comprise the majority of ISKCON members. The potential for such conflict is in keeping with the difficulties that have already cropped up in integrating the Indians into ISKCON's communities. Many devotees have negative feelings about the presence of the Indians in their communities. Cultural differences provide one source of tension, and many devotees have expressed the opinion that the Indians are not seriously committed to their Krishna-conscious beliefs and see them as having sold out already in various ways to a western lifestyle. Although it is difficult to predict the consequences of such future conflicts, it seems possible that this kind of hostility could result in the two sides parting ways, with the Indians establishing their own temples separate from those of ISKCON.

## Financial Resources and Preaching: Differentiation and Specialization

One problem that has remained with ISKCON throughout much of its North American history has involved the interrelationship between finances and preaching. ISKCON's development throughout the seventies and early eighties has centered on problems of gathering sufficient financial resources to maintain the organization, while at the same time to fulfill the movement's religious mission of preaching and recruitment. My discussion of *sankirtana* highlighted the ways in which these two organizational goals have come into conflict in the past, resulting in ISKCON's facing attack from both the outside and the inside. By trying to combine both of these goals through the practice of *sankirtana*, ISKCON spoiled its public image and invited formal and informal efforts to limit its influence in America.

Without question, the most immediate challenge facing ISKCON is to develop profitable business enterprises capable of supporting its American communities. It seems clear that ISKCON's economic policies must be developed in order to allow the movement's missionary activities to remain independent of money making. ISKCON's future, therefore, appears to involve increasing differentiation and specialization. Each of these trends is in fact already underway. As one ISKCON leader explained:

We now have to face the realities of the eighties and at least for the time being keep our book distribution separate from our financial maintenance. While there was a trend in the seventies for these to be one and the same through *sankirtana*, and that to be the ideal, things have changed. Public reaction turned sour toward our book distribution and the separation seemed necessary, where you could give out a book free without having to pressure the person in any way. We are looking more and more toward stratification of membership. We will have to assign the financial responsibilities for more accepted forms of business to devotees who have those natural abilities and who can be trained to do that. This system will take the burden off those persons who are going out and meeting the public [on *sankirtana*]. So that those meeting the public can do so in a very pure-hearted way. The only intention being giving the book, giving Krishna Consciousness. . . . So that attitude is there now to a good extent, since we increasingly have that separation of financial maintenance from book distribution (Philadelphia 1982).

As this statement suggests, ISKCON is in the midst of a major transformation involving differentiation and specialization of functions. This development, in combination with ISKCON's increasingly heterogeneous membership, more inclusive structures, and bureaucratic forms of power and authority suggest that its sectarianism may be giving way to denominationalism. In the devotees' own terms, the system of *Varna-Asrama* is now unfolding.[1]

Even though processes of differentiation and specialization are taking place, two questions still remain: How will ISKCON raise the economic resources needed to support its communities in the future? And, relatedly, how will the movement direct its missionary activities in the decades ahead?

ISKCON's economic strategies, for the most part, are more community-specific than movement-wide. While there are certain economic practices that are used throughout ISKCON in America and much of the world, most ISKCON communities have devised their own economic strategies in light of local talents and opportunities.

The most widely used economic strategy of the early eighties, and one which promises to remain important in the years to come, involves selling products in public places (i.e., *picking*). ISKCON members have taken on the role of salespersons, selling items such as candles and oriental art. The devotees present themselves to the public at such times as candlemakers or as the distributors of fine art, not as ISKCON members. This economic strategy avoids provoking the public's negative attitude toward the movement and helps to insure that these efforts will be economically successful. The separation of preaching from finances through paraphernalia sales has also freed the devotees from the internal conflicts that had resulted from previous *sankirtana* tactics, as the leader of one community explained:

> The thing is, some devotees actually prefer doing candles or art work. For example, I have devotees right now who sell paintings, who would much rather do that because they can dress as a businessman. They can talk like a businessman and they feel much more confident doing that than representing Krishna in a parking

lot, or *Hare Nam* [public chanting] situation. So specialization became a part of the movement and many people liked it, they felt
more comfortable. Like myself I had pangs of consciousness all
along about our *sankirtana* tactics. But, now, one day I could do
candles, sell candles door to door, collect a few hundred dollars,
then the next day, I would go out and distribute my quota of books
with no pressure. I was very happy to have that division. On the
one hand, I was selling candles, and it wasn't a lie, we presented
ourselves as candlemakers, which we were. And then we could go
out the next day and without using the change-up or anything, I
didn't have to lie to people, I could say 'Here take a book. Hare
Krishna' (Philadelphia 1982).

Instead of selling items that had little or no connection to the movement's religious or cultural heritage, as was done in the past, there
now is a growing interest in selling products that have a more direct
connection to India and to Eastern culture. Borrowing from the patterns of successful businesses in Europe, some ISKCON communities in
America are laying plans for opening up small businesses to sell oriental rugs and other Eastern art objects. These business enterprises
would avoid publicizing their connection with the Hare Krishna movement and their purpose would be expressly financial.

Beyond these movement-wide economic policies, individual communities have developed strategies directed toward raising money.
Devotees in several ISKCON communities, for example, have become
involved in various aspects of the computer business. One devotee,
residing in an ISKCON community in the northeast, is helping to support the community there through the sale of computers. In this and
other communities, a small number of devotees have become computer programmers working with local businesses. In the late seventies, the computer facilities at the movement's incense factory, Spiritual Sky Scented Products, were being leased by local businessmen on
a time-sharing basis.

Another source of income for ISKCON's communities has been the
sale of vegetarian food. In 1983, ISKCON owned and operated eleven

vegetarian restaurants in communities throughout America. In other locations (e.g., Denver and the Port Royal, Pennsylvania, farm community), natural candies are being produced and sold to local health food stores. On a smaller scale, some ISKCON communities send devotee women into public places to sell cookies and vegetarian foods of one sort or another. In California, for example, ISKCON members can be seen selling soda and food to travelers who stop at roadside rest areas; they also sell at zoos and in other public locations in that state. It is likely that these large- and small-scale efforts to sell vegetarian food to the public will continue in the future because the devotees view such activities as having indirect spiritual benefits (i.e., the people who consume such foodstuffs gain spiritual advancement because the foods were first offered to Krishna). Since the devotees' customers remain largely unaware that they are buying from ISKCON, this economic strategy promises to remain successful at least in the near future.

Other efforts to raise money to help support individual ISKCON communities are widely various. ISKCON's farm communities, of course, are able both to feed their members and to sell the surpluses (vegetables, corn, dairy products, etc.). In other communities, devotees are involved in small businesses such as landscaping and the making and selling of jewelry. In at least some instances, devotees are working jobs outside the movement, as security guards, in clerical positions, and in other such semi-skilled and unskilled positions to help support themselves and the local ISKCON community. Should ISKCON's developing economic policies fail to provide stable sources of income, it is entirely possible that men householders will be required to seek further outside employment to help support the movement. This kind of development, however, would have major consequences for ISKCON's structural and ideological future in America.

One other, potentially major, source of revenue for the movement comes from ISKCON's expanding congregation of Indian members. Since many of ISKCON's Indian supporters are professional and business people, they possess the resources to help finance ISKCON's communities. In the Detroit ISKCON community, for example, the Indian people provide a major share of financial support. In 1982, Indian members in that community contributed $100,000 to the Bhaktivedanta Book Trust Fund. In other communities, such as Chicago, Los Angeles, and New York, Indian people likewise contribute money to the movement, although their contributions fall short of actually supporting these communities to a substantial degree. As the leader of one ISKCON community explained, Indian contributions provide only a minor source of funds in support of his community:

> I know that the overhead in this community is something around $25,000 a month. The fact is that we can't depend on our congregational members, and I'm talking here of the Indian people, for much more than about a grand [$1,000] a month. So we have to see them in that light[2] (Philadelphia 1982).

In sum, while the growing congregations of Indian life-members may come to provide a major source of financial support for the movement in the future, for now, they remain only a relatively minor source of support for only a few of ISKCON's communities.

As alternative money-making enterprises have been developed, ISKCON has placed less financial pressure on *sankirtana*, restoring it to its traditional missionary purposes. Although *sankirtana* devotees continue to collect donations and although in some isolated locations these financial donations remain important, by and large, *sankirtana* no longer serves as the movement's major money-making activity. As the leader of one ISKCON community explained in 1982:

> In the airport here, we have devotees going out there distributing literature each day, but since we now have other sources of income, our emphasis to them is not that you are doing this to maintain the temple. Other activities are doing that. Our emphasis to them is to have a very high degree of integrity in your approach. We don't allow the change-up. We want them to be very straightforward about their identities. This obviously means that there are not as many customers, but, nevertheless, we find that they are do-

ing nicely and are able easily, without pressure, simply to get a donation covering the cost of the book (Philadelphia 1982).

Unless the movement's new economic strategies fail miserably in the future, it is unlikely that ISKCON would ever put strong financial demands on *sankirtana* again. History has shown that the long-term negative effects outweigh any short-term economic gains.

## Public Definition

Perhaps more than any other single factor, ISKCON's public definition promises to have a strong influence on the movement's future in America. Throughout the seventies, ISKCON was viewed by many people in America as a threatening movement, which sought to exploit the public for financial gain. The resulting public backlash had far-reaching consequences for ISKCON everywhere. ISKCON has now begun to take steps to neutralize and turn around the public's view of the movement. As one ISKCON leader stated:

We have had to learn lessons the hard way. We have learned a lot of good lessons, that is for sure. We are just banking on the fact that we can change the bad public image that we have over the course of time. It's not going to happen overnight. I can see by the 1990s that we could have outlived that image and that there will be positive things that people will come to identify us with. . . . When they are no longer harassed by us in public places any more, they are going to forget. . . . There is a definite sensitivity among the leaders to changing our public image to a positive one. So I think it will happen, though it will certainly take some time to live down these past excesses [in *sankirtana*] from the latter part of the 1970s (Philadelphia 1982).

To help promote a more positive public image, ISKCON has initiated a number of programs and policies. The first major step in this direction involved the separation of preaching from finances in *sankirtana*.

In addition, three other programs have been adopted, which the movement hopes will have a positive impact on its public image in the future: (1) efforts to align the movement's goals and values more closely and visibly with the larger Hindu tradition; (2) social welfare programs (i.e., distributing food to the poor and needy); and (3) building a number of cultural and religious attractions in the hope of introducing large numbers of people in America to Krishna Consciousness.

## Aligning ISKCON with Hinduism

The increasing involvement of Indian people in ISKCON promises to increase the movement's legitimacy in the eyes of the public. In the past, ISKCON has called on its Indian supporters to denounce the actions of deprogrammers, who have kidnapped ISKCON members and subjected them to psychological and physical harassment (i.e., deprogramming). In addition, Indian supporters of ISKCON, on a number of occasions, have been called in to testify to the religious authenticity of the movement's beliefs, undermining anti-cult claims that ISKCON is no more than a contemporary religious concoction designed to deceive and exploit America's young people. On still other occasions, ISKCON has called on its Indian members to back claims that government officials have discriminated against the movement on religious grounds. For example, in 1980, the Indian community in Los Angeles came to ISKCON's aid when the city tried to keep the movement from staging its annual *Ratha Yathra* Festival in the beachside community of Venice. When charges of religious discrimination against the Hindu tradition were made, the city quickly backed down and allowed the festival to take place.

While ISKCON's Indian supporters have recently proven to be a valuable resource for the movement, in its early days ISKCON often eschewed formal ties with other Hindu groups in America. In part this deliberate separation derived from the movement's rejection of certain social and theological elements of orthodox Hinduism (e.g., the caste system, the narrowly defined role of women, and the belief that Krishna is the supreme God rather than one of many Gods). Perhaps of equal importance, however, was Prabhupada's desire to avoid having his movement seen as rigidly sectarian. Prabhupada believed that Americans held negative attitudes toward Hinduism, so he sought to avoid having ISKCON viewed as Hindu. He wanted Krishna Consciousness to be accepted by America as a universal religion, not as one culturally and spiritually bound to India.

It was only after the movement came under attack from the anti-cult movement that ISKCON strategically tried to accentuate its Hindu roots. In the face of strong public opposition, ISKCON began actively to seek formal ties with the larger Hindu tradition. As one ISKCON leader explained:

> In fact, it was even stated in the 1980 North American GBC meeting that the goal of the decade is to have our public image be that of a denomination by the end of the decade. In other words, we are no longer a cult, we are a denomination of the Hindu church. And, of course, it is a tactical strategy to have the Hindu community come forward and say what they really think about ISKCON. We are Hindus. We are part of the Hindu culture and therefore deserve the same kind of First Amendment rights as any religion. I mean, I admit that this is strategy. But this is also their feeling as well. I mean, when ISKCON is persecuted, they feel that they are being persecuted too (Philadelphia 1982).

By aligning itself with the larger Hindu community, the movement hopes to shed its image as a deviant cult and establish its legitimacy as a truly religious movement in the eyes of the American public. ISKCON hopes that it will be extended the rights and priviledges of any other religious faith in America.

*Social Welfare Activities*

In the most general terms, ISKCON has always been in the business of providing programs for the benefit of the larger society. The movement's weekly Sunday feast, while it is expressly concerned with recruitment and missionary activities, has nevertheless fed thousands of needy youth and other less fortunate people in America and around the world. Now, however, ISKCON has undertaken a food program that is specifically targeted at the poor. The Hare Krishna Food for Life Program was quietly inaugurated in 1982,[3] making use of food donated by the federal government to nonprofit organizations. While altruistic and missionary motives are involved in this project, the program was begun primarily to promote a more positive public image for ISKCON:

> One program that we are undertaking now is what we are calling the Hare Krishna Food for Life Program. This basically is a program meant to help our public image. But it isn't just a PR hype. Food distribution is a form of preaching also. A practical part of any religion is social welfare work. . . . Now, in America, with the recessionary economy and the unemployment like it is, and with social security being slashed, we saw an opportunity to really gain some improved public image by distributing food. . . . It will show people that we are a group with a concern for society. . . . It's a fact that the way to a man's heart is through his stomach. So hopefully, they will have a little more appreciation, be open to those things which they see as odd about us. You get phrases [from the people being fed] like: 'I don't care what other people say about you, but you're alright in my book.' 'You may look a little strange, but you really helped me out.' . . . I think this program will help people realize that we are a movement that is genuinely trying to help people (Philadelphia 1982).

ISKCON has a tradition of food distribution; these welfare programs will doubtless be continued and perhaps expanded in the future. Whether these programs will actually improve ISKCON's public image is less clear. Instead of coming to appreciate the movement's efforts, for example, the public may become indignant over the use of public foodstuffs indirectly to support the Krishna movement in America. It is just this possibility that has led the movement to keep this program under wraps until it is well established and hopefully until it is brought to the public's attention by appreciative community members and local politicians.

*Cultural-Religious Attractions*

Following the lead of other religions throughout history, ISKCON is now attempting to educate the public about its religious beliefs and way of life by building temples and other cultural attractions meant to attract large numbers of people into its communities. This effort is largely concerned with nurturing a more positive public definition, since the preaching at such places is kept low key and recruitment is not given a role of importance. As the devotee in charge of the movement's public affairs department remarked in 1983, the movement is moving into its "cultural phase" (Suplee 1983).

The beginnings of ISKCON's "cultural phase" started with the vision of Prabhupada's first disciple, who is a current ISKCON guru, who decided in the mid-seventies to build a palace of gold to honor ISKCON's founder. On his two-thousand-acre farm in the hills of West Virginia, he and his followers have built Prabhupada's Palace, a restaurant, and lodging for visitors, including guest houses and camp sites. The community is presently building the first of several planned temples, which will be situated on top of the many hills surrounding Prabhupada's Palace.

Initially, the efforts of West Virginia Guru and his followers met with mixed reactions throughout the movement. Several ISKCON leaders and a substantial number of devotees openly criticized the project because it diverted monies that might otherwise have gone to help support the financially troubled Bhaktivedanta Book Trust in the late seventies. Despite the criticism, West Virginia Guru continued to raise money for the project and he and his followers completed Prahupada's Palace in 1980. Now, the project at New Vrindaban is widely regarded as the greatest preaching and public relations success that ISKCON has ever produced. As one ISKCON leader explained, Prabhupada's Palace has been a monumental public relations success:

> The Palace is like a hook: the people come because it is such a far-out thing and yet when they are there, they are actually undergoing a spiritual experience. . . . People often go away saying: 'You know I always thought you guys were weird. Now I see that you

actually are alright.' Before, these peoples' experiences of the movement were limited to some goofy devotee on the street who tried to take them out of a couple of bucks. But now they can see this huge cultural, historical heritage is there. They see this work of art . . . Prabhupada's Palace. Without doubt, that Palace has done more towards changing the public opinion toward us than anything else. Many Americans, when they think of Hare Krishna now, they think of the Palace as well as these other things (Philadelphia 1982).

Since its opening, Prabhupada's Palace has become the second largest tourist attraction in the state of West Virginia. In the summer of 1982, over three hundred bus loads of tourists reportedly visited the community. Literally thousands of people have traveled to the hills of West Virginia to see Prabhupada's Palace and hear about Krishna Consciousness. The Palace and the efforts of the devotees at New Vrindaban have been hailed by state and local politicians, by local businessmen, and by members of the local community, because they have brought considerable tourist money into the state.

Following in the footsteps of the founders of Prabhupada's Palace, ISKCON completed another major cultural attraction in Detroit in the summer of 1983. The opening of the Bhaktivedanta Cultural Center drew widespread press coverage, especially since the project was largely supported by the grandson of Henry Ford and the daughter of the late Walter Reuther, president of the United Auto Workers. In an old mansion built by Lawrence Fisher, founder of Cadillac Motors, ISKCON built what has been described as a "Disney-like multi-media diorama exhibition," explaining the spiritual traditions of Krishna Consciousness. In the same complex is a vegetarian restaurant and a temple room (Suplee 1983). Like Prabhupada's Palace, the Bhaktivedanta Cultural Center is expected to attract numerous tourists. In recognition of this possibility, the state senate of Michigan passed a resolution calling the center an occasion for "glad rejoicing." The senate resolution celebrating ISKCON's new cultural center was presented by senate representatives at the grand opening celebration (Suplee 1983).

ISKCON has come to recognize the need to respect the dominant social values of the society and to be more accommodating in its relations with the outside world. The question still remains as to whether the movement can ultimately turn around its public definition and come to be accepted as a legitimate religious organization in the future. Can ISKCON gain public acceptance so that it can gain access to legitimate means of promoting its goals and objectives? As the ISKCON leader quoted earlier suggested, it is certainly possible that the movement's public image will eventually change, but such change will in all probability come about slowly. Public attitudes do undergo change; but should the movement remain in the public eye through bad publicity, either because of its own actions or because of the propaganda of the anti-cult movement, it seems likely that present public opinions will die very slowly. More than any other single factor, the continuation of the current public attitude toward the Krishna movement in America threatens to severely limit its efforts to gain legitimacy, and this would hinder its prospects for becoming a denomination. Although my discussion has uncovered a number of social forces pushing ISKCON in the direction of denominationalism, in the end, these influences will have little overall effect unless ISKCON is able to alter the public's image of it. Without gaining some degree of public acceptance, ISKCON cannot hope to reach the status even of a tolerated adjunct to other religious institutions in America.

## *ISKCON Outside of America: Present Growth and Future Prospects*

While this case study has focused on the range of social factors that have influenced, or promise to influence, ISKCON's history in America, it would be a gross oversight not to give at least a cursory description of the movement's expansionary efforts in other countries. My discussion will necessarily be more descriptive than analytical, raising more questions than it answers, for in fact ISKCON has received little scholarly attention outside of America. (But see Carey 1983 for a discussion of ISKCON in Britain.)

Because ISKCON had its beginnings in America before spreading to other portions of the globe in the early and mid-seventies, its international pattern of development has proved unique. Just at the time when ISKCON was facing decline in America during the late seventies, for example, the movement was experiencing considerable growth in Europe, Latin America, Asia, Australia, and Africa. Although the precise extent of this expansion remains unclear, there are a number of direct and indirect measures that suggest the degree of ISKCON's international success. I will briefly discuss three measures that indicate ISKCON's growth and expansion outside of America: (1) the growth rate in the number of ISKCON communities and preaching centers worldwide; (2) the relative growth rate of membership in the United States and internationally; and (3) the yearly volume of movement literature distributed in North America and internationally.

Table 10.1 indicates ISKCON's rate of growth as measured by the increase in the number of communities and preaching centers established by the movement between 1975 and 1983. The growth rate in Europe, Asia and Latin America has ranged from 200 percent to 400 percent. Although the rate of growth in Australia, New Zealand, and Africa has been somewhat less, it was still double that found in the United States and Canada during the same eight-year period. The movement's expansion in Europe in a number of cases involved purchasing historic properties and landmarks. ISKCON presently has communities at Croome Court in England, an estate in Florence, Italy, that was once home to Machiavelli, and an historic chateau near Paris, which at one time served as a retreat of Jean Jacques Rousseau (Gelberg 1982). In addition, ISKCON purchased dozens of producing farm communities on virtually every continent. All in all, ISKCON currently has a community or preaching center in virtually every major city in the free world and is busily going about the work of spreading Krishna Consciousness to "every town and village," as directed by Srila Prabhupada.

As shown in table 10.2, ISKCON's growth in overall membership since 1976 has mostly come from countries outside of the United States. After 1974, ISKCON's recruitment in the U.S. declined before leveling off in 1977, and then dropped once again in 1982. Just at the

Table 10.1.
Growth Rate of ISKCON Communities and Preaching Centers
Between 1975 and 1983

| Area of the World | 1975 | 1983 | % Growth |
|---|---|---|---|
| United States | 30 | 50 | (66%) |
| Canada | 6 | 8 | (33%) |
| Europe | 11 | 43 | (290%) |
| Australia/New Zealand/Fuji | 5 | 11 | (120%) |
| Africa | 5 | 10 | (100%) |
| India | 7 | 22 | (214%) |
| Asia | 4 | 12 | (200%) |
| Latin America | 8 | 40 | (400%) |
| TOTAL | 76 | 196 | (158%) |

NOTE: These data were compiled from the movement's monthly magazine *Back To Godhead*.

time that ISKCON's recruitment in the U.S. began to decline, the movement began to experience a considerable expansion in its international membership. In 1978 and in every year thereafter, ISKCON's international growth has been twice what it was in the U.S.

While ISKCON has attracted new members from every country in which it has spread, its expansion has been greatest in Europe and in South America. One inside observer estimates that the number of core members residing in ISKCON's communities in Europe has tripled since 1977 (Gelberg 1982). A more indirect measure pertaining to the movement's growth in Latin America is a 1981 GBC decision to increase the number of initiating gurus in that region from one to two. This decision was made because of the rapid growth in membership that the movement was experiencing in this region. The ISKCON guru in South America had reportedly initiated over one thousand disciples over the preceding three-year period.

Table 10.2.

Number of ISKCON Recruits in the United States and Internationally by Year

| Year | United States | International |
|------|---------------|--------------|
| 1970 | 35 | 1 |
| 1971 | 171 | 59 |
| 1972 | 157 | 47 |
| 1973 | 278 | 237 |
| 1974 | 272 | 244 |
| 1975 | 231 | 235 |
| 1976 | 178 | 234 |
| 1977 | 213 | 356 |
| 1978 | 215 | 526 |
| 1979 | 216 | 422 |
| 1980 | 223 | 598 |
| 1981 | 210 | 502 |
| 1982 | 151 | 576 |
| 1983 | 157 | 505 |

NOTE: The above figures were compiled from a list of devotee names contained in a yearly ISKCON publication *Sri Vyasa Puja*. Each year, devotees from each of ISKCON's communities in America and around the world inscribe their names as part of a tribute to ISKCON's founder, Srila Prabhupada. The tributes are published yearly by ISKCON's publishing company, The Bhaktivedanta Book Trust. For more details on how these figures were compiled, see note 7.7.

Another measure of ISKCON's influence outside of America is suggested by the volume of movement literature it distributes in foreign countries. As shown in figure 10.1, the volume of literature distributed internationally grew steadily between 1974 and 1979, when the overall total reached approximately twice the total distributed in America. After that, the volume of literature distributed internationally declined, but it still continued to outpace the volume in America.

Figure 10.1.
Average Volume of ISKCON Literature Distributed Weekly in North America and Internationally (1974–1982)

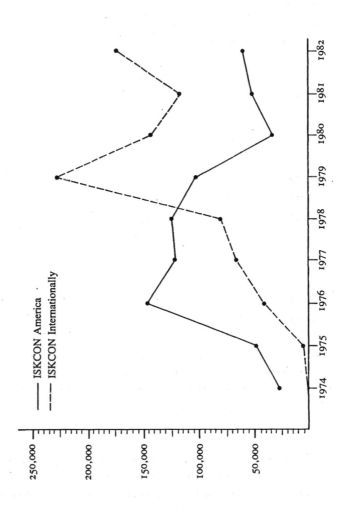

ISKCON America
ISKCON Internationally

While this kind of information points to considerable growth in the movement's influence and acceptance outside of North America, it is difficult without further research to interpret these findings in a meaningful way. ISKCON's expansion in America has demonstrated the way in which local conditions played a major role in the movement's growth. To attempt to analyze ISKCON's international growth without considering fully the range of cultural factors and conditions involved in each of these various settings is ultimately fruitless. Having acknowledged this, however, let me consider one aspect of ISKCON's international growth that in certain ways at least parallels the American pattern. This aspect concerns ISKCON's apparent success in attracting both the interest and active membership of people in Third World countries—especially in Latin America.

As indicated in table 10.1, in Latin America and in several other regions of the globe where ISKCON is expanding relatively rapidly, there are many Third World nations. In Latin America, ISKCON's growth has been greatest in Brazil, in Columbia and in Mexico, and to a lesser but still substantial degree, in Peru, in Guyana, in Chile, and in El Salvador. These countries are all Third World nations undergoing major cultural changes as a result of the pressures associated with modernization. Modernization has had the effect of fundamentally altering the very structure of these countries' institutions, and in the process restructuring the everyday lives of their citizens. As a result of this change, old cultural patterns, which have served to promote stability and predictability, are giving way to new ones, which produce feelings of anomie. These nations and their citizens face a transitional period, in which previous norms and values no longer apply, but new cultural forms capable of promoting stability are still lacking. Under these conditions, it is common for various religious sects and radical political movements to emerge, seeking to promote traditionalist ideologies (Etzioni and Etzioni 1964). One might hypothesize that the social context presented by Third World nations provides particularly fertile ground for ISKCON's expansionary efforts, in certain ways fertile ground not unlike that found in America during the 1960s and early 1970s. While the social factors promoting anomie, alienation, and frustration are clearly different in these cases, nevertheless, the ultimate consequences for peoples' potential participation in social movements are similar. These kinds of situations promote the purposes of social movements by: first, promoting structural availability among a substantial number of people (especially youth), who then become targets of the movements' recruitment efforts. Second, the pre-movement cognitive frameworks (i.e., grievances, values, interpretive schema) of those joining the Krishna movement has in many ways already been at least partially aligned with ISKCON's values and orientation. Because the lifestyle of Krishna Consciousness stresses traditionalist values and ways of living, it provides a reasonable alternative for at least some of the young people who come into contact with ISKCON, in the face of the disruptive changes taking place within their environment.

## Closing Thoughts on the Future of Hare Krishna

The history of Hare Krishna in America has been one of change and adaptation. ISKCON's ability to adapt to what have often been the most adverse circumstances points to the flexibility and ultimate resiliency of the movement. It is these qualities, combined with the deep faith and commitment of the devotees themselves, which will be the Krishna movement's greatest assets as it approaches the twenty-first century. Without question, the movement will face still further challenges ahead, as the ebb and flow of social forces turn against it and perhaps threaten its very survival. Conversely, the nature of the modern world virtually assures that conditions favorable to the Krishna movement and other new religions will arise again and again in the future, again to encourage their growth and increase their overall influence. For the many people of the world who welcome religious freedom and who see strength in religious diversity, we can only hope that the devotees of Krishna find the religious salvation they seek. All best wishes.

# Appendix: Transcription
# of the Appointment Tapes

## The May Tape

SATSVARUPA: Then our next question concerns initiations in the future, particularly at that time when you are no longer with us. We want to know how first and second initiation would be conducted.

SRILA PRABHUPADA: Yes. I shall recommend some of you, after this is settled up. I shall recommend some of you to act as officiating *acarya*.

TAMAL KRSNA: Is that called *rtvik acarya*?

SRILA PRABHUPADA: *Rtvik*. Yes.

SATSVARUPA: What is the relationship of that person who gives the initation . . .

SOURCE: "The Appointment That Never Was." Anonymous author, approximate date 1979–1980. Document of a counter-group of ex-members of ISKCON challenging the present leadership of ISKCON.

SRILA PRABHUPADA: He's guru. He's guru.

SATSVARUPA: But he does it on your behalf. ·

SRILA PRABHUPADA: Yes. That is a formality. Because in my presence one should not become guru, so on my behalf. On my order, *amara ajnaya guru hana,* he is actually guru. But by my order.

SATSVARUPA: So they may also be considered your disciples?

SRILA PRABHUPADA: Yes, they are disciples, but consider who . . .

TAMAL KRSNA: No. He is asking that these *rtvik acaryas,* they are officiating, giving *diksha,* the people who they give *diksha* to, whose disciples are they?

SRILA PRABHUPADA: They are his disciples.

TAMAL KRSNA: They are his disciples?

SRILA PRABHUPADA: Who is initiating. His grand disciple.

SATSVARUPA: Then we have a question concerning . . .

SRILA PRABHUPADA: When I order, you become guru, he becomes regular guru. That's all. He becomes disciples of my disciple. Just see.

## The June Tape

TAMAL KRSNA: Srila Prabhupada, we are receiving a number of letters now. People are waiting to get initiated. So, until now, since you were becoming ill, we asked them to wait.

SRILA PRABHUPADA: The local senior *sannyasis* can.

TAMAL KRSNA: *That's what we were doing formerly.* The local GBC *sannyasis* were chanting on their beads and they were writing to your Divine Grace. And you were giving a spiritual name. So should that process be resumed or should we . . . . (there is an interlude where Tamal Krsna discusses the spiritual master taking the disciples *karma,* and Srila Prabhupada's health). That's why we've been asking everybody to wait. I just want to know if we should continue to wait some more time.

SRILA PRABHUPADA: No. Senior *sannyasis.*

TAMAL KRSNA: *So they should continue to . . .*

SRILA PRABHUPADA: You can give me a list of *sannyasis.* You can do. Kirtanananda can do. Satsvarupa can do. So these three can do.

TAMAL KRSNA: So supposing someone is in America. Should they simply write directly to Kirtanananda or Satsvarupa?

SRILA PRABHUPADA: Nearby. Jayatirtha can do.

TAMAL KRSNA: Jayatirtha.

SRILA PRABHUPADA: Bhagavan. And he can do also—Harikesha.

TAMAL KRSNA: Harikesha Maharaja.

SRILA PRABHUPADA: Five, six men may divide. Who is nearest.

TAMAL KRSNA: Who is nearest. So persons wouldn't have to write to Your Divine Grace. They could write directly to that person. *Actually, they are initiating the person on Your Divine Grace's behalf. Those persons who are initiated are still your . . .*

SRILA PRABHUPADA: Second initiation. We shall think. Second.

TAMAL KRSNA: This is for first initiation. Okay. And for second initiation, for the time being they should . . .

SRILA PRABHUPADA: Again have to wait. Second initiation, that should be.

TAMAL KRSNA: Some devotees are writing you now for second initiation. And I'm writing them to wait awhile, because you are not well. So can I continue to tell them that?

SRILA PRABHUPADA: They can do second initiation.

TAMAL KRSNA: By writing you?

SRILA PRABHUPADA: No. These men.

TAMAL KRSNA: These men. They can also do second initiation. So there's no need for devotees to write to you for first and second initiation. They can write to the man nearest them. *But all these persons are still your disciples. Anybody who would give initiation is doing so on your behalf.*

SRILA PRABHUPADA: *Yes.*

TAMAL KRSNA: You know that book I'm maintaining of all of your disciples' names? Should I continue that?

SRILA PRABHUPADA: Hmmm.

TAMAL KRSNA: So if someone gives initiation, like Harikesha Maharaja, he should send the person's name to us here, and I'll enter it in the book. Okay. Is there someone else in India that you want to do this?

SRILA PRABHUPADA: India? I am here. We shall see. In India —Jayapataka.

TAMAL KRSNA: Jayapataka Maharaja?

SRILA PRABHUPADA: You are also in India. You can note down these names.

TAMAL KRSNA: Yes, I have them.

*(The list is read, and Srila Prabhupada adds two more names—Hrdayananda and Ramesvara.)*

SRILA PRABHUPADA: So without waiting for me, whoever you consider deserves. That will depend on discretion.

# Notes

## Chapter 1

1. This brief overview of ISKCON's historical roots, religious beliefs, and organization provide no more than a cursory introduction to the subject. For a more detailed account of the movement's historical roots and religious beliefs, see Judah (1974) and Gelberg (1983). For an excellent biography of the life of Srila Prabhupada, see Goswami (1980, 1981).

2. Statistics on membership are always difficult to substantiate reliably. Since I was first introduced to ISKCON in 1975, the movement has claimed to have five thousand members in America. Despite an overall loss in membership that occurred during the late 1970s, ISKCON continues to report a membership of five thousand. Estimates from devotees within ISKCON suggest that the total adult membership in America is currently nearer to two thousand.

## Chapter 2

1. Response to the questionnaire in Los Angeles was somewhat less than 50 percent. In other ISKCON communities surveyed, the response rate ranged from approximately 50 percent in New York to more than 90 percent for several of the smaller communities.

2. My troubles with the university did not stop there. Because ISKCON was in the middle of serious succession problems in 1980, which caused great factionalism, splintering, and the defection of many long-time devotees and the purging of others by the leadership (to be discussed in chapter nine), I felt it important that my dissertation not be made publically available at that time. My advisors and I petitioned the university to hold my dissertation out of circulation for a one-year period because of the likelihood that it would be used in the ongoing political struggle taking place within ISKCON. The university ruled against my petition and I was forced to wait for a full year before finally filing for my degree.

3. Harold Garfinkel has taken this approach to an extreme by encouraging his students to become trained in one of the professions as a way of gaining access to the everyday details that constitute peoples' work. In place of studies about work, which typify sociological accounts of the professions, Garfinkel is pushing instead for studies of work. These kinds of studies can only come from persons who have fully committed themselves to the work as practitioners (Garfinkel 1981).

## Chapter 3

1. Judah does not report the age of the devotees at the time they actually became ISKCON devotees. Even so, his data confirm the fact that the clear majority of the people participating in the movement during these early years were young.

2. Turner and Killian (1972:259–268) identify a number of factors that are necessary for individual misfortune to be transformed into a sense of injustice. Discontented individuals must come to view their situation as a collective misfortune for there to be an impulse toward action. Only when individuals feel a sense of group identity are they likely to also feel group pride and to assert their right to receive a better lot in life. But a group must also receive support from external sources, if its cause is to gain legitimacy. If the claims of any group

are to come to be accorded the status of a moral cause instead of an expression of self-interest, support and sympathy must be gained from others who have no direct stake in the group's objectives. Support from respected individuals and organizations within the society helps to define a group's cause as a problem of injustice; intellectuals often play a particularly important role in this function. Intellectuals change feelings of discontent into the rhetoric of injustice, and they do so with an authority that is given them because of their status in society. Finally, groups who come to view their misfortune as an injustice require a comparison or reference group. Discontented people must compare their circumstances with people they see as better off than they are, if they are to see injustice at work. Claims of injustice are based upon comparisons with other groups who are perceived to have greater "wealth, freedom, power or other benefits" (Turner and Killian 1972:266).

3. These findings on the involvement of ISKCON members in specific social movement organizations differ from the data presented in table 3.8. The data reported in the table reflect previous movement participation as either movement sympathizers or active members. By contrast, the above data on the devotees' participation in specific movement organizations refers *only* to active participation as core members. These data were compiled by having the devotees list chronologically all movements in which they had actually participated, prior to joining ISKCON.

4. Drug use among young American adults aged 18–25 years progressively increased throughout the decade of the 1970s (Kelleher *et al.* 1983). While marijuana use for this age group was less than 50 percent in 1972, the recreational and social use of this substance increased to nearly 70 percent by 1979. The use of hallucinogens increased from approximately 15 percent to 25 percent during this same period. Likewise the use of alcohol, cocaine, and every other major drug increased among young adults in America. While past drug use among ISKCON's membership is greater than the national average for their age group, these differences are perhaps less important than the increasing use of drugs in contemporary society as a whole.

5. A similar problem of interpretation arises regarding the accounts of ex-members of the new religions, especially those who have undergone deprogramming. Some of those who have left the new religions have joined forces with the anti-cult movement and are at work actively discrediting the cults. This usually involves denouncing the movement to which they were once committed in the most damning

fashion. Their new position as foes of the new religions leads these ex-members to reinterpret their original memberships in line with their present position. These reinterpretations by no means reliably reflect the motives that initially led them to join one of the new religions. They argue now that membership in the cult is not based on individual initiative and rational thought; the devious tactics of the cult and its members are held to blame for recruitment. Brainwashing instead of individual choice is made the explanation for membership. This method of accounting for their own prior actions restores their sense of competency in that "faulty" decision-making on their part was not responsible for their joining, but rather the sinister practices of the group itself were responsible. In sum, entering the movement involved one line of biographical reconstruction, while leaving it necessitates a totally different formulation. (See Durham 1981; Edwards 1979; Freed 1980; Underwood and Underwood 1979; and Wood and Vitek 1979 for the accounts of former cult members of their experiences in one of the new religions. Each of these ex-members retrospectively accounts for his or her involvement by arguing that he or she had been brainwashed by cult members. For a scholarly treatment of apostates and an analysis of the nature of their atrocity stories, see Bromley *et al.* 1979 and Bromley and Shupe 1981.)

6. Of course, social movements provide only one avenue by which people may seek to overcome their alienation and social tension. If troubles are seen as political or reformist in nature, they may choose to effect change through the established political process. If troubles are envisioned as personal and intrapersonal, psychotherapy may be seen as the reasonable remedial action. (See Lofland and Stark's (1965) and Richardson and Stewart's (1978) discussions of the general orientations used to deal with problems. See also Emerson and Messinger's (1977) discussion of the micro-politics of trouble.)

7. Affective bonds and intensive interactions in cults have been shown to be essential to membership and conversion processes (Lofland and Stark 1965; Snow and Phillips 1980); it is my argument here that similar relational factors are likewise crucial to the recruitment process and to the decision to join a particular movement organization. Along these lines, Barker (1980:394) reports that potential recruits who agree to attend one of the Unification Church's programs at a local center in Britain most often do so because they are seeking some kind of truth, or because they have an "interest in or curiosity about the person who has talked to them."

8. In fairness, I should note that the recruitment program in Los

Angeles during the middle seventies was not representative of similar programs in other ISKCON communities. The devotee in charge of the *bhakta* program in Los Angeles was known to be extreme in his approach to new recruits. While the events reported above may not be typical, they do reflect the general effort made by the movement to protect new recruits from outside influences during this period.

9. For a detailed discussion of the alignment process as it operates interactionally for recruits to ISKCON and also to the Nichiren Shoshu Buddhist movement, see Snow and Rochford (1983). I will discuss the problems that are posed for men and women recruits differently with regard to aligning their cognitive orientations with ISKCON's ideology in chapter five.

## Chapter 4

1. This life history of Devi is based on a six-hour taped interview conducted in Philadelphia in April 1983. Devi read and made corrections in the initial draft of the chapter in the spring of 1984. All quoted materials in this chapter come from this interview with Devi.

2. Devi married in the fall of 1983; she and her devotee husband moved to Washington, D.C., to assist in running the ISKCON community there.

## Chapter 5

1. To cite just a few examples among many: Jessie Bernard (1972) has demonstrated how men and women experience the institution of marriage in quite different ways. In a sense, marriage can be considered a different reality for husband and wife. Hochschild (1975) has shown the ways in which emotions such as love and anger are distributed differently between the sexes (anger being more often aimed downward at women by their husbands; love and compassion aimed upward from wives to their husbands). McCormack (1975) and Sapiro (1983) have argued that men and women ultimately live in two distinct political cultures.

2. Because this portion of my analysis relies on understanding men's and women's worlds in general, I believe that the analysis has more far-reaching implications for differential recruitment processes

than only those involved in participation in Hare Krishna. I see this discussion and analysis addressing the more general issue of how men and women come to participate in groups and movements of all kinds, although for now, this assertion can only stand as a claim, given the lack of research that has been done in this area.

3. In general, the social world of women can be characterized as largely *Gemeinschaft* in nature—valuing intimate face-to-face relations, and feelings of social solidarity—while men, on the other hand, inhabit a world that is more like a *Gesellschaft* way of life—stressing impersonal contacts and individualism, rather than group and community life. In fact, Tonnïes himself identified the *Gemeinschaft* with the female world, although in an overly sentimental fashion: "the realm of life and work in the *Gemeinschaft* is particularly befitting to women, indeed, it is even necessary for them" (quoted in Bernard 1981:28).

4. My characterization of women as marginal to the larger culture is not meant to stand as a moral or political value judgment. While I personally view the domination associated with the marginality of women in modern society as unjust, my discussion is not meant to constitute a moral enterprise. I leave that to other men and women more knowledgeable about these issues than I. I can't help but believe, however, that the dominance of the male world and worldview comes from clear acts of hegemony. In our society, the male worldview for all intents and purposes is the worldview of the culture. Sexism ultimately is the way in which men attempt to legitimize and safeguard their dominance over the prevailing ideas and values of people within the culture. Setting these issues aside, however, I want to argue that the marginality of women, whatever its roots and moral status, is an important force in shaping the social world of women in modern society.

5. While it is tempting to view the devotee women as marginal to the Krishna society because of the sexism implied by the movement's adherence to traditionalist sex roles, this view ultimately rests on an outsider's analysis (it is an assessment that rests on the assumption that women should be equal in all ways with men). Many, if not most, Krishna women see their role as complementary and ultimately equal to the role played by men. This is not to say, however, that all women easily and unquestioningly accept the movement's emphasis on traditionalist sex roles. Some devotee women initially find it difficult to accept their place within the Krishna lifestyle. For some, an inability to adapt to traditionalist sex roles becomes a factor in their decision to leave the movement. For many who stay to become committed members, the difficulties in coming to accept their status within the move-

ment stand as a major obstacle to their being able to align their cognitive orientations with the movement's ideology.

6. It should be noted that the contact between ISKCON members and the general public in airports and other public places often involves more than preaching and recruitment. As I will discuss in chapter seven, there has been a fundamental change in the nature of ISKCON's use of public places. From primarily pursuing preaching and missionary goals in public locations, ISKCON by the mid-seventies began increasingly to use public places for financial purposes. Even with this change, these locations continue to produce a substantial number of recruits, though perhaps not as many as in past years.

7. Another indication of the devotees' preferences for contacting men rather than women is suggested by the problems faced by a fellow student who assisted me in these observations. On a number of occasions, she tried to make herself a target for the devotees' attempts at contact. On only one occasion was she actually stopped by a devotee. Conversely, I was targeted over and over again by the devotees. I should note that our contacts with the devotees were not counted as part of the observations included in tables 5.2 and 5.3.

8. Levine *et al.* (1976) have found that men, who have presented themselves at individual homes (private spaces) as being lost and needing to use the telephone, met with considerably less success in gaining entry than their female counterparts. In most cases, the person at home was a woman, because the experiment was carried out during the daytime when women tend to be at home by themselves. In both towns and cities, women gained entry significantly more often than did men. These investigators concluded that "male (confederates) clearly were not trusted as often as females in both city and town, and this could be expected, since males are objectively more threatening than females" (1976:115).

## Chapter 6

1. The importance of social network ties have also been noted in relation to traditional religions (Stark and Bainbridge 1980) and for nonreligious groups and movements (Leahy 1975; Sills 1957). In addition, the role of social ties has been studied for a number of other social processes, including making job contacts (Granovetter 1973), seeking an abortionist (Lee 1969), the diffusion of medical innovations (Coleman, Katz and Menzel, 1966), seeking psychiatric treatment (Horwitz 1977), and the mobilization of political support (Sheingold 1973).

2. Sixty-seven of the devotees surveyed had had multiple contacts with Krishna Consciousness before joining ISKCON. I coded cases where social ties were involved along with other forms of contact (e.g., contacts in public places, self-initiated contacts, and others) as pertaining to either devotee or to nonmember networks, because it was the social tie that ultimately led to the decision to join.

3. While Judah does not report the community which the devotees in his survey joined, we can infer that the vast majority joined the movement in San Francisco, since only a handful of Prabhupada's disciples traveled from New York City to begin the temple there. Snow *et al.* (1980) present data that is more difficult to interpret: They do not report where the devotees they interviewed actually joined ISKCON, and a reasonable inference cannot be made, because by the mid-seventies, many had moved to other communities.

4. Recruitment in the New York and Boston ISKCON communities has also shifted away from public places toward devotee networks.

5. A similar attempt to build a congregation of less committed members has also been noted for the Unification Church. Barker (1980:393) reports that since 1978 there have been growing numbers of "Home Church" members in Britain: "These are people who accept the truth of the Divine Principle but who remain associate members living at home rather than devoting their whole lives to the movement."

## Chapter 7

1. Even though distribution of Prabhupada's books and public solicitation provided the primary source of revenue for ISKCON's communities, other monies came from the sale of Spiritual Sky incense. In 1969 in New York City, ISKCON began producing and distributing incense as a way of raising money to support the movement. The sale of incense was not, however, a major source of revenue for all of ISKCON's communities. Some communities chose to distribute incense, while others decided to rest their financial security solely upon the distribution of literature.

2. *Sankirtana* involves three types of activities in public places: Book distribution is the practice whereby devotees venture into airports and other public places to distribute for money Prabhupada's translations of the Vedic scriptures; *Hare Nam* usually involves a group of devotees going out in public to chant and preach. This activ-

ity may or may not involve literature distribution; and, *picking*, which will be discussed later in the chapter, involves selling products to the public for money. It generally does not involve literature distribution.

3. The decision to combine missionary activity with money making was made by ISKCON's founder, Srila Prabhupada. He instructed his disciples that book distribution would provide for ISKCON's financial needs and allow the movement to pursue its missionary goals at the same time. Prabhupada actively discouraged the development of other forms of business enterprise that might have helped support ISKCON. In fact, the ex-business manager of ISKCON's incense business, Spiritual Sky Scented Products, argued in a 1977 interview that the company's financial potential was never fully realized because Prabhupada had failed to support it.

4. In *Murdock* v. *Pennsylvania* (1942) the Supreme Court held that the Jehovah's Witnesses could not be held to a city ordinance requiring the purchase of a permit in order to conduct door-to-door solicitations and sales of religious literature. The fact that religious literature was sold rather than donated did not transform religious activity into a commercial enterprise, according to the court. While ISKCON was ultimately protected under the First Amendment, the movement nevertheless was forced initially to enter into litigation to secure its rights with regard to practicing *sankirtana* (*ISKCON* v. *Conlisk*, 1973; *ISKCON* v. *Rochford*, 1977; *ISKCON* v. *Evans*, 1977).

5. An additional factor that influenced ISKCON's decision to focus its distribution efforts in places like public airports was the gas crises, which began in 1974. A large portion of ISKCON's *sankirtana* revenue had been generated by teams of devotees traveling in vans across Canada and the United States, distributing literature and collecting donations. With the increase in gas prices, this strategy was no longer profitable.

6. Another indication of how much ISKCON made from its *sankirtana* practices is suggested by the financial report of the Berkeley ISKCON community, which cited *sankirtana* income of $1.1 million in 1977 and of $877,325 in 1978, according to its application for property tax exemptions in Alameda County (*Fresno Bee*, June 27, 1980).

7. While there is no reliable data available, one source suggests that recruitment in America peaked in 1973 and 1974. By 1976, ISKCON's yearly number of recruits had declined by approximately one-third from its 1973 high. Thereafter, the number of new recruits joining the movement each year leveled off. These recruitment trends

are reported in table 10.2. These figures were compiled from a list of devotee names contained in the yearly *Sri Vyasa-Puja* (1969–1983). Each year devotees from each of ISKCON's communities in America and around the world inscribe their names as part of a tribute to Srila Prabhupada on his birthday. The tributes are published each year by the movement's publishing company, The Bhaktivedanta Book Trust. I determined the number of new recruits by counting the persons listed who did.not have Sanskrit names (and were therefore uninitiated members). New recruits in the *Sri Vyasa-Puja* were identified by *bhakta* (for men) or *bhaktin* (for women) followed by their name (e.g., Bhakta John or Bhaktin Jody). There are a number of methodological problems associated with this data source, though I do believe the data compiled provide for a general understanding of recruitment trends. The method of counting only bhaktas and bhaktins without question underestimates the actual number of recruits to ISKCON in any given year, especially during ISKCON's early years. If a recruit remained in the movement for only part of a year, leaving before the *Sri Vyasa-Puja* was completed, s/he would not have been included. Moreover, during ISKCON's early years in America (especially 1966–1972) Srila Prabhupada often initiated new recruits within a relatively short time period, often in as little as a few weeks (Goswami 1980). Because of the number of new initiates defecting from the movement, Prabhupada instituted a policy whereby each recruit was required to wait at least six months before taking initiation. What this means with regard to the issue at hand is that many of the persons listed in the *Sri Vyasa-Puja* with Sanskrit names during the early years were in fact new recruits. Despite these obvious limitations, I have chosen to include these data from the *Sri Vyasa-Puja* because they represent the only source available pertaining to ISKCON's recruitment efforts over time.

8. Beginning as early as 1971, ISKCON members began to experiment with various strategies to increase their literature distribution and, thereby, the amount of money that could be raised through donations. The first major innovation was the introduction of "sales mantras." Instead of standing on the street and offering people passing by a copy of the movement's magazine, *Back to Godhead*, the devotees came upon the idea that people would be more likely to stop and talk if a printed card with the Hare Krishna mantra was offered first. Only after the person took the card and stopped would the devotee then offer the magazine. This simple strategy resulted in ISKCON members distributing substantially more literature and therefore raising more money as well. As one devotee explained: "Instead of a devotee being

able to bring home $10, he could now bring home $25 or $30, by that simple change. So then you could distribute so many more magazines and also fix up your temple and do so many things to preach Krishna Consciousness" (Philadelphia 1982).

9. In recent years, the devotees have continued, and refined, this method of public place solicitation. During the Christmas season of 1979, the devotee Santas in Los Angeles further enhanced their credibility by distributing Jesus coloring books to the people they confronted in public. Even after the holiday season, these coloring books were used to raise money for the children's school to be relocated in northern California.

10. The people interviewed by airport staff were selected randomly. At the time of the study, ISKCON members were distributing books as well as other nonreligious items to people in the airport terminal.

11. The practice of *picking* as a means of raising money originally developed very early in the movement's history. In 1969 and 1970, devotees in San Francisco and a few other ISKCON communities would occasionally go into the streets and distribute sticks of incense for donations. This practice was not performed very extensively, however, because Prabhupada at this time was laying more and more stress on distributing literature. A major difference between *picking* as it was developed in 1977 and as it was practiced in this earlier period was that the devotees distributing incense did not attempt to hide their involvement with ISKCON. On the contrary, they were as much hoping to find people interested in hearing about Krishna Consciousness as they were in raising money to help support the community.

12. Messinger (1955) notes a similar development within the Townsend movement as this group faced decline in the late 1930s and early 1940s in the United States. As the movement lost mass support, it faced growing financial difficulties. To bring money into the organization, members were urged to purchase a variety of consumable goods bearing the Townsend name (e.g., Townsend candy bars, toilet soap, and health foods). Purchase of these items did not signify any degree of commitment to the Townsend movement or its goals and ideology. As Messinger argues, this period in the movement's development involved "a striking shift from programmatic matters to concern(s) with promoting . . . product(s)" (1955:8).

13. ISKCON's public image as a threatening movement was also strongly influenced by two major controversies that received national media attention: In 1979, people claiming to be either current or former ISKCON members were charged by authorities in California with

possession and smuggling of drugs (*Los Angeles Times*, 1979). ISKCON officials denied any movement involvement, claiming that the people involved were not members in good standing. In 1980, a major controversy emerged that had far-reaching consequences for ISKCON's public image. Law enforcement officials in a community north of San Francisco uncovered what was described as "a cache of weapons and ammunition" in an ISKCON farm community (*Los Angeles Times*, 1980; *New York Times*, 1980). The leader of the community, who was one of the ISKCON gurus appointed by Srila Prabhupada prior to his death in 1977, was arrested and charged in the case. While these charges were later dropped, the incident had a significant impact on ISKCON's public image, following as it did closely on the heels of the tragedy at Jonestown in 1978. Irrespective of the facts in either of these cases, the media coverage they generated further influenced the public's view of ISKCON. The weapons incident, in particular, was used repeatedly by the anti-cult movement in its efforts to discredit ISKCON and the other new religions.

14. Another factor that entered into the decision to rely on book distribution and *picking* as major means of financial support had to do with the nature of ISKCON's members. As discussed in chapter three, 80 percent of the devotees possessed no employment skills whatsoever at the time they joined the movement, or their skills were limited to unskilled and semi-skilled jobs (e.g., clerks, mechanics). One Krishna devotee accounted for ISKCON's success in raising money in public places by commenting in a 1981 interview: "You have to remember that many of us came out of the counterculture and more than anything we were street-wise. *Sankirtana* was a natural for a lot of us."

15. The public's awareness of ISKCON members' work in public settings was influenced by several factors: 1) Insofar as ISKCON claims to have distributed 100 million pieces of literature by 1982, many members of the public had first-hand experience with the devotees' *sankirtana* tactics and actively sought to avoid further contacts; 2) The media's coverage of ISKCON often described Krishna members' deceitful *sankirtana* tactics (*Fresno Bee*, 1980; *Los Angeles Times*, 1976; NBC, 1979); 3) There have been a variety of formal and informal efforts by the authorities in charge of public facilities subject to ISKCON's *sankirtana* practices to inform their patrons of the devotees' presence and purposes. In a number of locations (e.g., the Los Angeles International Airport, Sea World in San Diego), signs warning the public of the Krishna activites were displayed around the facilities' entrances. At the Denver Zoo in 1980, I observed an employee stand-

ing outside the exit at closing time, warning zoo patrons as they left that ISKCON members were awaiting them and requesting that they not contribute any money; and, 4) anti-cultists have sought to disrupt ISKCON's *sankirtana* efforts in public settings by approaching people talking with a Krishna member and informing them of the identity of their contact (Bromley and Shupe, 1980).

16. It should be noted that while ISKCON's decline as a social movement organization was strongly influenced by the events I have described, it is entirely possible that the movement would have faced decline in any case. Virtually all of the major new religions faced a decline in recruitment and overall membership by the end of the 1970s. The Unification Church (Bromley and Shupe 1981; Lofland 1977), the Children of God (Davis 1981), Transcendental Meditation (Bainbridge and Jackson 1981), and The Divine Light Mission (Downton 1979), for example, all faced declining membership by the end of the decade. But while these other movements became what Zald and Ash (1966) refer to as becalmed movements, ISKCON faced the additional possibility of organizational failure, because of the internal crisis of legitimacy that arose over its *sankirtana* tactics. A becalmed movement is one that achieves a support base and organizational stability, but which ceases to grow; a failing movement organization loses members because its legitimacy as a instrument for realizing the movement's goals becomes discredited in the eyes of a portion of its membership (Zald and Ash 1966: 334–335).

## Chapter 8

1. For a brilliant analysis of the problems encountered by religious institutions and their belief systems in the face of modern pluralism and secularization, which is characteristic of modern industrial society, see Peter Berger's discussion of secularization and the problem of plausibility (1969:127–171). Berger discusses the crisis of theology in the modern age that comes from religious institutions having to exist within a social milieu that no longer takes their definition of reality for granted. In this sense, religious institutions in the modern age are required to engage in ideological work aimed at legitimizing their right to define the nature of reality as against disconfirming and competing plausibility structures. The present discussion of ISKCON draws upon Peter Berger's analytic framework, but the level of analysis is more in

line with what Bennett Berger (1981) refers to as a problem in the micro-sociology of knowledge.

2. Snow and Machalek (1982) in a most insightful paper on the nature of unconventional beliefs argue that sociologists often project a "scientific attitude" onto the belief systems they study. Such an approach, due to the disbelief inherent in science and the scientific attitude, looks cynically at unconventional beliefs (i.e., it asks, "How could they believe that?"). While the scientific attitude makes disbelief a topic of inquiry from the inside, that is, from the perspective of those who practice such beliefs, the more natural attitude is belief. Because religious adherents view worldly circumstances as generally consistent with their beliefs, it is not surprising that most of them do not dissect the policy of their religious leaders, looking for faults and inconsistencies between organizational practices and ideology.

3. Another factor that entered into the decision of at least some devotees to remain within ISKCON despite basic differences they had with the leader's *sankirtana* policies had little to do with ideology. Some devotees who expressed ideologically based explanations for their remaining with the movement—often in an off-hand fashion —also mentioned their considerable emotional investment in the movement and talked about how trying to become reintegrated back into the society would pose formidable problems of adjustment. Just as people sometimes stay in marriages or work situations that they no longer value because of the uncertainty of alternatives, some devotees chose to stay on with ISKCON for similar reasons.

4. While spiritual adaptors continued their membership in ISKCON on largely spiritual grounds, this is not meant to imply that organizational adaptors were any less concerned with spiritual and theological matters than others were. In fact, the ideological work of ISKCON's leaders was cast in theological terms. The difference between the two types of response is that spiritual adaptors essentially came to reject ISKCON's status as a spiritual enterprise, viewing it largely as a self-serving organization. Organizational adaptors, on the other hand, continued to endorse the direct links between Krishna Consciousness, Prabhupada, and ISKCON. In sum, there was no differentiation between ISKCON and the Krishna belief system for organizational adaptors, while this linkage was broken in the minds of spiritual adaptors.

5. My discussion has centered on the nature of ISKCON members' ideological work, but what this work ultimately means in any objective framework is debatable. In the case of those devotees who de-

fected from the organization, it is unclear, for instance, whether their ideological justification for that reflects purist attitudes or self-serving rationalizations. Seen from within ISKCON, the ideological work of defectors represents rationalizations that bear little relationship to their "real" reasons for leaving the movement. Committed ISKCON devotees point to the inabilities of defectors to live up to a strict Krishna-conscious lifestyle and argue that this is the "true" basis for their leaving. By contrast, the ideological work of most defectors explicitly places blame on the organization for their decisions to leave it. I am in no way trying to settle this issue, in part because I suspect it defies accurate assessment. Personally, however, my conversations with and knowledge about a number of people who have defected from ISKCON leads me to believe that both individual rationalizations and purist standards are at work.

6. It is generally understood that the correlation between peoples' attitudes and their behavior is far from exact or consistent. While people hold various attitudes and beliefs in good faith, circumstances often demand that these cognitive orientations remain flexible. To a large degree, our living practices and every-day behavior are the outcome of a dialectical relationship between beliefs and circumstances. For a most insightful discussion of these processes, see Bennett Berger (1981).

7. The defining characteristics of a sect and a denomination were derived from a review of the extensive literature on the church-sect model. The six contrasting characteristics I have noted are not meant to be an exhaustive list of the qualities that distinguish the two forms of organization. Instead, I have attempted to identify the most central defining qualities of each. For a more detailed discussion of the church-sect distinction, see Bainbridge and Stark (1980); Brewer (1952); Hill (1973); Johnson (1963); Martin (1962); Pope (1942); Wilson (1959,1961,1967); and Yinger (1957,1970).

8. A number of other studies have also challenged the church-sect model of movement change along similar lines. Robertson's (1967) study of the Salvation Army, and Isichei's (1967) investigation of English Quakerism, for example, suggest that prosperity and success do not necessarily result in a shift from sectarianism to denominationalism. In both of these cases, the group was able consciously to resist pulls toward denominationalism, despite their general success. In a somewhat different way, Bryan Wilson's (1983) research on the Seventh-Day Adventists suggests that this group became a denomination

only after the predicted Second Coming of Christ in 1843 failed to occur. Failure, rather than success, was clearly instrumental in the Adventists' shift from a sect to a denominational form of organization.

## Chapter 9

1. The two conversations which serve as the basis for this account of ISKCON's reorganization appear in the Appendix.

2. The movement's literature recognizes that advanced devotees may experience ecstatic symptoms, whereby they display physical behaviors that are out of the ordinary (e.g., crying uncontrollably). Such behaviors are often looked upon as spiritually induced and not a matter for questioning as was done in Foreign Guru's case. In fact, many Indian people who witnessed Foreign Guru's behavior reportedly interpreted it as a sign of his great spiritual energy. One Indian man reportedly commented: "Finally ISKCON is showing its true potential to produce a great *prima bhakta*" (a realized and spiritually potent devotee of Krishna Consciousness).

3. The order of *sannyasa* requires that all sense gratifications be renounced completely. When married, this injunction involves ending all family responsibilities and having no further involvement or contact with one's wife.

4. It should be noted that after conferring with his guru Godbrothers, Bombay Guru ultimately gave up his claim to be the true *acarya* following Srila Prabhupada.

5. I should stress here that even though the guru controversies led to a formal change in policy regarding the role of ISKCON's gurus, all the gurus were not in agreement with the change of policy. Several continued to feel that the authority of the guru could not be limited by the GBC. So even though formal agreement was reached, the potential for conflict and splintering remained. Only subsequent events, which I discuss later in this chapter, actually solidified the principle of GBC authority.

6. These data should not be interpreted as showing a lack of spiritual sincerity on the part of the disciples of the new gurus. Many if not most devotees experience difficulties in living up to the Krishna-conscious philosophy and lifestyle, especially during the early period of membership. Many in fact leave the movement as a result of these difficulties. The point of this table is to demonstrate the impact of organizational changes on the commitment of Prabhupada's disciples,

relative to the factors that have influenced the commitment of the disciples of the new gurus.

7. The following statement explains the distinction between ISKCON and UPA-ISKCON, as these terms are used by those challenging the movement under the new leadership:

> Actually, serious misconceptions have not overtaken ISKCON, they have overtaken what *appears* to be ISKCON. ISKCON itself is pure and perfect. It is beyond such defects. It survives no matter how many members it has, or does not have, on this insignificant planet. The International Society for Krishna Consciousness [ISKCON] is just that: an international society dedicated to the philosophy and principles of Krishna Consciousness. ISKCON is not an elite group of so-called leaders. If any person is ISKCON, then that person is the founding-*acarya* of ISKCON, our bonafide spiritual master, His Divine Grace, Srila Prabhupada. In the Sanskrit language, when something only appears to be something, which it actually is not, the word that stands for the reflected entity is prefixed by the Sanskrit term "upa." . . . Serious philosophical misconceptions have not overtaken ISKCON. Serious philosophical misconceptions are instead embedded in UPA-ISKCON. UPA-ISKCON is any society that appears to be ISKCON, but which does not actually represent and act according to the philosophy and principles of ISKCON as it is (unpublished document of ex-members of ISKCON 1980).

8. In retrospect, one might claim that these devotees defected from ISKCON, but this does not seem to have been their initial purpose. Rather, those joining forces with Maharaja, as later events demonstrated, were actually attempting to bring him within ISKCON.

9. In the spring of 1982, three additional gurus were appointed by the GBC. After the defection of Foreign Guru, there remained a total of thirteen ISKCON gurus.

## Chapter 10

1. Under the system of *Varna-Asrama*, there are different types of citizens in society, each performing a different role to maintain the society as a whole. There are four classes of people within *Varna-Asrama* society: The *brahmanas* who comprise the teachers or intellectual class; the *ksatriyas* who are the administrative leaders; the

*vaisyas* who are society's business men and farmers; and, the *sudras* who are the common laborers. Crosscutting these four divisions in society are four *asramas*: The *brahmacari*, or the students, the *grhasta*, or householder, the *vanaprastha*, or retired persons, and the *sannyasi*, or the person in renounced life (Prabhupada 1974). With the exception of the *vanaprastha asrama*, perhaps, the three other *asramas* have been part of ISKCON's structure since the early years. However, until recently there has been very little differentiation and specialization on the basis of class: essentially all of ISKCON's members have been *brahmanas*, to the exclusion of the other three classes within *Varna-Asrama* society.

2. In England and South Africa, where there are relatively large numbers of ISKCON members originally from India, the movement has received rather extensive financial support. In both countries, ISKCON has actively sought the support of the Indians through the movement's life member program.

3. The major reason that ISKCON's leaders have decided to keep the Hare Krishna Food For Life Program under wraps for now is the fear that the anti-cult movement will try to undermine these efforts. As one of ISKCON's leaders told me: "We are trying to be quiet, until we really have the thing working. We don't want to make it well known, because the anti-cult movement would like to undermine the whole thing. I mean the anti-cult people have a lot of underground people who are just watching our every move so they can discredit us. So we have to have some savvy in that regard, keep it low key" (Philadelphia 1982).

# Bibliography

Adams, Bert
  1968.  *Kinship in an Urban Setting.* Chicago: Markham.
Adelson, Joseph
  1971.  "The Political Imagination of the Young Adolescent."
    *Daedalus* 100 (Fall):1013–1050.
Bainbridge, William, and Jackson, Daniel
  1981.  "The Rise and Decline of Transcendental Meditation."
    *The Social Impact of New Religious Movements.* Bryan
    Wilson (ed.), New York: The Rose of Sharon Press,
    pp.135–158.
Bainbridge, William, and Stark, Rodney
  1980.  "Sectarian Tension." *Review of Religious Research* 22
    (December): 105–124.
Barker, Eileen
  1980.  "Free to Choose? Some Thoughts on the Unification
    Church and Other New Religious Movements." *Clergy
    Review* 65:356–368, 392-398.

1981. · "Who'd be a Moonie? A Comparative Study of Those Who Join the Unification Church in Britain, *The Social Impact of New Religious Movements.* Bryan Wilson (ed.) New York: The Rose of Sharon Press, pp.59–96.

Becker, Howard S.
1963. *Outsiders.* New York: The Free Press of Glencoe.

Becker, Howard S., Geer, Blanche, Huges, Everett C. and Strauss, Anselm L.
1961. *Boys In White: Student Culture In Medical School.* Chicago: University of Chicago Press.

Beckford, James A.
1975. *The Trumpet of Prophecy: A Sociological Study of Jehovah's Witnesses.* New York: Oxford and Halsted Press.
1978. "Accounting for Conversion." *British Journal of Sociology* 29 (2): 249–262.

Bell, Robert R.
1981. *Worlds of Friendship.* Beverly Hills: Sage.

Bensman, Joseph and Lilienfeld, Robert
1979. *Between Public and Private.* New York: Free Press.

Berger, Bennett M.
1981. *The Survival of a Counterculture.* Los Angeles: University of California Press.

Berger, Peter L.
1969. *The Sacred Canopy: Elements of a Sociological Theory of Religion.* Garden City, New York: Doubleday and Co.

Berger, Peter and Luckmann, Thomas
1966. *The Social Construction of Reality.* New York Doubleday and Co.

Bernard, Jessie
1972. *The Future of Marriage.* New York: World.
1981. *The Female World.* New York: The Free Press.

Best, Joel and Luckenbill, David F.
1982. *Organizing Deviance.* Englewood Cliffs, N.J.: Prentice-Hall.

Bibby, Reginald W. and Brinkerhoff, Merlin
1974. "When Proselytizing Fails: An Organizational Analysis." *Sociological Analysis* 35:189–200.

Bittner, E.
1973. "Objectivity and Realism in Sociology." *Phenomenologi-*

*cal Sociology: Issues and Applications.* George Psathas (ed.) New York: Wiley, pp 109–125

Blum, Alan and McHugh, Peter

1971.   "The Social Ascription of Motives." *American Sociological Review* 46:98–109.

Blumer, Herbert

1951.   "Collective Behavior." *New Outline of the Principles of Sociology.* A.M. Lee (ed.) New York: Barnes and Noble, pp.166–222.

Bodemann, Y. M.

1978.   "A Problem of Sociological Praxis: The Case for Interventive Observation in Field Work." *Theory and Society* 5:387–420.

Booth, A.

1972.   "Sex and Social Participation." *American Sociological Review* 37:183–192.

Brewer, Earl

1952.   "Church and Sect in Methodism." *Social Forces* 30:400–408.

Bromley, David and Shupe, Anson

1979.   *"Moonies" in America: Cult, Church, and Crusade.* Beverly Hills: Sage.

1980.   "Financing the New Religions: A Resource Mobilization Approach." *Journal for the Scientific Study of Religion* 19(3):227–239.

1981.   *Strange Gods: The Great American Cult Scare.* Boston: Beacon Press.

1982.   "The Archetypal Cult: Conflict and the Social Construction of Deviance." Paper presented at the Meeting of the Society for the Scientific Study of Religion, Providence, R.I. October.

Bromley, David G., Shupe, Anson D. Jr., and Ventimiglia, Joseph C.

1979.   "Atrocity Tales, the Unification Church and the Social Construction of Evil." *Journal of Communication* 29 (Summer):42–53.

Brooks Gardner, Carol

1981.   "Passing By: Street Remarks, Address Rights, and the Urban Female." *Sociological Inquiry* 15(3–4):328–356.

Burris, Val

1983.   "Who Opposed the ERA? An Analysis of the Social Basis of Antifeminism." *Social Science Quarterly*, 64 (2) (June):305–317.

Carey, Sean
  1983.  "The Hare Krishna Movement and Hindus in Britain." *New Community*.

Cavan, Sherri
  1972.  *Hippies of the Haight*. St. Louis: New Critics Press.

Clark, John
  1979.  "Cults." *Journal of the American Medical Association*. 242 (3):279–281.

Cohen, Albert K.
  1955.  *Delinquent Boys: The Culture of the Gang*. New York: The Free Press of Glencoe.

Coleman, J., Katz, E. and Menzel, H.
  1966.  *Medical Innovation: A Diffusion Study*. Indianapolis: Bobbs—Merrill.

Conway, Flo and Siegelman, Jim
  1978.  *Snapping: America's Epidemic of Sudden Personality Change*. New York: Lippincott.

Daner, Francine
  1976.  *The American Children of Krsna: A Study of the Hare Krsna Movement*. New York: Holt, Rinehart and Winston.

Davis, Rex
  1981.  "Where Have the Children Gone?" Paper presented at the Conference on New Religious Movements, Lincoln, England.

Davis, Rex and Richardson, James
  1976.  "The Organization and Functioning of the Children of God." *Sociological Analysis* 37 (4):321–339.

Devi Dasi, Sitarani
  1982.  "What's the Role of Women in Krsna Consciousness?" *Back to Godhead* 17(12):11–13,26.

Douglas, J.D.
  1976.  *Investigative Social Research: Individual and Team Field Research*. Beverly Hills: Sage.

Downton, James
  1979.  *Sacred Journeys: The Conversion of Young Americans to Divine Light Mission*. New York: Columbia University Press.

Durham, Deanna
  1981.  *Life Among the Moonies: Three Years in the Unification Church*. Plainfield, N.J.: Prentice-Hall.

Edwards, Christopher
1979.  *Crazy for God.* Englewood Cliffs, N.J.: Prentice-Hall.
Ehrenreich, Barbara
1981.  "The Women's Movement: Feminist and Antifeminist."
         *Radical America* 15 (Spring):93–101.
Ellwood, Robert S.
1983.  Forward to *Hare Krishna, Hare Krishna.* Steven J.
         Gelberg (ed.) New York: Grove Press, pp.11–13.
Elshtain, Jean Bethke
1974.  "Moral Women and Immoral Man: A Consideration of the
         Public-Private Split and its Political Ramifications." *Politics and Society* 4:453–474.
Emerson, Robert M.
1981.  "Observational Field Work." *Annual Review of Sociology*
         7:351–378.
1983.  *Contemporary Field Research.* Boston: Little, Brown.
Emerson, Robert and Messinger, Sheldon
1977.  "The  Micro-Politics  of  Trouble."  *Social  Problems*
         25:121–134.
Enroth, Ronald
1977.  *Youth, Brainwashing and the Extremist Cults.* Grand Rapids: Zondervan.
Etzioni, Amitai and Etzioni, Eva
1964.  *Social Change: Sources, Patterns and Consequences.*
         New York: Basic Books.
Feuer, Lewis
1969.  *The Conflict of Generations.* New York: Basic Books.
Fine, Gary A. and Kleinman, Sherryl
1983.  "Network and Meaning: An Interactionist Approach to
         Structure." *Symbolic Interaction.* 6(1):97–110.
Flacks, Richard
1967.  "The Liberated Generation: An Exploration of the Roots
         of Student Protest." *Journal of Social Issues* 23(3):52–75.
Freed, Josh
1980.  *Moonwebs: Journey Into The Mind of a Cult.* Toronto:
         Dorselt Publishing.
Freeman, Jo
1979.  "Resource Mobilization and Strategy: A Model for Analyzing Social Movement Organization Actions." *The Dynamics of Social Movements.* Mayer Zald and John
         McCarthy (eds.) Cambridge, Mass: Winthrop Publishing,
         pp.167–189.

*Fresno Bee*
1980.   "Krishna Cult Members Hustle Millions in Cash From Public." June 27.

Gamson, William
1975.   *Strategy of Social Protest.* Homewood, Ill: Dorsey.

Garfinkel, H.
1967.   *Studies in Ethnomethodology.* Englewood Cliffs, N.J.: Prentice-Hall.
1981.   Lectures in ethnomethodological methods. Unpublished. University of California, Los Angeles.

Garner, Roberta Ash
1972.   *Social Movements in America.* Chicago: Rand McNally College Publishing Co.

Gelberg, Steven J.
1982.   ISKCON after Prabhupada: An Update on the Hare Krishna Movement. Paper presented at the 1982 Annual Meeting of the American Academy of Religion, New York, N.Y.
1983.   *Hare Krishna, Hare Krishna.* New York: Grove Press.

Gerlach, Luther and Hine, Virginia
1970.   *People, Power and Change: Movements of Social Transformation.* Indianapolis: Bobbs-Merrill.

Goffman, Erving
1963.   *Behavior In Public Places.* New York: The Free Press.
1977.   "The Arrangement Between the Sexes." *Theory and Society* 4(3):301–331.

Goswami, Satsvarupa dasa
1980.   *Planting the Seed.* Los Angeles: Bhaktivedanta Book Trust.
1981.   *Only He Could Lead Them.* Los Angeles: Bhaktivedanta Book Trust.

Granovetter, Mark
1973.   "The Strength of Weak Ties." *American Journal of Sociology* 78:1360–1380.

Gurr, Ted
1970.   *Why Men Rebel.* Princeton: Princeton University Press.

Hacker, Helen
1951.   "Women as a Minority Group." *Social Forces* (October) 30:60–69.

Harrison, Michael
1974.   "Sources of Recruitment to Catholic Pentacostalism." *Journal for the Scientific Study of Religion* 13:49–64.

Heirich, Max
   1977.   "Change of Heart: A Test of Some Widely Held Theories
           about Religious Conversion." *American Journal of Sociol-
           ogy*, 83 (3):653–680.
Hill, Michael
   1973.   *A Sociology of Religion*. London: Heinemann.
Hochschild, Arlie Russell
   1975.   "The Sociology of Feeling and Emotion: Selected Possi-
           bilities." *Another Voice*. Marcia Millman and Rosabeth
           Moss Kanter (eds.) Garden City, N.Y.: Anchor Books,
           pp.280–307.
Horwitz, Allen
   1977.   "The Pathways into Psychiatric Treatment: Some Differ-
           ences Between Men and Women." *Journal of Health and
           Social Behavior* 18:169–178.
Horowitz, Irving and Liebowitz, Martin
   1968.   "Social Deviance and Political Marginality." *Social Prob-
           lems*, 15:281–296.
Isichei, Elizabeth
   1967.   "From Sect to Denomination among English Quakers."
           *Patterns of Sectarianism*. Bryan Wilson (ed.) London:
           Heinemann, pp.161–181.
Johnson, Benton
   1963.   "On Church and Sect." *American Sociological Review*
           28:539–549.
Johnson, Gregory
   1970.   "Counter-culture in Microcosm: A Study of Hare Krishna
           in San Francisco." Unpublished manuscript.
   1976.   "The Hare Krishna In San Francisco." *The New Religious
           Consciousness*. Charles Glock and Robert Bellah (eds.)
           Los Angeles: University of California Press,. pp.31-51.
Judah, Stillson
   1974.   *Hare Krishna and the Counterculture*. New York: Wiley.
Jules-Rosette, B.
   1975.   *Vision and Realities: Aspects of Ritual and Conversion in
           an African Church*. Ithaca: Cornell University Press.
Kanter, Rosabeth
   1972.   *Commitment and Community*. Cambridge: Harvard Uni-
           versity Press.
   1977.   *Women and Men of the Corporation*. New York: Basic
           Books.

Kelleher, Maureen, MacMurray, Bruce K. and Shapiro, Thomas M.
1983. *Drugs and Society.* Dubuque: Kendall/Hall Publishing Co.

Keniston, Kenneth
1967. "The Sources of Student Dissent." *Journal of Social Issues* 23 (3):108–137.
1968. *The Young Radicals: Notes on Committed Youth.* New York: Harcourt, Brace and World.
1971. *Youth and Dissent: The Rise of a New Opposition.* New York: Harcourt, Brace and World.

Kirby, R. and Corzine, J.
1981. "The Contagion of Stigma: Fieldwork Among Deviants." *Qualitative Sociology* 4 (1):3–20.

Klapp, Orrin
1969. *Collective Search For Identity.* New York: Holt, Rinehart and Winston.
1972. *Currents of Unrest.* New York: Holt, Rinehart and Winston.

Komarovsky, Mirra
1946. "Cultural Contradictions and Sex Roles." *American Journal of Sociology* 52:184–189.

Kuhn, Thomas
1970. *The Structure of Scientific Revolutions.* (Postscript) 2nd ed., Chicago: University of Chicago Press.

Leahy, Peter
1975. "The Anti-abortion Movement: Testing a Theory of the Rise and Fall of Social Movements." Unpublished Ph.D. dissertation. Department of Sociology, Syracuse University.

Lee, N.H.
1969. *The Search for an Abortionist.* Chicago: University of Chicago Press

Levine, Marshall E., Vilena, Julio, Altman, Doris and Nadien, Margot
1976. "Trust of the Stranger: An Urban/Small Town Comparison." *The Journal of Psychology.* 92:113–116.

Lofland, John
1966. *Doomsday Cult.* Englewood Cliffs, N.J.: Prentice-Hall.
1977. "Becoming a World-Saver Revisited." *American Behavioral Scientist* 20:805–819.

Lofland, John and Stark, Rodney
1965. "Becoming a World-Saver: A Theory of Conversion to a Deviant Perspective." *American Sociological Review* 30:862–874.

*Los Angeles Times*
   1976.   "The Hare Krishna Cover-up." March 19.
   1979.   "11 Linked to Krishna Cult Indicated in Narcotics Case."
            November 6.
   1980.   "Hare Krishna Arsenal Discovered at Ranch." March
            16.
   1984.   "Seeking Rights for Little People." June 24. (San Diego
            edition).
Lynch, Frederick R.
   1978.   "Toward a Theory of Conversion and Commitment to the
            Occult." *Conversion Careers: In and Out of the New Reli-
            gions*. James Richardson (ed.) Beverly Hills: Sage.
Martin, David
   1962.   "The Denomination." *British Journal of Sociology* XII
            (1):1–4.
McCarthy, John and Zald, Mayer
   1974.   "Tactical Considerations in Social Movement Organiza-
            tions." Paper presented at the Annual Meeting of the
            American Sociological Association, August.
McCormack, Thelma
   1975.   "Toward a Nonsexist Perspective on Social and Political
            Change." *Another Voice*, Marcia Millman and Rosabeth
            Moss Kanter (eds.) Garden City, N.Y.: Anchor Books,
            pp. 1–33.
Mehan H. and Wood, H.
   1975.   *The Reality of Ethnomethodology*. New York: Wiley.
Messinger, Sheldon
   1955.   "Organizational Transformation: A Case Study of a De-
            clining Social Movement." *American Sociological Review*
            20:3–10.
Michels, Robert
   1962.   *Political Parties*. New York: The Crowell-Collier Pub-
            lishing Co.
Millman, Marcia and Kanter, Rosabeth Moss
   1975.   *Another Voice*. Garden City, N.J.: Anchor Books.
National Broadcasting Corporation (NBC)
   1979.   "Prime Time with Tom Snyder." July 1. New York: Na-
            tional Broadcasting Corporation.
*New York Times*
   1980.   "Krishna Arms Caches Draw Police Scrutiny in Califor-
            nia." June 9.

Pope, Liston
  1942.   *Millhands and Preachers*. New Haven: Yale University
          Press.
Port Authority
  1976.   "Portland International Airport Study on the Activities of
          Hare Krishna Members." Portland, Oregon.
Prabhupada, A.C. Bhaktivedanta
  1972.   *Bhagavad-Gita As It Is*. New York: MacMillan Publish-
          ing Co.
  1974.   *A Varna-Asrama Society*. Los Angeles: Bhaktivedanta
          Book Trust.
Richardson, James
  1980.   "Conversion Careers." *Society* 17 (3):47–50.
  1982.   "Financing the New Religions: Comparative and Theoreti-
          cal Considerations." *Journal for the Scientific Study of Re-
          ligion* 21 (3):255–268.
Richardson, James and Stewart, Mary
  1978.   "Conversion Process Models and the Jesus Movement."
          *Conversion Careers: In and Out of the New Religions.*
          James Richardson (ed.) Beverly Hills: Sage, pp.24–42.
Robertson, Roland
  1967.   "The Salvation Army: The Persistence of Sectarianism."
          *Patterns of Sectarianism*. Bryan Wilson (ed.) London:
          Heinemann, pp. 49–105.
Rochford, E. Burke, Jr.
  1976.   "World View Resocialization: Commitment Building Pro-
          cesses and the Hare Krishna Movement." Unpublished
          M.A. thesis. Department of Sociology, University of Cal-
          ifornia, Los Angeles.
  1982.   "Recruitment Strategies, Ideology, and Organization in
          the Hare Krishna Movement." *Social Problems*. 29
          (4):399–410.
*Sankirtana Newsletter*
  1974–
  1982    Los Angeles: Bhaktivedanta Book Trust.
Sapiro, Virginia
  1983.   *The Political Integration of Women: Roles, Socialization
          and Politics*. Chicago: University of Illinois Press.
Schutz, Alfred
  1971.   *Collected Papers I: The Problem of Social Reality*. The
          Hague: Martinus Nijhoff.

Scott, Marvin and Lyman, Stanford M.
1968. "Accounts." *American Sociological Review* 33:46–62.
Sheingold, Carl
1973. "Social Networks and Voting: The Resurrection of a Research Agenda." *American Sociological Review* 38: 712–728.
Shupe, Anson and Bromley, David
1979. "The Moonies and the Anti-Cultists: Movement and Counter-Movement in Conflict." *Sociological Analysis* 40(4):325–334.
1980. *The New Vigilantes: Anti-Cultists, Deprogrammers, and the New Religions.* Beverly Hills: Sage.
Sills, David L.
1957. *The Volunteers.* Glencoe, Ill.: Free Press.
Smelser, Neil
1962. *Theory of Collective Behavior.* New York: The Free Press.
Singer, M.T.
1979. "Coming Out of the Cults." *Psychology Today* 12 (January):72–82.
Snow, David A.
1976. "The Nichiren Shoshu Buddhist Movement in America: A Sociological Examination of its Value Orientation, Recruitment Efforts, and Spread." Ann Arbor, Michigan: University Microfilms.
1979. "A Dramaturgical Analysis of Movement Accommodation: Building Idiosyncrasy Credit as a Movement Mobilization Strategy." *Symbolic Interaction* 2(2):23–44.
Snow, David A. and Machalek, Richard
1982. "On the Presumed Fragility of Unconventional Beliefs." *Journal for the Scientific Study of Religion* 21:15–26.
Snow, David A. and Phillips, Cynthia
1980. "The Lofland-Stark Conversion Model: A Critical Reassessment. *Social Problems* 27:430–447.
Snow, David A. and Rochford, E. Burke, Jr.
1983. "Structural Availability, the Alignment Process and Movement Recruitment." Paper presented at the Meeting of the American Sociological Association, Detroit, August.
Snow, David A., Zurcher, Louis Jr. and Ekland-Olson, Sheldon
1980. "Social Networks and Social Movements: A Micro-

structural Approach to Differential Recruitment." *American Sociological Review* 45:787–801.

1983.   "Further Thoughts on Social Networks and Movement Recruitment." *Sociology* 17(1):112–120.

Sorokin, Pitirim

1950.   *Altruistic Love: A Study of American "Good Neighbors" and Christian Saints.* Boston: Beacon Press.

Stark, Rodney

1982.   "New Religious Movements: Genesis, Exodus and Numbers." Unpublished manuscript. University of Washington, Seattle.

Stark, Rodney and Bainbridge, William S.

1980.   "Networks of Faith: Interpersonal Bonds and Recruitment to Cults and Sects." *American Journal of Sociology* 85:1376–1395.

Suplee, Curt

1983.   "The Temple of Tomorrowland: Heirs of Detroit's Assembly Line Investing in Hare Krishna." *The Washington Post* May 27.

Thorne, Barrie

1979.   "Political Activist as Participant Observer: Conflicts of Commitment in a Study of the Draft Resistance Movement of the 1960s." *Symbolic Interaction* 2(1):73–88.

Tiger, Lionel

1970.   *Men In Groups.* New York: Vintage.

Travisano, R.

1970.   "Alterations and Conversion as Qualitatively Different Transformations." *Social Psychology Through Symbolic Interaction.* G.P. Stone and M. Garverman (eds.) Waltham, Mass: Ginn-Blasidell, pp.594–606.

Turner, Ralph and Killian, Lewis

1972.   *Collective Behavior.* Englewood Cliffs, N.J.: Prentice-Hall.

Turner, Victor

1977.   *The Ritual Process.* Ithaca, New York: Cornell University Press.

Underwood, Barbara and Underwood, Betty

1979.   *Hostage to Heaven.* New York: Clarkson N. Potter.

Wallis, Roy

1977.   *The Road to Total Freedom.* New York: Columbia University Press.

Warren, C. A. B.
1974. *Identity and Community in The Gay World.* New York: Wiley.
Weber, Max
1968. *Economy and Society.* New York: Bedminster Press.
Weiss, L. and Lowenthal, M.F.
1975. "Life-course Perspective on Friendship." *Four Stages of Life.* M.F. Lowenthal, M. Thurnher, and D. Chiribotga (eds.) San Francisco: Jossey-Bass, pp.48–61.
Wilson, Bryan
1959. "An Analysis of Sect Development." *American Sociological Review* 2(2):3–15.
1961. *Sects and Society.* London: Heinemann.
1967. *Patterns of Sectarianism.* London: Heinemann.
1983. "Factors in the Failure of the New Religious Movements." Paper presented at the Fourth International Conference on New Religious Movements, Berkeley, California, October.
Wilson, John
1973. *Introduction to Social Movements.* New York: Basic Books.
Wolff, K.
1964. "Surrender and Community Study: The Study of Loma." *Reflections of Community Studies.* A. J. Vidich, J. Bensman, M.R. Stein (eds.), New York: Wiley, pp.233–263.
Wood, Allen T. and Vitek, Jack
1979. *Moonstruck: A Memoir of my Life in a Cult.* New York: William Morrow.
Wood, James
1974. *The Source of American Student Activism.* Lexington, Mass.: Lexington Books.
Wright, Paul H.
1982. "Men's Friendships, Women's Friendships and the Alleged Inferiority of the Latter." *Sex Roles* 8(1):1–20.
Yinger, J. Milton
1957. *Religion, Society, and the Individual.* New York: MacMillan.
1970. *The Scientific Study of Religion.* New York: MacMillan.
Zald, Mayer
1970. *Organizational Change: The Political Economy of the YMCA.* Chicago: University of Chicago Press.

Zald, Mayer and Ash, Roberta
    1966.    "Social Movement Organizations: Growth, Decay, and Change." *Social Forces* 44:327–341.

## Cases Cited

*Heffron* v. *ISKCON*, 49 U.S.L.W. 3802, 1981.

*Murdock* v. *Pennsylvania* 319 U.S. 105, 63 S. Ct. 870, 87 L. Ed. 1292, 1942.

*ISKCON* v. *Barber, Young, and Garlick*, 506 N.Y. 147, 1980.

*ISKCON* v. *Conlisk*, 374 ILL. 1010, 1973.

*ISKCON* v. *Evans*, 440 U.S. 414, 1977.

*ISKCON* v. *Rochford*, 425 ILL. 734, 1977.

*ISKCON* v. *State Fair of Texas*, 461 TX. 719, 1978.

## Unpublished Documents

1980    (Untitled document) Governing Body Commission response to criticism. August.
1980    "When You Hear Someone Say . . . " Mimeographed paper.
1980    "The Appointment That Never Was." Mimeographed paper.
1980    "The Spiritual Master Never Deviates." Mimeographed paper.
1980    "Guru is Never Appointed." Mimeographed paper.
1981    Untitled letter from Members of Los Angeles ISKCON community to [Western Guru].

# Index